Art Therapy for Racial Trauma, Microaggressions and Inequality

of related interest

Cultural Humility in Art Therapy
Applications for Practice, Research, Social Justice, Self-Care, and Pedagogy
Louvenia C. Jackson, PhD
Foreword by Dr Melanie Tervalon
ISBN 978 1 78592 643 3
eISBN 978 1 78592 644 0

Using Art Therapy with Diverse Populations
Crossing Cultures and Abilities
Edited by Paula Howie, Sangeeta Prasad, and Jennie Kristel
Foreword by Mercedes B. ter Maat and Gaelynn P. Wolf Bordonaro
ISBN 978 1 84905 916 9
eISBN 978 0 85700 694 3

Therapy in Colour
Intersectional, Anti-Racist and Intercultural Approaches by Therapists of Colour
Edited by Dr Isha McKenzie-Mavinga, Kris Black, Karen Carberry and Eugene Ellis
ISBN 978 1 83997 570 7
eISBN 978 1 83997 571 4

ART THERAPY FOR RACIAL TRAUMA, MICROAGGRESSIONS AND INEQUALITY

SOCIAL JUSTICE AND ADVOCACY IN THERAPY WORK

CHIOMA ANAH, Ed.D.

Forewords by BETH GONZALEZ-DOLGINKO, Ed. D. AND ALAN GREEN, PhD

Jessica Kingsley Publishers
London and Philadelphia

First published in Great Britain in 2025 by Jessica Kingsley Publishers
An imprint of John Murray Press

2

Copyright © Chioma Anah 2025

Forewords © Beth Gonzalez-Dolginko and Alan Green 2025

A CIP catalogue record for this title is available from the British Library and the Library of Congress

ISBN 978 1 83997 833 3
eISBN 978 1 83997 834 0

Printed and bound in Great Britain by CPI Group

Jessica Kingsley Publishers' policy is to use papers that are natural, renewable and recyclable products and made from wood grown in sustainable forests. The logging and manufacturing processes are expected to conform to the environmental regulations of the country of origin.

Jessica Kingsley Publishers
Carmelite House
50 Victoria Embankment
London EC4Y 0DZ

www.jkp.com

John Murray Press
Part of Hodder & Stoughton Ltd
An Hachette Company

The authorised representative in the EEA is Hachette Ireland, 8 Castlecourt Centre, Castleknock Road, Castleknock, Dublin 15, D15 YF6A, Ireland

This book is for my mother, Mrs. Rose Ijeoma Anah, my true north.

November 13, 1939–September 2, 2021

*In the ultimate raffle of life, having you as my mother was
a platinum ticket, and the greatest honor of my life. Forever
and a day...Ndinne Baby...Odogwu nwanyi, obi diya.*

And, for my father, Mr. Raphael S. Anah.

*It is rare to have one Iroke tree as a parent; strong, resilient, yet loving.
However, to have two was, and is indeed, a divine blessing. Thank you for
planting the seed of knowledge and education in my mind and nurturing it. I
celebrate you as the patriarch of the Anah/Azonwanna family and legacy and
I'm so happy that you know how much you are loved, adored and cherished.*

Psalm 91, vs 4-7 (New International Version)[1]

He will cover you with his feathers,
and under his wings you will find refuge;
his faithfulness will be your shield and rampart.

You will not fear the terror of night,
nor the arrow that flies by day,

nor the pestilence that stalks in the darkness,
nor the plague that destroys at midday.

A thousand may fall at your side,
ten thousand at your right hand,
but it will not come near you.

---

1   Psalm 91 retrieved from www.biblegateway.com/passage/?search=Psalm%2091&version=NIV

Contents

Acknowledgments 11

Foreword by Dr. Beth Gonzalez-Dolginko 14

Foreword by Dr. Alan Green. 17

Preface 19

Introduction 21
Racism hurts us all   21
Art therapy, anti-racism and healing   22
The purpose and rationale for this book   25
Who this book is for, and ways of using the book   27
Important things to keep in mind when reading this book   27
Obstacles and reactions to learning about racism   29
Chapter 1: Art and Healing   30
Chapter 2: The History, Origins and Evolution of Racism   31
Chapter 3: Microaggressions   31
Chapter 4: Special Study: Results and Findings   31
Chapter 5: Inequality, Social Justice and Advocacy   32
Chapter 6: Intersectionality: Black Women in Art Therapy   32
Chapter 7: Theoretical Frameworks for Understanding Racism, and
Interventions and Implications for Art Therapy Clinical Practice   32
Chapter 8: Healing and the Way Forward   33

1. **Art and Healing**. 35
Multicultural counseling and therapy (MCT) defined   37
Art as a healing intervention to personal and social oppression   37
Irene's work and the therapeutic process   42
Introduction and assessment   44
Broaching: Race, ethnical and cultural exploration   45
Locus of control and locus of responsibility   47

Art work and process   47

Therapy with the culturally diverse, and the Trump administration's contributions to oppression and fear   48

Summary   52

2. The History, Origins and Evolution of Racism   55

Racism defined   55

Racial trauma   58

Understanding racial trauma in the context of art therapy   61

Ways to be anti-racist and dismantle White supremacy in art therapy   62

A brief early history of racism: Colonialism and the origins of racism   64

The evolution of racism in the United States   67

Denial, minimization and distortions of the existence of racism   72

The eradication of American history—slavery—2023 and beyond   73

Summary   74

3. Microaggressions   76

What are microaggressions?   76

Racial microaggressions   77

Taxonomy of racial microaggressions   78

Environmental microaggressions   83

Psychological dilemmas of racial microaggressions   84

Psychological effects of racial microaggressions   86

Physical effects of racial microaggressions   88

The realities of racial microaggressions   89

Gender-based microaggressions   90

Sexual-orientation microaggressions   92

4. Special Study: Results and Findings   95

Introduction   95

Instrumentation   96

Tables: Results and findings of the study   96

Section I: Experiences of racial microaggression themes   108

Section II: Reactions/Responses to racial microaggressions   124

Section III: Impact and consequences of racial microaggressions   126

Section IV: Collages—experiences of racial microaggressions and visual metaphors   132

Section V: Coping with racial microaggressions in the workplace   142

Section VI: Collages—coping with racial microaggressions in the workplace, visual metaphors   148

Section VII: How to combat racial microaggressions in the workplace   157

Section VIII: Participant thoughts about this study   159

Summary and conclusion   160

5. **Inequality, Social Justice and Advocacy** 162

What is social justice advocacy?   162

Art therapists' roles as agents of change   165

Art therapy: A call to action for social justice and advocacy   167

Summary   172

6. **Intersectionality: Black Women in Art Therapy** 173

What is intersectionality?   173

Intersectionality: Black women in art therapy   175

7. **Theoretical Frameworks for Understanding Racism, and Interventions and Implications for Art Therapy Clinical Practice**. 194

My Iroko Tree of Identity and Pathway Towards Healing—exercise explained   198

Section I: Exploring internalized racism   199

Section II: Exploring and understanding racial identity   200

Section III: Critical race theory and art therapy considerations   214

Section IV: Clinical considerations and recommendations for art therapists developing cultural responsiveness when practicing with clients   216

Summary   218

8. **Healing and the Way Forward** 219

Section I: What wounds need healing?   220

Section II: True racial allyship—being a co-conspirator or accomplice   221

Section III: Who is a culturally competent art therapist? What competencies are important for culturally responsive practice?   223

Section IV: Ways to increase cultural awareness and unlearn anti-Black racism   225

Section V: Healing artwork   227

Section VI: The way forward for art therapists and the field   227

Summary   232

Glossary. 233

References. 237

About the Author. 248

Subject Index 249

Author Index 255

Acknowledgments

A great many people contributed, in one way or another, to this book. It is based on research conducted for my doctoral degree from 2012 to 2014. Since then, the data from my dissertation has given rise to many articles and national, state and local conference presentations, leading finally to the publication of this book.

My very first debt and honor is to my late mother, Mrs. Rose Ijeoma Anah, my champion and North Star who convinced me that I had several books in me, and that I should write. And, my dear father, Mr. Raphael Anah, who through unconditional love and sheer willpower, fighting through his own insurmountable grief and loss, encouraged me to continue the book when Mummy died, as I was certain that I had no strength to do so. Her death has been a soul-crushing loss to all of us, and we are all forever changed by it. My love for you both continues to run so deep, and I am eternally grateful for your love. Mummy, I feel you with me every second of the day, encouraging and loving me. Thank you for guiding me through this book. I miss you sorely.

I am grateful to Dr. Day-Vines, Professor and Associated Dean at Johns Hopkins University (JHU), for introducing me to Cose's (1993) book, *The Rage of a Privileged Class*, while meeting with me before I began my doctoral dissertation. Although I didn't really know it then, that meeting would be the genesis of this book.

Jane Evans has my gratitude for offering me a home at Jessica Kingsley Publishers after attending my 2018 American Art Therapy Association conference lecture in Miami, Florida. Also, to Elen Griffiths and Maudisa King, who took over my care, and edited me so capably, with just the right amount of patience to bring the book to reality.

To the six participants in the "special study" chapter, I thank you for trusting me with your stories and voices.

To Beth Gonzalez-Dolginko, for being on my doctoral dissertation committee, and writing a beautiful foreword, I am thankful. Many thanks to Dr. Alan Green, for his mentorship during his time at the Counseling Department at JHU, and for his foreword.

In the course of writing this book, I have often called on friends and colleagues for advice and perspective. Among those to whom I am particularly indebted are art therapists Gwendolyn Short and Charlotte Boston. Thank you both so much for such a rich and powerful contribution to the book.

I thank those many individuals who, along the way, supported and encouraged me. To *ENVISAGE* (Canadian Art Therapy Magazine) and Counselors for Social Justice (Shon D. Smith), thank you for publishing my articles on racial microaggressions and social justice advocacy. To my Fall 2023 Diversity and Social Justice in Counseling students at JHU School of Education, Yahellah, Yusma, Amora, Bethann, Becca, Debbie and, of course, Kyla, Terry and David, who contributed to the healing chapter of the book, you are amazing.

Deep gratitude to Dr. Benjamin and Mrs. Nwanyinna Opara (my Aunty Inna) and family. Thank you for safe harbor when I arrived in the United States from England to attend college and beyond, and for nursing me through my initial stages of grief when my mother died. I will forever be grateful.

I owe a great debt to the legacy and strength from my late grandparents, Lucy Adure Anah Azonwanna (Nee Anokam), John (Anamemena) Anah Azonwanna, Chief Inspector Michael Ajoku Madufor and Lady Juliana MmezieOke Madufor.

For a lifetime of unwavering unconditional love and support, I give thanks to my family. Everything good in my life exists because of your love and care. I would like to acknowledge, with gratitude, the love and support of my brothers and sisters, Chuks, Okey, Ugos, Ebis and Inma. Thank you for helping me keep my mental equilibrium and ensuring a safe space to land, always. Our collective grief and resilience kept me going and this book would not have been possible without all of you.

I was born right at the end of the Nigerian civil war, and my name, Chioma—meaning *God is good* in Igbo—signified blessings following a devastating time. It was a thanksgiving to God for the deliverance from the brutality of the Biafran war. This book is also dedicated to the lives lost in the Biafran war.

Thank you to my father for his heartfelt and scholarly contribution to the book about his experiences during the Biafran war. I know recalling those horrors was challenging for you during our interview, and I am thankful for your strength and perseverance.

To all my Nigerian, British and American family and friends, I am who I am because of all my experiences with you.

Finally, I give thanks to all the clients with whom I have worked throughout the years, who have taught me more than books and have given me purpose in my life and work.

NOTE: Some of the names in this book have been changed and the identities of the individuals whose stories are told in this book have been fully disguised to protect the confidentiality and the sacredness of the art therapy and counseling relationship. Some case studies and all the interviews included in this book are from experiences of my clients, research study participants, friends, family, students and those actively involved in social justice advocacy. Some have given permission to use their stories and real names, and others have asked for their names to be changed. All stories and anecdotes have been thoughtfully and deliberately selected to illustrate experiences of racial trauma, racial microaggressions and inequality, and of the importance of art and art therapy as a vehicle for healing and restoration.

Foreword

—— DR. BETH GONZALEZ-DOLGINKO ——

Systemic racism runs deep in our society and culture. It impacts family, education, food, shelter and healthcare. When I look at the systems we are mired in, it makes me think of the molasses swamp in the classic board game of Candyland™. With beauty and brightness all around, the player must pass the molasses swamp that appears so dark, compared to the rest of the board, and the threat is of getting stuck there forever. That is what systemic racism is—a molasses swamp that gets a hold of you and keeps you from getting anywhere that might be better. But it's always there, and after a while, we stop noticing it except as part of the rest of the board.

Sometimes, the world notices the molasses swamp and progressively tries to change the situation. Some things change; many things don't. But the shadow of the molasses swamp is ever present. Even if people are "woke," the shadow tickles the back of their reality and perception—lingering, both consciously and unconsciously. And when this shadow emerges with ugly remnants of systemic racism, that is microaggression.

Dr. Anah has devoted much of her professional career and research to studying, presenting and publishing on microaggression. I have known her for 30 years, since she was a graduate student in the Creative Arts Therapy Program at Hofstra University in Hempstead, New York. Dr. Anah was an outstanding, passionate, dynamic student. She was clearly a leader in her class and, academically, at the top of the group. She always questioned and invited discussion in the classroom in pursuit of knowledge. Her work was, and continues to be, scholarly and thorough.

In 2012, I was honored when Dr. Anah vetted me to be part of her dissertation committee for her doctorate degree. Her intention was to use art directives with her subjects as part of her data collection, and we would qualitatively analyze the artwork for results. Her study on microaggression was cutting edge. Dr. Anah incorporated extensive research with an art directive (collage) and group and individual interviews with African American men, who were all professionals with advanced degrees, to create a masterful and informative opus regarding the subjects' experiences with microaggressions in all aspects of their lives. It is a significant contribution to the field of counseling, art therapy and racial consciousness.

Dr. Anah continued to spread the message about systemic racism and microaggression through the presentations at the American Art Therapy Association Conferences on subjects including the experiences of racial microaggressions and coping skills among professional African American men (2015); the Baltimore uprising and her healing artwork after the killing of Freddie Gray (2016); and reflections of an artist's journey as a social justice activist (2018).

The decision by Dr. Anah to include art, and her background as an art therapist, in her research touched a note of intersectionality that resounds nicely with her work. Art therapists have been viewed as lesser than in many professional circles, even though psychoanalytic pioneers like Carl Jung incorporated art into some of their work. There has been an overall general acceptance of art therapy by other mental health professionals at this point. With this, the art therapy community's awareness has slowly grown to realize that we are part of systemic racism and must make moves towards including content in education programs, and understanding and implementing cultural competence.

A brief report in *Art Therapy: Journal of the American Art Therapy Association* (Johnson, Deaver & Doby-Copeland, 2021) discussed a qualitative study addressing the lack of racial and ethnic diversity in American graduate art therapy programs. Seven current art therapy students or recent graduates of color from one predominantly White institution participated in individual semi-structured interviews and a group meeting. Four overarching themes emerged: Courses, Internships, Affective disruptions and Differences. Participants addressed concerns that there was limited course content incorporating the contributions of pioneers of color, and uneven exposure to course content designed to increase racial/cultural self-awareness, and preparation for cross-cultural interactions.

In response to the Tennessee HB 1840 Law allowing counselors to decline services to clients whose desired goals of therapy or their behaviors conflict with counselors' beliefs, Donna Kaiser, then editor of the *Journal of the American Art Therapy Association*, published a special issue on ethics, law and cultural competence in art therapy (2017). She referred to Elkins and Deaver (2015), who reported that, compared to other professions, art therapy had been and still was primarily comprised of an unusually high percentage of White people. A further reference to Carr (2016) noted that this extensive

Whiteness leads to embedded systems of structural racism and oppression that perpetuate the silencing of marginalized voices in discussions, deliberations and action plans, thus continuing White power and privilege.

Language is enmeshed with microaggressions and comes out with venom, subtly and not so subtly. Kapitan and Kapitan (2023) discuss that language shapes and constructs our world around us through communication and perception. It shapes how we understand the world, each other and ourselves. Words maintain "cultural norms and values regarding which experiences and identities are considered valuable, normal, and powerful and which are considered abnormal, pathological, and even nonhuman" (Kapitan & Kapitan, 2023, p.65). The authors urge therapists to consider the power of the words they use and be mindful of language that perpetuates the status quo and does harm. Rather than focusing on censorship or being politically correct, therapists can use words to disrupt oppression in language by centering on care and not doing harm. This liberatory mental model sets the stage for a practice free from all forms of violence and respectful of and honoring all life, all identities and experiences.

Dr. Anah has continued to pursue the cause of social justice through publishing, lecturing, presenting, university teaching and participating in social action committees in her professional organizations. This publication is a culmination of decades of work and research, but it is certain that it is not the end of the line, only a stop along the way of Dr. Anah's lifelong research. And, definitely, looking at the molasses swamp in the rearview mirror.

Foreword

—— DR. ALAN GREEN ——

In these times of great racial trauma, this book is an essential text for everyone working with Black and other culturally diverse clients, especially Black and White art therapy students, practitioners and counselors. *Art Therapy for Racial Trauma, Microaggressions and Inequality* has been a long time coming—a comprehensive book about racism, with clear guidelines about best practices for working with Black clients. Dr. Anah has drawn on her decades of experiences as a Black woman, practitioner and educator to write a clear and extraordinary book.

I first met Chioma about 25 years ago when she came to Johns Hopkins University for the Certificate of Advanced Graduate Studies (CAGS). She had completed her master's in art therapy at Hofstra, and she wanted another graduate program that would lead her closer to a doctorate, while advancing her studies with a 33-credit master's program in counseling. She was at that time very much about finding ways to heal those who were oppressed and marginalized. She was smart, driven, innovative and passionate, and this book has been decades in the making.

Art Therapy for Racial Trauma, Microaggressions and Inequality is replete with essential information and ideas clearly rooted in the historical context of slavery and its ongoing consequences of racism. Dr. Anah addresses the scourge of racism and the long-standing problem of White supremacy at the heart of the United States. We learn about the consequences of colonialism, and hear her father's own words about the horrors he witnessed during the Nigerian-Biafran war. We learn about the devastating harm racial trauma can cause Black people, and other culturally diverse populations, and the continued damage it does to their psyche and self-concept. We learn ways to be anti-racist and dismantle White supremacy. We learn about microaggressions and the importance of social justice advocacy for art therapists and other mental health practitioners and students-in-training, when working with Black and marginalized clients.

In Chapter 4, talking about her Special Study, Dr. Anah shares the results of her dissertation—powerful stories and narratives from African American men who have been subjected to daily racist assaults, and their coping mechanisms. It is something that everyone should read.

Readers of this book will find that Dr. Anah has given us all food for thought, in a way that demands self-reflection as well as healing from racism. This book is a major contribution to the art therapy field, as well as the multicultural/diversity/social justice counseling field, and should be required reading for every art therapist, supervisor, student, researcher and mental health professional looking to improve their cultural competence when working with Black people and other culturally diverse populations. History will remember the things we tried to change in times of great racial struggle, and history will remember Dr. Anah in her efforts to speak out and move the professional of art therapy towards racial, ethnic and cultural awareness, self-reflection and healing.

Preface

There have been very few books by art therapists on the inexhaustible themes of racial trauma, microaggressions and inequality. Anti-racism and anti-Blackness seem to be a sparse area of inquiry in art therapy, yet many of us working in the field of art therapy—professionals, supervisors and students-in-training included—have experienced some of these assaults, and have clients who have also experienced them, sometimes daily. The genesis of this book came from my 2014 dissertation, and a need to hear the voices and stories of Black men who had experienced the trauma caused by racism. No one really likes to confront the issue of anti-Black racism, but we must. As an organization and a people, we cannot be "anti-racist" if we do not work to acknowledge the depth and ubiquitous aspect of anti-Blackness. Anti-Blackness does not always mean White supremacist beliefs, attitudes and behaviors, but also, well-intentioned people, with minimal cultural humility, who feel they do not need to further understand the nuances of Black culture within the context of the power dynamics of the dominant culture. Racial microaggressions are insipid, and understanding their importance as a real and unique source of inquiry, as a way to improve the therapeutic effectiveness of the services we provide culturally diverse clients, is vital.

We cannot get anywhere if there are misleading untruths about the historical narratives surrounding colonialism, slavery and the history of racism, and the fact that native people have suffered significantly from the injustices of colonization—violence, stolen resources, forced assimilation and instability. We cannot get anywhere if states are systematically trying to wipe clean the atrocities of slavery and the origins of racism. Violent acts of human destruction in history that are not recognized and atoned for are bound to repeat themselves.

This book works unapologetically to center an important, yet often overlooked, aspect of art therapy training, practice and research. Racism and White supremacy are in our collective consciousness, and addressing these forces in art therapy requires more scholarship and deeper understanding. This book works in taking action to develop real strategies for learning the history and origins of racism, understanding one's own racial biases and identity, acknowledging others' racial experiences and, with the healing quality of art therapy, beginning the journey of racial healing and finding the way forward. I encourage more conversations around racism and racial trauma in an effort to dismantle its damaging effects and provide more culturally responsive art therapy services, and a just and safe world for clients who are Black, Indigenous, marginalized or from otherwise culturally diverse groups. Healing and understanding are our way forward because *racism hurts all of us.*

Dr. Chioma Anah, Baltimore

Introduction

Racism hurts us all

I can't breathe. Mama, mama, mama, mama.
I can't believe this man. Mom, I love you. I love you.
Mama, I love you. I can't do nothing.
My face is gone. I can't breathe man. Please! Please,
let me stand. Please, Man I can't breathe...
I can't breathe. Ah! I'll probably just die this way...
I can't breathe. Please, I can't breathe. Shit.
I will, I can't move. My knee, my neck.
I'm through, I'm through. I'm claustrophobic.
My stomach hurts. My neck hurts. Everything hurts. I need some
water or something, please, please? I can't breathe officer.
You're going to kill me, man.
Come on, man. Oh, oh. I cannot breathe. I cannot breathe. Ah!
They'll kill me. They'll kill me. I can't breathe. I can't breathe. Oh!
Ah! Ah! Please. Please. Please.

(Last words of George Floyd, 2020, filed in District
Court, State of Minnesota, 7/7/2020)

The United States seems to move from waves of yet another reckoning with anti-Black racism and White supremacy, to long periods of apathy in which most White Americans minimize the existence of racism, particularly anti-Black racism. In May 2020, as the world quarantined and tried to grapple with, and make sense of, the COVID-19 pandemic, we watched in utter shock and horror the video of George Floyd, a Black man, lying face to the ground, pleading and calling out for his mother, while police officer Derek Chauvin's knee was pinned to his neck for 8 minutes and 46 seconds, until he spoke his last words. This murder, broadcast worldwide all over news outlets and social media, sparked protests and civil unrest as cries for social justice and equality for Black lives filled the streets of Minneapolis, other states and nations all over the world. Another unarmed Black American had been murdered by police. In February 2020, we also saw a video of Ahmaud Arbery in Georgia, a Black man, being murdered at the hands of White vigilantes, again fueling mass protests worldwide and demands for change. We also saw videos of the murder of Breonna Taylor (March 13, 2020) by police officers.

However, these events did not mark a turning point, as since June 2020 we have witnessed numerous murders of Black people motivated by White supremacy and racism, specifically anti-Black racism. On Saturday, August 26, 2023, three Black people in Jacksonville, Florida, were assassinated by a 21-year-old White supremacist who "hated Black people," in the words of the local sheriff. These racist murders did not appear in a vacuum, as the dehumanization of Black people, and hateful words and sentiments, deeply rooted in the United States, history of slavery and racism, came first. The killing of Black men and women continues today.

Racism has been defined by Singh (2019) as a system of oppression that places reliance on the beliefs that one race or group is superior to another based on biological and physical characteristics. White supremacy, a key influencer of racism, assumes that *White people* are superior to *Black people* and *people of Color*, an assumption that is completely inaccurate, as no race is greater than another (Singh, 2019). Our world is steeped in racism and anti-Blackness, and the racial reality and worldview of many Black Americans today is that racism is alive and well. This worldview is not without merit when we closely examine the tragic events of murder precipitated by racism in the last decade. The consequences of racism continue to be visible in all facets of American society; of huge concern is how laws, policies and societal norms have been the root of race-based inequality and discrimination. If we as a nation are to rid ourselves of such tragic events, it is important to examine the role of racism, and our ambivalence and inability to compassionately and empathically discuss difference and race openly, honestly and respectfully. This book unabashedly discusses the root cause of racism and injustices and recognizes that sticking to the status quo continues to destroy us. Racism hurts us all.

Art therapy, anti-racism and healing

There is power, both spiritual and therapeutic, in art making. My own healing from daily systemic racism and gender bias, and the death of my dear mother, has, among other healing strategies, been facilitated through the process of art making. I believe that art can be a significant form of hope and healing, so the power of art therapy as a healing tool is not a notion that has been foreign to me. Moon (1994) described art therapy as an effective tool to facilitate therapeutic growth, while Liebmann (2004) posited that art therapy utilizes art to communicate feelings and personal expression, which is available to everyone, with no artistic talent required. Payne (1993) described art therapy as a creative process that focuses on non-verbal communication in which the art therapist works to facilitate a safe environment for their client's emotional expression. According to the American Art Therapy Association (AATA) (2017), art therapy has been used to foster self-esteem, improve cognitive and sensory-motor functions, enhance social skills, improve insight, cultivate emotional resilience, resolve conflicts and distress and advance societal and ecological change. In my practice and professional experience, I have witnessed art therapy stand as a powerful vehicle to promote social justice and advocacy and heal the wounds of those who have been racially, ethnically and culturally oppressed. In times of intense sociopolitical turmoil, art therapists hold a unique role in facilitating healing. The power of art therapy for those who have experienced racial trauma, microaggressions and inequality lies within the idea that art and the creative process allow clients to engage in both personal exploration and self-expression. The actual creation and process of art making can help provide individuals with power, choice and freedom, which are all experiences of agency often lacking in those who have been marginalized in society.

The American Art Therapy Association, founded in 1969, is one of the leading art therapy membership organizations in the world. It is important to note that the field of art therapy is largely populated by cisgender, White, heterosexual women, and largely shaped by both *patriarchal* and *Eurocentric* theories and discourse (Talwar, Iyer & Doby-Copeland, 2004). Elkins and Deaver (2015) report that White art therapists continue to control and influence art therapy history and theory, which negatively affects art therapists, Black clients and clients of Color. This dominant Whiteness limits art therapists in their social skills, self-awareness and ability to engage in meaningful dialogue about racism and oppression with their clients or colleagues (Hamrick & Byma, 2017). Art therapists who reject or deny racism or oppression risk inflicting psychological harm on their Black clients, as well as fail to help their White clients and colleagues achieve racial self-awareness (Hamrick & Byma, 2017).

To successfully work with clients, art therapists and other healing professions must acknowledge the historical influences of oppression, current racist acts and events, and their psychological harm to Black people and people of Color and their communities. Day-Vines *et al.* (2007), in their article regarding the importance of *broaching* with clients, stated, "It is incumbent upon the counselor to recognize the cultural meaning of phenomena assigned by the client and to translate cultural knowledge into meaningful practice that results in client empowerment" (p.402). In addition, White art therapists should have honest discussions about responses and reactions to racism, privilege and oppression. This book encourages art therapists to acknowledge and work on their own bias, as well as develop awareness and skills to assist marginalized clients with enhancing their agency to access and effect change. There also seems to be a dearth of resources and training opportunities regarding Black, Indigenous and other culturally diverse populations, which is harmful to the clients of those communities who seek art therapy. Thus, it is important to understand how art therapy students and practitioners can better foster multicultural, anti-racist, social justice competencies in the effort to dismantle anti-Blackness and eradicate racism. If art therapy is to live up to its definition, art therapists must develop culturally responsive clinical practices, anti-racist values and social justice competencies.

Some art therapy scholars have called for more cultural competency (Awais & Yali, 2013; Gipson, 2015; Talwar *et al.*, 2004; ter Maat, 2011). Despite these calls, art therapy practice still falls short on focusing on anti-racism and White supremacy. When I presented my paper and workshop on racial microaggressions at the 2015 AATA Conference , I learned that I had been the first to concentrate my presentation on the topic of racial microaggression. I have since presented in 2016 and 2018 on racial microaggressions, racism and intersectional identities as they relate to art therapy. I was encouraged to see a paper on microaggressions being presented by Jayashree George, DA, ATR-BC, LMFT, SEP (2023) and a panel on "Art in response to antiracism" by Valicenti *et al.* (2023) at the 2023 AATA Conference in San Diego. Although this is encouraging, more papers, workshops and panels are needed on racial microaggressions, racial trauma, racism, anti-Blackness, White supremacy and art therapy for social justice advocacy.

To counteract the dearth of literature examining multicultural content such as racism, art therapists Charlotte Boston and Gwendolyn Short have also discussed cultural competency, as we will see in Chapter 6. There are a few art therapists today calling for more anti-racist competencies in art therapy. In her article "A colorful canvas," AATA member Louvenia Jackson (2020) discusses the importance of AATA members and practitioners in developing anti-racism work to support their clients. She asks questions of educators, practitioners and members that support an awareness of an anti-racism agenda in art therapy against White supremacy. And in his February 26, 2020, essay "Antiracist approach to art therapy: Re-examining core concepts," American Art Therapy Association member Jordan S.

Potash (2020) reinforces three strategies for art therapists to become more responsive and understanding when working with the culturally diverse. He challenges art therapists to work on developing an anti-racist perspective, to re-examine core art therapy concepts and pursue systemic change.

Art therapists cannot ignore the social and political sources of oppression and the trauma experienced by those with marginalized identities. The counseling and art therapy professions have evolved over the years by recognizing and acknowledging advocacy engagement as an important role for professional counselors. Given our ongoing unsettling social and political climate, it seems fitting that this trend should continue to play a key role in the evolution of the art therapy and other mental health fields. Professional counselors and art therapists stand to gain from familiarizing themselves with some of the salient terminology associated with the social justice advocacy movement. This book does that by also offering a definition of terms at the back of the book. The norms of White supremacy pervade our individual and professional consciousness, resulting in the importance of moving the profession towards a more "culturally responsive" therapy.

The purpose and rationale for this book

Racial relations continue to be tense and most people are cautious about talking about race or disclosing their views and feelings about racism. This book focuses heavily on anti-Black racism and anti-Blackness, given the pervasive multifaceted enactments of violence and hatred directed towards Black people and Black communities. Webster's dictionary defines "inequality" as social disparity and disparity of distribution and opportunity (www.merriam-webster.com, s.v. "inequality"). Black people are systematically cut off from power, privilege and opportunity and denied any legitimacy to occupy space, rendering them invisible. In this book, information is offered that can guide art therapists in working with individuals who are culturally diverse, whose background and life experiences differ from their own. I have offered robust guidance on how to develop anti-racist therapy equipped to heal racial trauma and encourage individuals to engage in their own racial healing. It has been my experience that art making and creativity are ways of gaining understanding of the factors that contribute to racial trauma, which in turn leads to healing and provides the courage to explore what life changes need to be made. I have found that clients sharing their racial trauma and microaggressions through art making feel less intimidated than sometimes telling their stories aloud, as they don't often know how to put the aggression they have experienced into words.

There are several implications for the art therapy profession that can be drawn from this book. The mission of this book is to change the status quo and challenge the discipline of art therapy in tackling anti-Blackness and structural racism, by providing racially responsive services to Black and diverse individuals, families and communities. Art therapy must move towards being an anti-racist field.

The fundamental premises of this book can be enumerated as follows:

1. In a climate where Black history and African American history are being banned from being taught in schools, and diversity, equity and inclusion (DEI) programs are being attacked and cut, it is important to remember our brutal history of colonialism and slavery in order to facilitate a journey of healing.

2. As an effort to increase focus on anti-racism in therapy work, this book challenges the expectations for art therapists to disrupt the White supremacy culture that permeates art therapy theory and practice. It calls for the decolonization of art therapy shaped by theory that is largely Eurocentric and patriarchal. It addresses the knowledge gap of racism in art therapy, fills the void in its literature and practice and provides a new perspective and insight for art therapists to practice from a culture-specific and anti-racist social justice framework.

3. The therapeutic relationship can mimic race relations in the United States, and art therapists are not immune from inheriting racial biases. It is possible that they can unintentionally inflict micro-aggressions on their diverse clients, which can lead to premature therapeutic termination. This book calls for art therapists to develop multicultural competencies and responsiveness, which means an awareness of their own cultural identities, power, privilege, oppression, knowledge and skills in working across cultures (Sue *et al.*, 2019). This book guides art therapists in making it second nature to understand human behavior in a sociopolitical and cultural context.

4. This book works to offer a "best practices" resource that provides models for anti-racism and social justice advocacy that can inform theory and be incorporated into art therapy practice as well as research. It aims to utilize functional frameworks that work in the treatment and empowerment of Black and other culturally diverse clients.

Who this book is for, and ways of using the book

This book is aimed primarily at art therapy students-in-training, practitioners, professionals, educators and others in a wide variety of mental health professions, as well as supervisors providing guidance for working with diverse populations in the therapy field.

It can be used as a textbook for any course that covers multiculturalism, diversity and social justice. In every chapter, there are opportunities, questions and exercises geared towards self-reflectivity, discussion and art making. Instructors and professors can use these sections with their students-in-training for more clarification and practice of knowledge from each corresponding chapter.

Important things to keep in mind when reading this book

- The basic premise of this book is that racism exists, and it is woven into the fabric of the United States and the world.

- In the spirit of choosing words with care, I have chosen to use the term *N-word*, rather than using its full racial epithet in this book. The full word has been used to express hostility, anti-Blackness and racial animus towards Black people. Although some Black people use it interracially, the connotations are different among Black people than when White people direct it towards Black people. When other people use it in their narratives, I have chosen to leave it in to honor the authenticity of their voices.

- Black people in the United States are not a *monolith*. In fact, Eugene Robinson's book, *Disintegration: The Splintering of Black America* (2010), proposes *four Black* groups: (1) The Transcendent, which includes wealthy Blacks like Oprah Winfrey and Michael Jordan; (2) The Abandoned, which includes the underclass; (3) The Emergent, which includes children of parents from the African diaspora, and biracial people, like Barack Obama; and the last group (4) The Black Mainstream, "a middle-class majority with full ownership stake in American society" (Robinson, 2010, p.5). Robinson (2010) goes on to posit, "It was increasingly clear to me that there was not just one Black America—that there were several, and that we had to distinguish among them if we were to talk intelligently about African Americans in the twenty-first century" (p.20).

- There are several complex racial identities and experiences; however, as you will find in this book, I use the terms *Black American/African*

American, and sometimes *people of Color*, and *White people*. The use of *Black* is to reference individuals, people and communities who are Black. You will notice that I use the terms Black American, Black people and African American interchangeably or synonymously—and although this is imperfect, it aims to recognize Black people as a group in society. Please note that this may hold different meaning for individual clients, and as art therapists we must understand how clients self-identify. The term *African* is used to describe a person from the continent of Africa.

- I also sometimes use *Black, Indigenous/Native Alaskan, Asian, Latinx and other non-Black people of Color and/or Black and non-Black people of Color* to acknowledge anti-Blackness and how White supremacy and racism affect those who are not White. I also use *Black people, and other culturally diverse populations*, to sometimes highlight not combining these different communities' experiences into one whole. I do not use the acronym BIPOC (Black, Indigenous and People of Color) in this book. However, I have allowed the term when used by guest narrators.

- I capitalize Color in people of Color, when it is used, because it is a racial and ethnic group of non-White people in the United States. I have sometimes used people of Color in the book to show solidarity among oppressed racially and ethnically minoritized groups.

- Although an unstable social construct, I use the term *White*. You should also notice that I do not use the term *Caucasian* to describe the race of White people. This is an inaccurate term to describe White people. The term Caucasian was used by German Professor Johann Friedrich Blumenbach in 1795 for his favorite skull from the Caucasus Mountains in Russia. He gave the group to which he belonged to as a European the same name as the region of his beloved skull.

- I also use White *EuroAmerican* or *European American* to also describe the race of a White person.

- In this book, I use the term *Latinx* as a gender-inclusive term to refer to Spanish-speaking individuals with ancestry in Mexico, Cuba, Puerto Rico and the Dominican Republic, and to non-Spanish-speaking individuals from South and Central American countries living in the United States.

- I use the term *Asian Americans* to refer to people with origins in Southeast and East Asia, or the Indian subcontinent, with shared ethnic, cultural, linguistic and historical connections who reside in the United States.

- I use *minoritized* rather than *minority* throughout this book to signify that people are not born into a minority status, rather they are rendered minorities due to specific social situations and institutional environments that uphold privilege and White superiority. The term "minority" is seen as a disempowering term.

- I highlight that healing from racism can be achieved through changing your personal and interpersonal interactions, and that action is required for art therapists to be anti-racist.

Obstacles and reactions to learning about racism

Racism is such a difficult topic to talk about and even more complex to write about. No matter what, there will be critics about what is being said or written. If the then President Barack Obama's seemingly non-polarizing and moving speech following the acquittal of George Zimmerman for the murder of Trayvon Martin could garner outrage and a ridiculous backlash because he dared identify with a Black teenager when he was supposed to be the president for ALL Americans (he stated, "when Trayvon Martin was first shot, I said that this could have been my son. Another way of saying that is Trayvon Martin could have been me 35 years ago" (Obama, 2013)), then I understand the zeitgeist and racial tension in which I write this book. I also understand that not everyone will be thrilled in the art therapy community about me pointing out the glaring *ethnocentric monoculturalism* of the field.

Reading this book might be, at times, difficult and uncomfortable, and elicit powerful emotions for many of you. Talking about racism has the capacity to touch hot buttons in all of us and cause cognitive, emotional and behavioral *dissonance* (Sue *et al.*, 2019), and this book is heavy in its unapologetic raising of anti-Black racism and systematic oppression. Many would classify me as a "race baiter," "divisive," even "racist"—which is a distraction from the point of this book. I've heard people say "People like you, who constantly talk about race, are the racist ones" and "You people just wouldn't let something go that happened a long time ago." I say that being honest and holding authentic discussions about race and racism is courageous, and it is okay to feel both positive and negative feelings when reading this book. If you experience any of these emotions, it is extremely important that you lean into those feelings. Recognize and have the courage to explore where you feel resistance and defensiveness. If you are honest, authentic and courageous, you will find that you learn so much about yourself, which will only enhance and enrich your path to becoming a culturally responsive art therapist. As a Black, female professor, who has been tasked to teach a Diversity and Social Justice in Counseling course, I have experienced and encountered students who have exhibited some or all of these resistant behaviors. I have also experienced students being incredible, appreciative of and humbled by what they are learning. I will share some of my students' experiences from my Diversity course in Chapter 8.

One last thought—systemic racism and oppression exist, and success, power and equality are not solely dependent on personal responsibility but are due to systemic and institutional failures that have made it difficult for Black people and other marginalized groups. It is important to stop blaming Black people for conditions that they did not create, and instead ask what you can do to lend a hand. As art therapists and mental health practitioners, the path to becoming more culturally responsive is filled with self-reflexivity and understanding your own biases and the differing worldviews of those with different identities from you. I am asking for all of you to consider this in the spaces in which you practice, making sure therapeutic safety, validation, empowerment and change are central to your work with Black and other culturally diverse clients. Becoming culturally sensitive and responsive is a lifelong process, which requires curiosity and openness to create conditions that maximize the optimal development of the client and client systems, which also facilitate racial healing.

Note: Artwork featured in the book will be available online for readers to download at https://library.jkp.com/redeem using the code CQXSRUU

Chapter 1: Art and Healing

Art can be an effective avenue of communication and expression, especially when words fail in terms of traumatic experiences. Art and creativity are catalysts for conversations about race, coping with individual and collective trauma from racial bias and injustice, healing, understanding, forgiveness, self-awareness and therapy. The visual possibilities inherent in the use of art provide a tangible way to explore race/ethnicity and culture. The spatial character of a drawing, painting or collage can describe many nuances of a person's experience. Art facilitates creativity, it's useful for working with unconscious thoughts and feelings, and it produces a tangible product that can be examined at a later stage, if the client is not ready to process those feelings during that time. This chapter shares the case study of Irene Hendricks (fictional name). It highlights her therapeutic journey of oppression, validating her voice and empowering her, and leading her towards a racial healing path through three of her artworks.

Chapter 2: The History, Origins and Evolution of Racism

It is important to understand that race is an inaccurate social construction to describe who you really are because it is based on other people's perceptions of your race or what it might be. It is also important to understand that racism affects all of us—we all suffer from racism and White supremacy, and we all have the power to change and heal from it. What is racism, anyway? In this chapter, I suggest that in order to define racism, we have to understand its history, the similarities and differences between race and ethnicity, and the evolution today, with the killing of George Floyd, the Black Lives Matter movement, police shootings of Black Americans, the voting rights law, and the ban on teaching African American history by many southern states. There is a brief overview of the history of racism, definitions of racism, the horrors of colonization of many African countries, and a rich and scholarly description of what it was like during the Nigerian civil war from my father, Raphael Anah.

Chapter 3: Microaggressions

Microaggressions are the everyday slights and put-downs, insults and invalidations directed towards groups who are socially devalued by well-intentioned people, who are often unaware that they have engaged in biased or harmful behaviors or unwilling to hear such personal stories of pain and suffering (Sue *et al.*, 2019). Whether it be racism, sexism or homophobia, those in power tend to ignore such uncomfortable topics. This chapter focuses more on racial microaggressions and highlights the psychological damage and physical impact these have on Black people and other culturally diverse populations.

Chapter 4: Special Study: Results and Findings

In this chapter, I share the results of my in-depth individual interview and art-based focus groups from my 2014 qualitative doctoral research study *Experiences of Racial Microaggressions and Coping Skills Among African American Professional Men* (Anah, 2014). Six purposefully selected African American professional men from various disciplines participated in this study and they share their stories, as well as provide a visual representation through collages that address their experiences of racial microaggression and their coping styles. Their names have been changed; however, their narratives and specific quotes have been left verbatim.

Stories wield power and are sacred. The participants' narratives have been shared with full consent. In this study, the participants were given a safe space to share their experiences of discrimination and pain, with validation and affirmations. It was also important for the participants to explore their coping and self-care strategies in this study. They were purposeful in their storytelling, and knew that their personal narratives would provide a greater good to effect change.

This study helps art therapists to understand how racial microaggressions are a constant for African American men, how they can manifest as a presenting problem in therapy, and what there is to learn from a client's racial microaggressions.

Chapter 5: Inequality, Social Justice and Advocacy

This chapter focuses on defining social justice and advocacy. There are case studies (fictional) to illustrate how art therapists can work successfully with diverse clients utilizing a social justice advocacy lens and framework.

Chapter 6: Intersectionality: Black Women in Art Therapy

This chapter looks at the work of Kimberlé Crenshaw, who coined the word "intersectionality" to highlight how people suffer discrimination on several fronts of their intersecting identities. Two seasoned art therapists, Charlotte Boston and Gwendolyn Short, have been very generous in discussing their experiences in their varying positions as professionals in the field of art therapy. They share their experiences as Black women in art therapy, illuminating their struggles and challenges with social barriers, racism and sexism, as well as their unique and transformative ways of coping, surviving and thriving. Strategies for empowerment, success, mentoring, advocacy and professional growth are also shared.

Chapter 7: Theoretical Frameworks for Understanding Racism, and Interventions and Implications for Art Therapy Clinical Practice

This chapter focuses on a combination of theoretical frameworks for understanding and explaining racism, with implications for art therapy clinical practice. The frameworks explored include internalized racial socialization, racial identity models and critical race theory. This chapter also provides clinical considerations and recommendations for art therapists developing cultural responsiveness when practicing with culturally diverse clients.

Chapter 8: Healing and the Way Forward

Although this process works differently, both Black people, other culturally diverse groups and White people internalize racism. How do we all heal from racism? This chapter explores racial healing strategies, and posits a way forward in dismantling racism.

This chapter discusses the importance of allyship and co-conspirators in the fight to dismantle racism. It also highlights resources to enhance racial understanding and healing, as well as featuring artwork and excerpts from my students-in-training and their thoughts about the Diversity course and racial healing.

Chioma Anah

Chapter 1

Art and Healing

In today's climate in our country, which is...riddled with burgeoning racism..., we need art, and we need art in all forms. We need all methods of art to be present, everywhere present, and all the time present.

—MAYA ANGELOU (HANKS, 1990)

FIGURE I.I: "OUR STRUGGLE IS THE STRUGGLE OF A LIFETIME" BY CHIOMA ANAH, © 2018 (MIXED MEDIA ON PAPER, ORIGINAL SIZE: 11" X 14")

This artwork was part of a presentation given at the 49th AATA Conference on November 3, 2018, titled "Still I Rise: Reflections of an Artist's Journey as Social Activist." It was also used in the Winter 2019 publication of The Canadian Art Therapy Association Online Magazine, *ENVISAGE*, titled *Art and Social Activism* (Anah, 2018b). Artwork inspired by John Lewis' Twitter post during the height of the Trump presidency: "Do not get lost in a sea of despair. Be hopeful, be optimistic. Our struggle is not the struggle of a day, a week, or a year, it is the struggle of a lifetime. Never, ever be afraid to make some noise and get in good trouble, necessary trouble" (John Lewis Twitter post, June 27, 2018).

THE HEALING POWER OF ART: THE CASE AND ARTWORK OF IRENE HENDRICKS

Irene Hendricks (a pseudonym) is a 24-year-old African American female of dark skinned complexion, who identifies as a bisexual woman and is able-bodied. Irene has just graduated from a predominantly White university and will be attending the same university for graduate school. She self-referred to my practice three years ago in the second semester of her sophomore year, with a diagnosis of anxiety disorder. At the time of intake, Irene stated, "It's hard to keep up sometimes, and I don't always have a lot of Black people to relate to." She also stated that she felt she had a lot of "pressure" as she felt a sense that she was representing her whole community by becoming a mathematician. Irene was the first female in her family to go to college, and work towards a graduate degree. She stated that her student adviser was a "White man" who "doesn't get me," and had frequently dismissed her concerns.

Six months after her initial visit, the COVID-19 virus changed all our lives and required us all to quarantine. She was now in her junior year, and at this time, class protocols regarding the virus and education had not been solidified, which exacerbated Irene's anxiety. At one point, she wanted to "quit" school and didn't think she could keep up: "there's just too much happening." Her mother had lost her job, and her father had incurred a disability that made it impossible for him to work. She reported being "scared" because she was witnessing people around her get sick and be hospitalized from COVID-19. Her grandmother, who had been struggling with diabetes, subsequently passed away from COVID-19.

When George Floyd was killed, she reported that her anxiety level was exacerbated by the trauma, and she felt compelled to protest. She stated, "It's so upsetting to see time and time again Black people who look like me being handcuffed and getting killed by the very people who are supposed to protect us."

Irene was consumed with excessive worry about her current life circumstances and many sociopolitical traumatic circumstances beyond her control. She was struggling with the uncertainty of the COVID-19 pandemic, the workload of being a junior in college while also dealing with the upheaval of the pandemic, systemic oppression, racial microaggressions and sexism, and the racial trauma associated with the murder of George Floyd.

Multicultural counseling and therapy (MCT) defined

Multicultural counseling and therapy can be defined as both a helping role and a process that uses modalities and defines goals consistent with the life experiences and cultural values of clients; recognizes client identities to include individual, group, and universal dimensions; advocates the use of universal and culture-specific strategies and roles in the healing process; and balances the importance of individualism and collectivism in the assessment, diagnosis, and treatment of client and client systems.

—SUE & TORINO, 2005, P.6

The definition of MCT broadens the roles of mental health practitioners to include teaching, consulting and advocacy—the client is seen not just as an individual, but someone within their systems and culture. This includes utilizing modalities that are consistent with clients' racial, ethnic, cultural, gender and sexual-orientation backgrounds, acknowledging the individual as well as the universal dimensions of diverse clients, and working from a culture-specific framework with diverse clients, which includes looking at intergenerational stress and other culturally relevant concepts.

Art as a healing intervention to personal and social oppression

Art such as painting, drawing, poetry, music and dance is a great tool for personal healing and growth. Participation in the arts has been found to reduce stress, depression and anxiety and assist in the process of healing (Ganim, 1999; McNiff, 2004). As Liebmann (1990) so appropriately stated, "A picture is often a more precise description of feelings than words and can be used to depict experiences which are 'hard to put into words' (p.13). The creative process allows clients to explore their self-expression and gain better understanding of factors contributing to their stressors (Chambala, 2008; Liebmann, 1990). Expression, in the form of creating color and design, is often more advantageous than just depending on words when communicating (Liebmann, 1990). For decades, artists have reflected on the social ills of their times through their art and poetry. Artists are observers, social critics of the world around them; they are natural agents of change, particularly in times of great unrest and turmoil (Anah, 2018a). Throughout history, art has been utilized as a tool to communicate and raise awareness of the injustices and inequalities of the world and effect positive social change. Many artists have called for racial and social change, as I have stated in past publications:

Artists like Adrian Piper were calling out racial oppression, and other artists like Favianna Rodriguez who produces art to highlight the immigrant justice movement, or Kerry James Marshall, a great storyteller, whose paintings show what it means to be Black in America, highlighting Black stereotypes, and boldly advocating for racial and social change and justice. (Anah, 2018a)

From my experiences as an art therapist, practitioner and educator, I have witnessed the process of art and creativity being a catalyst for conversations about race, coping with individual and collective trauma from racial bias and injustice, healing, understanding, forgiveness, self-awareness and therapy. I have shared my journey regarding racial oppression and healing through seminal pieces from my artwork, in presentations at the American Art Therapy Association Conferences: Still I rise: Reflections of an artist's journey as social activist (2018b) and Baltimore Uprising/Freddie Gray: An artist's creative journey towards clarity and healing (2016b). I have created work that intersects with sociopolitical activism and causes (Figure 1.1). As an art therapist, I have leaned on an approach that is client-centered, trauma-informed, feminist and oriented towards social justice and advocacy for clients. Art and creativity are also important to the portrayal of human experiences, as they relate to race-related stress and anxiety. Art making has the ability to make the invisible visible, and generate healing through its process. I have found that art making can be used as a vessel for empowerment, as a way to lift up the community, society and people. It is important to remember that the process of art making requires self-reflection, which is the cornerstone of art psychotherapy.

As a practitioner, I have found that when trauma disrupts one's personal life, art can be used as a tool to process the trauma and work towards healing, which makes art therapy an important treatment modality to foster resilience and change. Using these approaches, I worked with Irene, through the process of her artwork, to voice her experiences of racism, to explore her fears and anxiety about societal upheaval that impacted her well-being and those of her loved ones, to validate her narratives involving her intersectional identities (Black, female, bisexual), to examine her responses to her racial trauma, and to build a sense of power, agency and action that also led to healing in a safe therapeutic environment. I made sure Irene felt validated and "seen" in our therapeutic work.

The following three art pieces presented here are a reflection and social commentary on Irene's experiences as a Black, bisexual woman with systemic oppression, racial microaggressions and sexism; her struggles during the COVID-19 pandemic and her response to the killing of George Floyd; and the consequences of historical racism. Irene also shared her observations about the daily injustices suffered by individuals, groups and communities living on the margins of society. The materials used in these pieces were chosen by Irene and included poster board, watercolor paints and Crayola watercolor paints; the size of each artwork is 8" x 10".

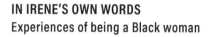

IN IRENE'S OWN WORDS
Experiences of being a Black woman

My experience as a Black woman has been filled with ups and downs and many challenges. Yes, there's a uniqueness attached to being Black and bisexual and feeling like part of a company; however, it has been very difficult.

Being a Black woman, I have been stereotyped by society as being constantly angry, unpredictable and irrational, like I might snap at any time. I don't really talk very much about being bisexual—I'm still trying to figure that out, but there are some things here in this picture. This is the reason I picked red to depict my body in the picture and show what the world sees when they see me—angry. The spats of red, green, orange and yellow around me are the various events in my life experience as well as some rainbow colors for being bisexual. Some of those colors represent both happiness and excitement, as well as some anger at times. Those spats of color and events in my life are represented in my painting above my shoulders because I try to keep everything at eye level; however, sometimes the events I face are above me and catch me off guard.

My hair is purple because in Africa that color is the symbol of royalty, bright and noticeably different from all the other colors I use—because I wear it as a crown exposing my curls to the world.

The background below my shoulders is darker than the background above me because I feel there is just so much uncertainty in front of me that it grows darker and darker than the events that have already happened around me. I wear the darkness on my shoulders to be prepared for what may happen in the future, which constantly is on my mind.

Based on my skin color and my dark skin tones, I have painted my mouth as prominent but crossed shut, to defy the stereotypes of being a "loud Black woman." I'm still trying to find my own voice and not perpetuate the stereotype like the one society has already placed on me. The Black mark on my chest over my heart represents the uncertainty and sadness I have inside me, because of the fear I have in becoming what they are trying to make me be. I am trying my best to hold it together and not succumb to the ever-growing emotions that I try unsuccessfully to keep at bay.[1]

Experience as a Black woman during the time of COVID-19

COVID for me was hard and life-changing; I lost my grandmother to COVID within the first month of the pandemic. It was devastating and I coped horribly; unless you were my bed, TV, liquor or my two friends that I was together with before the pandemic started, then my

---

1   All images are available to view in color online: please visit https://library.jkp.com/redeem

world was empty and off limits to everything else. I was closed off, I was lost, and paid no real attention to things still going on around me. I didn't feel like myself. The gray at the bottom of the picture symbolizes that. My isolation didn't stop the world from changing around me, and in the picture, there is a big red thick line to symbolize the differences between my mindset and what was happening around me. I could see through social media that unless you had money, or your skin tone was five shades lighter than mine, then your life was going to be terrible during the pandemic. I could see that there were other people, mostly White, who had it made, the stars and the moon still shined around them, and their lives weren't changing as dramatically as mine was. Then you had people who looked like me, who had sadness, anger, confusion and anxiety visible all over them due to their daily struggles, with no way of leaving or escaping where they were.

On the right side of my painting, you see how empty the outside is, and the arrows at the bottom are still directions we still have to follow when we go out. Everything is bare, although people need human contact, but the yellow arrows again are giving us directions that human contact is not allowed. The rainbow lights in the upper-level right corner, on top of the building, are on a newer floor of the building, and it is the only one with the lights on and those in that building are the privileged few who can party and live their lives as if nothing has happened. It is night time and the moon is lighting up the way for those who are isolated—there is some hope. In the red building on the right, where the isolated people are, there is the blue window on the left of the house representing sadness, the darker red of the house representing anger and the gray representing confusion and anxiousness.

The George Floyd killing, black man dying, police brutality during COVID-19—and healing

The George Floyd killing, Black men dying and police brutality during COVID-19 showed me the faultiness of my educational upbringing regarding race and racism. I was taught to be okay with the fact that people who looked like me went through daily racism and trauma. I have since learned that this is not okay and extremely wrong. Slavery was very wrong, and I acknowledge that on the left side of my artwork.

The events that took place during COVID-19 made me step out of the false information I learned at school and follow this yellow brick road to the Truth about racism. In the picture, you see me walking towards the yellow brick road. Along the road are people who don't look like me, who are friends and allies, who understand the importance of their voice, the importance of laws and how they affect us Black people every day of our lives.

My ancestors were not slaves who came to America, but people turned into slaves for the benefit of others. Most importantly, along this road is the knowledge that Black Lives Matter, which means that our lives are just as important as the people who don't look like us and don't have to deal with the problems that we face daily.

Again, I'm in the picture wearing a black shirt because I'm a proud blank canvas ready to learn along the road. My hair is purple to symbolize my royal ancestry of Africa. My eyes are bright white to symbolize them being wide open to see the truth along this path of knowledge and understanding.

Irene's work and the therapeutic process

Ghiselin (1952) suggests that the creative process is the process of change, of development, of evolution, particularly in times of extreme emotional pain and world crisis, and that creating requires attention during times of disaster and pain. There were racial and cultural factors that contributed to Irene's pain that needed examining. Black people living in the United States are not monolithic. As a Black, female, cisgender clinician, I may have shared some of the same racial experiences with Irene as a Black woman but I did not presume to understand her exact experiences due to our age difference, cultural upbringing, socioeconomic status and other identities, nor her experiences as a bisexual woman. As Irene's art therapist, it was important for me to be aware of my own assumptions and biases, understand Irene's worldview and her community, as well as find appropriate interventions for Irene's presenting problems, and to be a culturally competent and responsive therapist. In their textbook *Counseling the Culturally Diverse*, Sue *et al.* (2019) define cultural competence as:

> a lifelong process in which one works to develop the ability to engage in actions or create conditions that maximize the optimal development of client and systems. Multicultural counseling competence is aspirational and consists of counselors acquiring awareness, knowledge, and skills needed to function effectively in a pluralistic democratic society (ability to communicate, interact, negotiate, and intervene on behalf of clients from diverse backgrounds), and on an organizational/societal level, advocating effectively to develop new theories, practices, policies, and organizational structures that are more responsive to all groups. (p.39)

In the American Counseling Association (ACA)'s Multicultural and Social Justice Counseling Competencies (MSJCC) (Ratts *et al.*, 2016), it is suggested that counselors must engage in social justice action on both an individual and a systemic level as well as be aware of their biases, values and stereotypes. They must acknowledge the worldview of their client, consider the cultural context of the client and how this might affect the client-therapist relationship, as well as develop appropriate interventions to work with their diverse clients that are rooted in social justice and advocacy (Ratts *et al.*, 2016). The American Art Therapy Association' (AATA)'s (2013) *Ethical Principles for Art Therapists* includes a detailed section on Art Therapy Multicultural and Diversity Competence (Principles 7.0–7.7). Talwar (2015) suggested that a social justice vision should be central to art therapy services. It was important to Irene's therapeutic process to develop the appropriate interventions to help her with her presenting problems. It was also important to discuss race and ethnicity with Irene during the counseling process—did the center of focus reside in her experiences of microaggressions, her fear and the loss she was feeling around her during COVID-19, or her desire to protest the injustices and inequity of Blacks/African Americans following the death of George Floyd? What changes were needed at an institutional level for Irene to feel "seen" and develop a balanced perspective between her and her school? How could I assist Irene with challenging the status quo and prevailing beliefs of the institution? Knowing that institutions are very powerful entities, how could I empower Irene to challenge the system with minimal punitive action? I also needed to find more effective long-term solutions for Irene.

Introduction and assessment

Irene came in for therapy due to anxiety regarding racial and social issues outside her control that she couldn't make sense of. Her mental health problem seemed to have escalated at an alarming rate during the COVID-19 pandemic, and had worsened after the death of her grandmother, the tragic killing of George Floyd, and the racial and social justice unrest in the country. The country was, and still is, experiencing a great degree of stress and trauma, and Irene was experiencing a loss of community and stability in many areas of her life. Irene was also dealing with emotional pain from her experiences of being a Black woman and a bisexual woman. It was important for me to honor the frameworks she brought into the session, and work to incorporate them in the therapeutic process. According to Sue *et al.* (2019), it is important for therapists to be *emic* and *culturally responsive* as they work to consider the cultural context in which the therapy is occurring. In my work with Irene, I was aware of my cultural realities as well as her own.

In a 2018 article in the Counselors for Social Justice newsletter, "Art therapy and social justice intersectionality: Interview with Dr. Chioma Anah and Molly Watkins," I explain how art therapy can be impactful with clients experiencing cultural and racial oppression:

> It is very important for art therapists to understand social structures that give power to others and oppress others. Also, to fully understand their biases so that they are careful not to silence the voices of their marginalized clients. I hold the unique position of being both an art therapist and a professional counselor. Art therapists truly hold a unique position to facilitate healing with clients experiencing racial microaggressions, oppression and marginalization. I have the unique position as an art therapist and a professional counselor to help facilitate healing with clients faced with systemic, historical, and racial trauma. (Anah, 2018a)

Art making was utilized as an intervention to process Irene's anxiety and racial trauma, over a period of six weeks in the confines of my private practice office. Irene attended one 90-minute session per week. Each session was conducted in a similar format, following the initial intake session, assessment, informed consent, diagnosis and case conceptualization, and of course rapport building with the client. Informed consent provided Irene with information regarding the course of therapy before she committed to treatment, which also consisted of reviewing and signing a consent to present or publish the case. Irene also reviewed and signed an additional consent for her and her work to be included in this book. We also discussed the art-making process as a therapeutic tool and talked about any questions, including expectations and any possible feelings this process might release.

There is great diversity among Black people, and African Americans are not monolithic. I worked to assess Irene's values and her feelings about mental health treatment, and explore how she viewed her problems and whether she saw any resolutions to those problems. As a clinician, I chose to recognize Irene's race, ethnicity and cultural background, but also other variable and social identities such as her gender, bisexuality, educational achievements and social class, while making genuine connections and building therapeutic rapport.

Broaching: Race, ethnical and cultural exploration

Broaching with the client was also conducted in the first session. Day-Vines *et al.* (2007) coined the term broaching:

> To refer to the counselor's ability to consider the relationship of racial and cultural factors to the client's presenting problem, especially because these issues might otherwise remain unexamined during the counseling process. (p.401)

Broaching is an effort by the art therapist to explore the complexities of race, ethnicity and culture with the client. In essence, as an art therapist, I deliberately and intentionally made efforts to discuss those racial, ethnic and cultural (REC) concerns that might impact Irene's presenting problems; failure to broach the client's REC concerns effectively could sabotage the therapeutic relationship (Day-Vines *et al.*, 2007).

Broaching was used on an ongoing basis, in this case to help strengthen the therapeutic process to acknowledge racial, ethnic, cultural and other differences between the client and the therapist and help build therapeutic rapport, as well as respond to the sociopolitical and sociocultural concerns of the client during treatment (Day-Vines *et al.*, 2007). I shared with Irene that I am a Black, cisgender, heterosexual woman who is able-bodied and from an upper-middle socioeconomic status background living in America, with a different upbringing, but some shared racial experiences. Here is an example of my broaching style with Irene (some parts adapted from Day-Vines *et al.*, 2020).

- I am a Black, cisgender, heterosexual woman. How do you feel about working with someone like me?

- Although we are both Black women, and we may have some experiences in common, I do not assume that our experiences are completely the same. We do not share the same ethnic backgrounds and upbringing and we are from different age groups and generations.

- If at any point you feel that I have misunderstood you in any way, I want you to feel comfortable enough to let me know. I promise to do the work in understanding more clearly those parts of your identity that are different from mine.

- I want you to feel comfortable in sharing your racial, ethnic and cultural experiences.

- I wonder if you'd like to describe what your experiences have been as a Black woman, and the first person in your family to graduate from college, and now to go on to graduate school?

Such questions and awareness showed that I was interested in Irene as a racial being, and I was interested in exploring her experiences. Broaching with Irene was an ongoing process throughout therapy. Irene was immediately at ease and told me that she was comfortable with me as her therapist and she was glad that I was able to broach the subject of racial and cultural factors with her, as her former therapist did not, which made her question her credibility and competence. Irene stated that she never returned to her former therapist after the first session. Irene reported that she felt safe and able to disclose her racial issues with me. She also reported feeling empowered during the therapeutic process. Additionally, Day-Vines *et al.* (2020) proposed the Multidimensional Model of Broaching Behavior (MMBB) to describe the specific context in which counselors broach, which is not just exclusive to issues of racism and discrimination. I was able to set the tone and climate of the therapeutic space for Irene to openly share about several other topics and issues in her life. The MMBB dimensions are 1. intra-counseling, 2. intra-individual, 3. intra-racial, ethnic and cultural, and 4. inter-racial, ethnic and cultural (Day-Vines *et al.*, 2020). For instance, I used all four broaching dimensions with Irene on an ongoing, dynamic and fluid way during the sessions:

1. *Intra-counseling dynamics:* I explored our differences and acknowledged that I would not always understand her experiences.

2. *Intra-individual dynamics:* I explored her multiple social identities—mainly her race, gender and sexual orientation—and there was an integration of her intersectional identities.

3. *Intra-racial, ethnic and cultural issues:* I explored issues she presented with people with whom she shared a common heritage but had different values and personal beliefs. In this instance, Irene shared about one of her Black male friends who had different values surrounding the lesbian, gay, bisexual, trans, queer, questioning, intersex, asexual

and more identities (LGBTQIA+) community and frequently made derogatory and negative comments about them, which made it difficult for her to share her own sexuality with him.

4. *Inter-racial, ethnic and cultural issues:* We discussed issues between her and people from other racial, ethnic or cultural groups. Here I facilitated discussions regarding racism and discrimination, including racial microaggressions, inequality and her experiences of oppression as well as institutional racism. In addition, we discussed social justice advocacy interventions, such as acknowledging Irene's experiences, working on empowerment to gain control over her life, identifying strategies for combating oppression, and providing resources to facilitate change (Ratts *et al.*, 2016). Further, I was able to use individual art therapy efforts with advocacy interventions in order to disrupt institutional racist barriers that impacted her life.

Locus of control and locus of responsibility

We explored Irene's *locus of control* and *locus of responsibility* within the reality of her racial experiences and sociopolitical realities. In her locus of control, we looked to see her internal control (IC), which refers to the belief that reinforcements are contingent on our own actions and that we can shape our fate. Or external control (EC) refers to the belief that reinforcing events occur independently of our actions and the future is determined more by chance and luck (Sue *et al.*, 2019). Locus of responsibility was the degree of responsibility or blame placed on the individual (internal R) or system (external R). Blame on an individual allows for the effects of the system, especially for minoritized clients, to be overlooked or not considered in counseling (Sue *et al.*, 2019). Irene reported that she had an internal locus of control (IC) and external locus of responsibility (ER). She believed she was able to shape events in her own life if given a chance. She did not accept the idea that their present state was due to their own inherent weakness. She was realistic about the challenges and external barriers of discrimination. She participated in the George Floyd protest and other activism protests, and stressed her racial identity. She had pride in her racial and cultural identity.

Art work and process

We had processed her initial thoughts and feelings surrounding her anxiety and experiences of microaggressions in school, and her problems regarding family life. Week three began the art-making sessions. We had discussed art making, its therapeutic qualities and any concerns she would have pertaining to the process during the initial and assessment stage, and we also discussed it again. Regarding Irene's choice of art materials, although she was familiar with basic art supplies and techniques, I did not want her to get overwhelmed with several art media options. Instead, I kept the materials simple and limited and gave her the option to choose the art material she wanted. She used poster board, watercolor paints and Crayola watercolor paints. She noted that she liked how "fluid" the materials were, which, she stated, helped her work "flow with my thoughts." Irene found it more natural to transfer her emotions onto her painting with her chosen art media. The main goals of the session were to listen to Irene's experiences as a Black woman, and to communicate through the process of art making. The art directive was to create an image about her experiences as a Black woman and bisexual woman. After spending 20–30 minutes creating the artwork, Irene was asked to share her image, and a discussion of her painting and experiences followed. For homework, Irene was asked to write about her experiences and the artwork created.

In week four, the session was conducted in a similar format, but the directive was to create an image of her experiences during COVID-19, with homework. During this session, Irene also processed the death of her grandmother, and homework included writing about her grandmother. Week five was similar again; however, the directive was to create an image reflecting her reactions and responses to the killing of George Floyd. Homework was given to journal about her experiences and the artwork created in the session. In week six, we processed the homework given. Irene's work and narrative were thought provoking, inspirational and healing for her, and served as an emotional educational intervention regarding her experiences with racism and the collateral damage of COVID-19. Throughout her sessions, Irene was provided with racially affirmative therapy, keeping in mind the need for healing in my therapeutic approach. In the sessions, I assisted Irene with developing self-knowledge, strength, resistance and ability for critical consciousness. I worked to teach her new and positive coping strategies to deal with her presenting problems. I also validated and normalized Irene's reactions to her experiences of sexism, racism and oppression.

Therapy with the culturally diverse, and the Trump administration's contributions to oppression and fear

There are some unique challenges in group differences when working with marginalized populations. Sue *et al.* (2019) caution us to recognize that "multiculturalism" and "diversity" are broad terms that include race, gender, class and many other sociodemographic groups in our society in order to validate the visibility and uniqueness of a group, and there are unique histories and challenges affecting each group. Sue *et al.* (2019) report:

> It is critical when counseling diverse clientele, you actively work to avoid succumbing to stereotypes... Instead, your task is to develop an in-depth understanding of each client, taking into consideration their unique personal background and worldview. By doing this, you will be in a position to develop an individually tailored treatment plan that effectively addresses presenting problems in a culturally sensitive manner. (pp.282–283)

It is imperative that European American art therapists address race with Black clients and clients of Color, and listen and validate their narratives and experiences of racism. Granello and Wheaton (1998) and Day-Vines *et al.* (2007) suggest that not broaching the subject of race and culture can force a dominant cultural standard on minoritized clients. Art therapists must explore the extent to which racism affects a client's life experience, and maintain ongoing broaching throughout the therapy process (Day-Vines *et al.*, 2007). To avoid early termination and to recognize the nuances about race and culture assigned to a culturally diverse client, White art therapists must provide a safe environment for their clients, built on trust and validation, which works to empower the client. Recognizing that there are cultural differences across geographic areas, here I offer a few strategies for working with the Latinx population, Asian Americans and Native Americans, Indigenous people, and Alaska Natives.

It is fair to state that, in 2016, when Donald Trump was elected President of the United States, he proceeded to unleash racist and xenophobic rhetoric and gave permission to other people who supported and followed him to be outwardly racist about a myriad of different groups in society. His racist rhetoric and policies continue to affect us, and we will be dealing with them for decades to come. According to Human Rights Watch (2017):

> The election of Donald Trump as president in November 2016 capped a campaign marked by misogynistic, xenophobic, and racist rhetoric and Trump's embrace of policies that would cause tremendous harm to vulnerable communities, contravene the United States' core human rights obligations, or both. (p.633)

As President, Trump continued his verbal assaults; he has called Muslims "criminals" and "rapists," fought to build a wall to separate Mexico from neighboring states and kept minors inhumanely separated from their adult parent or relative, according to Human Rights Watch (2017). Trump was no supporter of Obama's Deferred Action for Childhood Arrivals (DACA) program, which would allow children brought by their parents or guardians illegally to the United States, known as "dreamers," to avoid deportation. While in office, Trump labeled the entire continent of Africa and its countries as "shitholes." O'Keefe and Gearan (2018) in their article in *The Washington Post* stated:

> In responding to President Donald Trump's controversial statements about immigrants from Haiti and African countries, United Nations human rights spokesman Rupert Coville said in a briefing in Geneva "There is no word one can use but 'racist.' You cannot dismiss entire countries and continents as 'shitholes,' whose entire populations, who are not White, are therefore not welcome." (para 9)

Trump, instead, wanted the United States to seek immigrants from countries like "Norway" rather than from Mexico or Africa (O'Keefe & Gearan, 2018). The Trump administration's approach and attitude towards immigrants from non-White countries, DACA, refugees and its general anti-Black immigration policies have continued to evoke fear and uneasiness within the immigrant communities all over the United States (Sue *et al.*, 2019). It is highly unlikely that immigrants will report abuse or crime or even seek therapy based on their immigrant status. When immigrants or refugees seek therapy, art therapists will have to take on several roles that will include assisting to advocate for their client in areas of healthcare, employment, education and mental health services, in addition to working with them regarding *acculturation* issues, family dynamics and language barriers.

Kuhlberg, Pena and Zayas (2010) posit that the family unit and maintaining interpersonal relationships within the family are central to the Latin American culture. Issues affecting Latinx individuals and families include language barriers, lack of acculturation, and conflicting views about the roles and expectations of family members (Baumann, Kuhlberg & Zayas, 2010), immigration, spiritual and religious values, poverty, inadequate housing, food and fear of deportation. Art therapists will encounter individuals and family members dealing with isolation and depression (Santiago-Rivera *et al.*, 2008). Art therapy techniques such as collages that utilize family portraits and photos are helpful in addressing issues of identity and heritage, and encourage cultural esteem and pride (Mauro, 1998). Assessment of the acculturation level of the client and family members and possible referral to a Spanish-speaking therapist will be important for the provision of culturally appropriate treatment.

During the COVID-19 pandemic, which was devastating for humanity, Donald Trump called the virus the "China" virus. The singling out of China contributed to an environment in which an increase in domestic terrorism and hate crimes against Asian people occurred. This included a series of shootings that left six Asian women dead in Georgia (Reja, 2021).

> A new study suggests that former President Donald Trump's inflammatory rhetoric around the coronavirus, which is believed to have originated in China, helped spark anti-Asian Twitter content and "likely perpetuated racist attitudes." The Asian American community has experienced a striking rise in incidents of hate since the onset of COVID-19, according to officials and advocates, and critics say the former president's repeated use of "China Virus" and other terms helped fuel an environment of hatred. (Reja, 2021)

With Asian Americans, art therapists must be aware of the stressors and pain regarding the increase of hate crimes caused by information stating that the COVID-19 virus originated in China in late December 2019, with Wuhan being the epicenter of the pandemic (Ahmadi *et al.*, 2020). Hate crimes against Asian Americans have escalated since 2020, particularly in cities like New York and Los Angeles (Yam, 2021). Effective art therapy techniques used in working with Asian American clients have included collage and image making (Yates *et al.*, 2007).

With Native Americans, Indigenous people and Alaskan Natives, art therapists must be aware of the historical root of their problems that involve stolen land and resettlement, genocide, social injustice and colonialism. Art therapists should become familiar with key books referring to working with Native Americans, Indigenous people and Alaskan Natives, including *Healing the Soul Wound: Trauma-informed Counseling for Indigenous Communities* by Eduardo Duran (2019). In my work, I recognize their continued resiliency and hope for the future. I express gratitude, and honor them and the land we presently occupy. Here is my land acknowledgment recognizing the United States' brutal history and legacy of colonialism.

> I want to acknowledge that the land that I now occupy, the United States of America, was the original home and traditional territory of Indigenous peoples and many more tribal nations, some of which no longer exist.
>
> I recognize the barbaric brutalization of Indigenous/Native people, including the killings, raping, genocide and separation of families, and the stealing, occupation and claiming of their land. The history and legacy of slavery and colonialism are shameful, and I acknowledge the generations of forced labor and exploitation of people that helped build and establish the United States.
>
> I honor the lives and the land of Indigenous, enslaved and immigrant people and recognize their loss and resilience. I commit to honor them and

create a future that is founded on gratitude, hope, respect and justice for all people, as I work towards healing the wounds of injustice. (Anah, 2023)

Summary

Art, used as an intervention tool in art therapy, has the power to facilitate change and assist the healing process for clients who have experienced trauma and oppression. Multiculturalism in the field of mental health has had a renaissance in the past decade given our current sociopolitical climate, which has disproportionally affected marginalized and minoritized groups. Like any other helping professionals, art therapists are expected to be aware of these social changes. More and more culturally diverse clients are having the same experiences as Irene, and art therapists have the unique opportunity and responsibility to provide a safe space for them to process pain and empower them. Broaching becomes an important way to build rapport and create a pathway for honest and meaningful dialogue about clients' experiences with racism and social injustices. Cultural sensitivity requires ongoing training and practice, supervision, consultation and research as more information and literature are needed on appropriate ways for art therapists to work with culturally diverse clients. Art therapists should make lifelong commitments to address individual, institutional and societal injustices and be aware of our own biases that may unintentionally discriminate against others/our clients. By listening, validating Irene's racial trauma experiences and facilitating ways to enhance agency and power, I was able to help Irene to work successfully on healing her racial traumas and move towards altering her systems.

QUESTIONS ABOUT IRENE'S WORK

1. How do you think the race and culture of both Irene and me (the therapist) impacted on the process, product and relationship within the therapeutic dynamics?

2. What were some of the striking images in Irene's work? What does Irene's work say about her use of images, color and language?

3. Exploring the nature of Irene's artwork, what invisible attribute of her racial trauma did she make visible in her work?

4. What other racial traumas and experiences of inequality need to be processed with Irene?

5. What were some of Irene's personal coping strategies both in her work and her narrative?

6. What is Irene's racial healing prognosis?

DISCUSSION QUESTIONS

1. Is Irene exaggerating or being oversensitive or paranoid in her experiences of how difficult it is to be a Black woman? A bisexual Black woman?

2. Although both client and therapist were Black women, why was broaching important?

3. As an art therapist of your race, how would you broach with Irene?

4. How would an art therapist work with a client with an external locus of control and an external locus of responsibility? What types of counseling interventions may be helpful for this type of client? How does this relate to race and racial identity?

5. How would an art therapist work with a client with an internal locus of control and internal locus of responsibility?

6. If you were an art therapist, how would you address this case?

7. As an art therapist, what would be your first focus for this case?

8. What art therapy techniques would you use with Irene? For what?

9. What information is missing in this case study?

COMMUNICATION STYLES

• Does your communication style reveal your stereotypes, biases, values and assumptions?

• Does your non-verbal communication style reflect your fears and stereotypes about your client's racial group?

• Does your therapeutic style help or hinder your ability to work with a culturally diverse client?

ART AND HEALING EXERCISE

Materials: Paper, paints, collage images, decorative items, fabric, yarn, glitter, tissue paper, markers, pencils, crayons, colored paper, colored pencils, magazines, scissors, glue.

Purpose: Awareness and healing.

Reflections and art-making response:

1. Reflect and respond to three major events that have occurred in your life in the past three years that require processing.

2. Reflect and respond to two sociopolitical or social injustices of your times.

3. Understanding that social injustice benefits no one and hurts all of us, reflect and respond to your thoughts about art therapists being social change agents by being involved in addressing issues of racism in order to improve the mental health of communities at large.

4. Reflect and respond to ways you would broach a session with a culturally diverse client, if you were a White art therapist?

5. In order to be culturally competent, it is important for the art therapist to develop an understanding of culturally diverse groups and develop skills that facilitate culture-specific therapeutic responses (Sue *et al.*, 2019). Reflect on some of your strategies for working with these groups in the United States: African Americans, White Americans, Indigenous/Native Americans, Latinx and Asian. Use the art process to express your response.

6. Create an art piece that reflects your experiences during the COVID-19 pandemic. What have you learned about your personal resilience? How has what you have learned about yourself improved your understanding of marginalized clients?

7. Reflect and respond to ways you can heal others after your own healing journey. Use the art process to express your response and journey.

Chapter 2

The History, Origins and Evolution of Racism

Racism defined

Although founded on the principles of equality and justice, the United States continues to be overshadowed by the consequences of slavery, as racism persists in permeating the very fabric of its society (Bell, 1992; Jones, 1997). Racism can be defined as the practice of racial discrimination through individual behaviors and societal and structural/institutional policies directed towards another race composed of beliefs about racial superiority and inferiority (Jones, 1997). Some of these institutional policies permeate everyday decisions made towards African Americans and perpetrate racial and gender inequalities for Black people and other minoritized groups. Mills (2017) favors this definition of racism:

> Racism is the belief that (i) humanity can be divided into discrete races, and (ii) these races are hierarchically arranged, with some races superior to others. The second would then refer to institutions, practices, and social systems that illicitly privilege some races at the expense of others, where racial membership (directly or indirectly) explains this privilege. (p.4)

Harper (2012), along with Jones (2000) and Harrell (2000), defines racism as:

> individual actions—both intentional and unconscious—that engender marginalization and inflict varying degrees of harm on minoritized persons; structures that determine and cyclically remanufacture racial inequality; and institutional norms that sustain White privilege and permit the ongoing subordination of minoritized persons. (p.10)

In much the same way, Pierce (1975) characterized racism as a public and mental illness that perpetrated the false belief that one's inferiority correlated with one's dark skin color. Franklin and Boyd-Franklin (2000) stated, "Racism gives permission to disregard or devalue those attributes that do not reflect their privileged status and to be reactive to those that pose a threat to them" (p.35). Delgado (1984) also reported that minoritized people view racism as "including instructional components that extend far beyond lynch mobs, segregated schools, or epithets like ['N-word'] or 'spick'" (p.571).

Singh (2019) defined racism as "a system of oppression that relies on beliefs that one race or group is superior to another based on biological characteristics, like skin color, facial features, and hair," with White supremacy being the key influencer to that ideology. Legal scholar Frances Lee Ansley (1989) defined White supremacy as a "political, economic and cultural system in which Whites overwhelmingly control power and material resources, and in which White dominance and non-White subordination exists across a broad array of institutions and social settings" (p.993). White supremacy is embedded in the 1787 Constitution of the United States, as Article 1, Section 2 asserts that enslaved Blacks could be counted as three-fifths of the number of White residents in a state for the purposes of Congressional representation (U.S. Constitution, Article 1, Section 2). White dominance and supremacy exist throughout the Western world. In his writings, Thomas Jefferson, prior to his change of heart and ultimate freeing of the slaves, proposed slaves as inferior and subhuman, lacking in intellect and incapable of deep or complex emotion, "their griefs are transient." He stated, "I advance it therefore as a suspicion only that the blacks, whether originally a distinct race, or made distinct by time and circumstances, are inferior to the whites in the endowments both of body and mind" (Jefferson, 1787/1954, p.143). Jefferson, for fear of retaliations from the slaves, proposed that they be deported back to Africa following their emancipation (Magnis, 1999).

Racism devalues, demeans and disadvantages African Americans and people of Color by treating them as second-class citizens and denying them equal access to opportunity (Sue *et al.*, 2019). The following quote gives you an idea of what it is like to live as an African American man in a society filled with daily covert and direct racist acts.

TOM REDD'S STORY

Being Black in America feels like a unique, unpredictable and chronic condition. I don't really think White people have an idea about what it is like to be a Black man and be constantly assessed and challenged just because of the way you look. I feel like based on the daily assaults we suffer, we've somehow inherited a culture where our life expectancy is short, and we are ravaged by chronic diseases and poor coping skills. Even as a professional, with all my education, every day it is something:

discrimination, racism, stereotypes and microaggressions. We now have "Karens" using "Black man" as a weapon, to continue the cycle of criminalization. And let me not start with our relationship with the police. The maltreatment is exhausting, and I'm often left feeling angry and sad. The racism is not even just from individual White folks, but the policies, and new laws are really taking us down. I don't know...it seems like a whole conspiracy to take you down or keep you at a level where you can be controlled. Every day, I deal with racist acts. There is no break from being Black. It's something, every single day. I really do want to feel hopeful, but I don't know. It's bleak out there.

There are multiple and competing definitions of racism that include individual, institutional, hostile and *aversive* racism (Carter, 2007; Dovidio & Gaertner, 2000). For the purposes of this book, I define racism in three parts:

1. As the unequal treatment, devaluing of human rights, denial of access and opportunities, violent attacks and actions by individuals, systems, institutions and society on Black and marginalized people.

2. Based and motivated by untrue racial stereotypes of inferiority rooted in slavery and White supremacy—both subtle and covert.

3. Causes significant harm and trauma to the psyche and self-esteem of Black people and people of Color.

In addition, racism is costly to White people in power (Spanierman *et al.*, 2008). I know that the cost of racism in no way is comparable to that faced by Blacks and minoritized people, and that White people benefit from racism and White supremacy; nonetheless, according to Kivel (1996), Whites do go through costs that include guilt over unearned privilege, irrational fear of Black people, distorted beliefs about racism and race and untrue reliance on stereotypes. However, Whites still benefit from racism. It is noteworthy to state that racism affects everyone in negative ways. In this context, I acknowledge the individual and institutional contributions to racism and its roots to White supremacy and the individual, institutional, societal harm it causes Black people and people of Color. I also recognize the psychosocial cost to the White community—hence, the idea that racism affects and hurts all of us. However, it is important to note that what racism and anti-racism is should not be charged to a sole arbiter, but rather, it should continue to be widely debated and discussed. There is an opportunity later in this chapter for art therapists and others reading this book to explore the question *what is racism?*

Racial trauma

Racism and oppression based on socially constructed racial hierarchies has detrimental consequences on the mental and physical health and safety of Black, Indigenous and other people of Color. The emotional and psychological consequences of racism are pervasive, enduring and harmful due to the assumption of superiority given to Whites (Pearson, Dovidio & Gaertner, 2009). In his book *Invisible Man*, Ralph Ellison (1952) described what it feels like to be an African American man: "I am an invisible man... I am invisible, understand, simply because people refuse to see me... When they approach me, they see only my surroundings, themselves, or figments of their imagination—indeed, everything and anything except me" (p.3). Franklin and Boyd-Franklin (2000) suggest that when African Americans are made to feel invisible, they demonstrate psychological conflicts in which they strive to become noticed, acknowledged and accepted.

The ongoing murders of unarmed Black people by racist vigilantes and police officers have emphasized the need to address the anti-Blackness at the core of our society (Bell *et al.*, 2021). *Anti-Black racism* is the structural and systemic power to dehumanize Black people. *Anti-Blackness* views "the Black person as socially dead—that is denied humanity and thus ineligible for full citizenship" (Dumas, 2016, p.12). Due to racism, African Americans must choose daily between whether to assimilate into the dominant White culture or their own African American culture (Franklin & Boyd-Franklin, 2000). In 1903, the African American intellectual W. E. B. Du Bois (2007), in *The Souls of Black Folk*, introduced the concept of *double-consciousness*, referring to the burdensome experience of Black Americans having to choose whether they want to function within an imposed identity categorized by White Americans, or work against it (Acuff, 2018). In his book, Du Bois (2007) writes:

> It is a peculiar sensation, this double consciousness...one ever feels his two-ness, an American, a Negro; two souls, two thoughts, two un-reconciled strivings; two warring ideals in one dark body, whose dogged strength alone keeps it from being torn asunder... The history of the American Negro is the history of this strife—this longing to attain self-conscious manhood, to merge his double self into a better and truer self. In this merging he wishes neither of the older selves to be lost. (pp.2–3)

This complex experience of the split of consciousness for African Americans while attempting to merge their true Black culture with that of the White dominant values and society has been shown to cause physical and psychological damage leading to *racial battle fatigue* (Smith, 2010; Smith, Allen & Danley, 2007; Smith, Hung & Franklin, 2011). Various other ethnic minoritized Americans also experience this double consciousness in their attempts to integrate into American society. Native Americans also experience it, as they were stripped of their native identities and forced to fit and integrate into the American way of civilization (Gingras, 2010).

Racial battle fatigue leads to racial trauma, and vice versa (Smith *et al.*, 2011). Carter (2007) defines racial trauma as the cumulative effect of discrimination, systemic racism and the manifestation of maladaptive behaviors that contributes to numerous mental health conditions, including depression, anxiety, low self-esteem, and hypervigilance. Many African Americans experience *racial trauma* due to the danger related to real or perceived experience of discrimination, threats of harm and injury, and humiliating and shaming events, in addition to witnessing harm to other *ethnoracial* individuals because of real or perceived racism (Smith, 2010). On his trauma model "the impact of racial trauma on African Americans," Smith (2010) proposed that recovery from trauma was possible if specific interventions to improve one's coping skills were used to assist in decreasing and avoiding re-experiencing the trauma. Smith proposed two phases of experiencing trauma. The first phase, the arousal phase, exposes how people respond and manage the threat. People who manage their trauma poorly tend to be more suspicious of others, are hypervigilant and feel more comfortable in their own social and racial circles (Smith, 2010). Signs of poor responses to racial trauma also include increased aggression—explaining the double-bind common to victims of racial trauma, anxiety, depression and being in a chronic state of danger (Smith, 2010). An example of *double-bind* in racial trauma is a Black man who experiences racist acts every day and responds to the trauma by drinking to get drunk every day after work, as a coping skill. Subsequently, the man is criticized and shunned by his family because he does "nothing but drink" when he comes home from work. Those who can manage and respond to threats and danger are able to be more controlled and plan better when faced with the emotions that accompany trauma (Smith, 2010).

The second phase is how well people who experience trauma cope. People with better coping skills when faced with trauma can learn from their traumatic experience and move on to live a more meaningful life (Smith, 2010). Clinical interventions used to treat racial trauma in clients include helping to encourage clients to tell their racial trauma stories in a safe space, helping to empower clients to have better control over their racial trauma, and educating clients regarding the trauma (Smith, 2010). I have found in my experiences with working with clients with trauma-related issues that using art to encourage visual narratives, in a safe therapeutic environment, where they can face the challenges of the trauma rather than avoid it, is a useful intervention. In my work, clients within these therapeutic spaces tend to gain their sense of self and power back and are better equipped to take control over their lives.

TOM REDD'S STORY CONTINUES

When you constantly see videos of police hunting and killing your people, it traumatizes you and drastically changes your ideas and sense of safety and what is truth. As weird as it sounds, even today, I really can't get that image of that monster kneeling on the neck of George Floyd out of my mind, with his hands in his pocket, *and* looking at the person videotaping him with a smirk on his face, like saying, "I dare you to do something." The thing is, we have been hunted down for centuries and some White folks really do think it's their birth right. America is wild. I did go out and protest. That helped a bit. But most of the time, I'm just super careful with everything these days. I don't go out past a certain time; I stay home with my family most of the time, which is actually nice.

Analysis of Tom Redd's story: Racial trauma, also known as race-based traumatic stress, is an accumulation of emotional, psychological and physical injuries from real and perceived racism (Carter, 2007). One of the key elements of racial trauma is the continued exposure to racial discrimination and racial violence. Although not present at the murder of George Floyd, Tom Redd has a detailed account from watching the news, recalling the smirk on the officer's face. Indirect exposure to racial violence or *vicarious trauma* can also cause emotional, psychological and physical distress (Singletary, 2022; Smith, 2010). Clearly, watching the video had triggered a traumatic response, and an injury in Tom that had affected his mental health. The symptoms of vicarious trauma are like post-traumatic stress disorder (PTSD) and include a compromised sense of safety, low self-esteem, a sense of loss of control, and an inability to trust (Kozlowska *et al.*, 2015). According to Carter (2007), racism creates psychological damage in the same way that being captive or violently attacked and tortured can create emotional damage. Tom Redd shared his fear and anxiety symptoms regarding messages from the media, feeling a loss of control and trust (of White people), and not feeling safe. He also offered coping mechanisms that included protesting, being hypervigilant and staying at home with his family.

Understanding racial trauma in the context of art therapy

Art therapists cannot ignore the effects of racism that cause harm to marginalized clients. The killings and police shootings of unarmed Black people, including Trayvon Martin in Florida, Michael Brown in Missouri, Philando Castile in Minnesota, Breonna Taylor in Kentucky, George Floyd in Minnesota, and many more, have created trauma for us, collectively. Erikson (1976) stated that *collective trauma* harms the very core of societal bonds:

> The collective trauma works its way slowly and even insidiously into the awareness of those who suffer from it...a gradual realization that the community no longer exists as an effective source of support and that an important part of the self has disappeared. (p.154)

In the wake of the killing of George Floyd, I witnessed a tenfold increase in the numbers of clients who came to my private practice for therapy related to racial trauma. Art therapists mostly play a role in addressing systems of oppression and power, and the impact these have on the lives of their clients who are Black, Indigenous and people of Color. Art therapists are charged by the AATA *Ethical Principles* to "safeguard the welfare of the individuals, families, groups and communities" with whom they serve (American Art Therapy Association, 2013). Art therapists have a responsibility for multicultural and diversity competence to "continually acquire cultural and diversity awareness of and knowledge about cultural diversity with regard to self and others, and to successfully apply these skills in practice with clients" (American Art Therapy Association, 2013, p.8).

Art therapists must first understand that racism is real and move away from the naive notions that racist acts only occur in isolation; they occur daily and racism is woven into the fabric of all sectors of society, and intersects with the client's other identities (e.g. age, gender, class). Some of the techniques I have used as a clinician and art therapist have included addressing the stigma and mistrust Black people have about mental health treatment. I have used ongoing *broaching* techniques to explore issues of race and diversity with clients (Day-Vines *et al.*, 2007), creating a safe and consistent environment for them based on building a trusting therapeutic rapport.

Art therapists are in a distinctive and extraordinary position to facilitate healing with clients experiencing harm and trauma. Clack (2018) highlights the importance of helping clients who have experienced racial trauma to refrain from blaming themselves for their emotions, but rather to make connections to the experiences in their lives. I have applied these interventions in my own work with clients, with positive responses and results. Art therapists must work with clients to first name their feelings and validate their reactions and responses to their racial traumas. In addition, art therapists should provide their marginalized clients with a safe space where they can build their autonomy and power, to effect change. Last, but certainly not least, art therapists must work to protect themselves against vicarious trauma caused by working with traumatized clients (Pearlman & Mac Ina, 1995). It can be helpful to work with a culturally informed supervisor to learn better ways to cope with the trauma narratives presented by clients.

Ways to be anti-racist and dismantle White supremacy in art therapy

There are some art therapists who have called for the dismantling of White supremacy in art therapy (Hamrick & Byma, 2017; Talwar *et al.*, 2004) and for art therapists to go beyond the four walls of their offices, to be anti-racist and work on being social justice advocates for their Black clients and clients of Color (Anah, 2019[AQ]; Jackson, 2020; Potash, 2020). In acknowledging that the field of art therapy is largely populated by cisgender, White, heterosexual women, and largely shaped by both patriarchal and Eurocentric theories and discourse (Talwar *et al.*, 2004), I propose and reinforce here ways in which White art therapists can become more anti-racist and aim to dismantle White supremacy.

1. Acknowledge that the Black community in the United States is not monolithic but shares some common experiences of racism. Racism exists individually, institutionally, socially, in laws and policies. They must be aware of the worldview of their Black clients and clients of Color who have experienced racism.

2. Work on their own biases, assumptions, racial stereotypes and worldviews, and accept that they have been part of a system of oppression and have benefited from their privilege—whether consciously or unconsciously.

3. Create a safe therapeutic environment where marginalized clients feel comfortable enough to talk about their stories and experiences of racism and oppression. Art therapists must demonstrate active listening, trust and judgment-free guidance.

4. Stories wield power and are sacred. White art therapists must create a safe space where Black clients and clients of Color can be emotionally vulnerable. This space must be void of judgment or minimization of racist experiences and be rich on strategies for coping and self-care for the minoritized client.

5. Accept the privilege and benefits of their Whiteness and utilize that awareness to enhance their clients' sense of power and self-esteem.

6. Understand that this process is ongoing and should continue and they should invest in anti-racist training and seek the support of other White colleagues working on this process of dismantling White supremacy, and actions that positively affect their clients' environments.

7. Contribute work to the AATA and Art Therapy Credential Board, in research, education, supervision, conference presentations and practice, that calls out racism of any kind and aims to dismantle White supremacy in art therapy.

8. Seek their own personal counseling to work towards processing their own emotions and avoid experiencing vicarious trauma caused by their clients' stories of racism and racial trauma, and deal with their guilt, anger and frustration associated with continued therapeutic engagement with marginalized clients.

Many *culturally responsive* counselors operate from an *emic* (culture specific) position and challenge universal assumptions. *Culturally competent* and culturally responsive art therapists must be aware of their own worldviews, their assumptions of human behavior, their biases and prejudices and their lack of knowledge regarding the diverse culture they serve (Sue *et al.*, 2019). It is also important for art therapists to process how racism has impacted their lives, particularly if they live with marginalized identities themselves.

SELF-REFLECTION FOR ART THERAPISTS

1. What is racism? How do you define racism?

2. What have been your experiences with racism? How has racism impacted your life? Have you experienced racial trauma?

3. Do you remember where you were when George Floyd was murdered? What were some of your coping skills?

4. Are you aware of any resources (e.g. faith or community-based organizations, or mental health resources) available to assist and support African Americans in your area?

5. How can you advocate for African Americans and their families?

6. As you reflect on your own power and privilege as a therapist, how would you treat an individual with racial trauma? How can you create a safe therapeutic space for healing while processing the client's racial realities?

A brief early history of racism: Colonialism and the origins of racism

History is often written by the victors. We should know history that is grounded in facts, not the winners' interpretation. For instance, in 1492, Christopher Columbus did not "discover the new world" of the Americas, but rather, landed in present day Bahamas, and later Haiti and the Dominican Republic, brutalizing the Indigenous/Native people, colonizing, stealing, occupying and claiming their land for the King and Queen of Spain (Zinn, 2005). Columbus believed in the superiority of White people and the inferiority of the Native people, causing the replacement and eradication of their culture—hence, the core tenet of colonialism.

> Neither cruelty, nor violence, nor torture will make me beg for mercy, because I prefer to die with my head raised high, with unshakeable faith... In my country's predestination rather than live in submission forsaking my sacred principles. My dear countrymen! In joy and in Sorrow I will always be with you. (Patrice Lumumba, first Prime Minister of the Republic of Congo (1958–1961), who was executed in a firing squad by Belgium/U.S. allies because he tried to stop them from looting his country's minerals)

Racism and White supremacy, according to Kendi (2019), found its roots in the slave trade of early 15th-century Europe. Before major European nations started colonizing Africa in the 15th century, most African nations were economically fruitful and traded with their neighboring countries (Kinney, 1971). The Portuguese under King John of Portugal sought to conquer African countries and take ownership of their land and riches. W. E. B. Du Bois stated, "Whiteness is the ownership of the earth for ever and ever!" (1995, p.454). Here, he highlights the link between White supremacy, racism and colonialism. Countries like Congo and Nigeria were susceptible to these attacks and colonialization due to their rich mineral resources. Racist ideas formed to justify the brutalities: Africans were thought to be "wild savages" and the White Europeans came to "civilize" and "Christianize" them (Fredrickson, 1987). Colonialism sought to control the language barriers, as the Europeans had assigned African language and tribes as "barbaric." Muslim traders who relied on the labor of enslaved Black people in African countries were attacked by King John of Portugal, who acquired all the riches of the Muslim traders. Thus began the White European enslavement of Africans and the acquisition of their land and resources (Hornsman, 1986). This looting and invasion of African countries caused irreparable damage for many African nations for years to come (Boyd-Franklin, 1989). *Maafa* is a Swahili word that translates to the "great disaster" or "unspeakable horror" and speaks to the African Holocaust of Enslavement and the mass slaughter of millions of Africans by White Europeans, North Americans and others, and the ongoing consequences for African peoples and the descendants of those who were enslaved (Merriam-Webster.com, "maafa"; Ani, 1994).

In Nigeria, particularly, the arrival of major European colonizers encouraged and fueled intense tribalism between the three main tribes—Igbos, Yorubas and Hausas—and class struggle. There was formation of political parties, mostly along tribal lines. Where there existed strong tribal affiliations, colonialism came to further exacerbate this division and create bitterness and hatred among the various groups. In Nigeria, the Hausas, Yorubas and Igbos who had lived in peace and harmony now became bad neighbors with a bitter class struggle (Anah & Anah, 2023–2024). Even after Nigeria gained its independence on October 1, 1960, the Nigerian leaders left behind continued to adhere to the colonial style of governance and to intensify tribalism, eventually leading to a devastating civil war only seven years later (Anah & Anah, 2023–2024). The war, which lasted for three years, was over the state of Biafra—the Igbo people in the Southeast of Nigeria—and the Nigerian government. My father, Mr. Raphael Anah, an Igbo man, a Biafran, was a witness to the Nigerian civil war, and the following is an excerpt from my interview with him.

THE CONSEQUENCES OF COLONIALISM IN NIGERIA—RAPHAEL ANAH (2023)

I was there with my wife and twin baby boys, and the brutality of this war that ended 53 years ago has left so many scars on me, both psychologically and physically, that I will never forget it.

The style of governance and the constitution crafted under the colonial rule intensified the struggle by the three main tribes for dominance of the Nigerian polity. The Constitution was not designed to deliver a stable government but was built on very weak foundations, such as the false population census conducted on the eve of the granting of independence to Nigeria on October 1, 1960. The arid north that was sparse in population was then designated as the most populous region in the country. Even after independence, the leaders who took over power were coerced by the British into making mere cosmetic amendments to both the style of governance and the Constitution, merely glossing over the crucial areas. It is no surprise, therefore, that less than seven years after, a brutal and genocidal war broke out between South Eastern Nigeria (declared the Republic of Biafra) and the Federal Government of Nigeria, preceded by two bloody military coups. The war was clearly fought along ethnic lines, and with the main objective to eliminate the Igbo Tribe.

At the time, I did not consider myself a Biafran, although my parents hailed from that territory. I was born and bred outside Biafra, and I thought that this conferred on me Nigerian citizenship and that I was safe where I had lived for over 30 years. I spoke the local language fluently. Unknown to me, however, a new nomenclature (indigene/non-indigene) had been introduced into the political lexicon to exclude my genuine claim to citizenship. I was, to them, a Biafran. Twice there was reconnaissance in my residence in Lagos by two suspected military personnel, which prompted me to send my wife with our three-month-old twins back to her parents in Biafra. I also had to relocate from my house to another area in town which I considered "safer," but three months later and because of constant harassment from my office, I had to escape by boat to join my wife and children without notifying my employers. We were there for the three brutal and barbaric years of war. The Igbo massacres were real.

The Nigeria-Biafra war was an unnecessary and perilous journey, but its echo was heard long before the first shots were fired. Apart from the concocted colonial census, there was the Aburi Agreement between Yakubu Gowon, the then Nigerian Military Head of State, and Odumegwu Ojukwu, the Governor of Eastern Nigeria. This Agreement was pivotal as it sought to restore hope and confidence in Nigeria remaining as one nation. After the two bloody military coups of 1966, the holocaust suffered by people of Eastern Nigeria living in the north, and the mass exodus to Eastern Nigeria of survivors of the holocaust, Nigeria's unity was in serious disequilibrium; the foundation was near collapse and required the complete restructuring that the Aburi Accord provided. The Aburi Accord was organized by General Ankrah of Ghana and supervised by him. However, the ex-colonial masters who were watching Nigeria with eagle eyes would not let the Accord be and worked to dismantle it.

An agreement "signed, sealed and delivered" by all the participants, and witnessed by General Ankrah, that was supposed to be made public within a few days of return to Nigeria, took Gowon some months to release, and then only to be repudiated. This triggered the defining and deafening slogan of "On Aburi We Stand" all over Eastern Nigeria. The "Republic of Biafra" was declared by popular acclamation of an assembly of all the major ethnic groups that made up Eastern Nigeria.

Nobody underrated the gravity or magnitude of the declaration of the Republic, and the serious consequences that would follow. But nobody was prepared for war on either side. Biafra had no weapons, and Nigeria's military arsenal lacked the heavy weapons of war. But Nigeria could always rely on its allies, and what started as mere "police action" escalated into full-blown military genocidal war when these colonial predators started pouring armaments into Nigeria. Nigerian soldiers killed thousands of Biafrans and burnt houses. You could see dead bodies in the rivers and lakes. Biafra had no weapons of war, no trained personnel, just determination to survive. Everyone believed that the war would be over in a matter of days; however, Nigeria unleashed bloody and ferocious attacks by sea, air and land, and used starvation tactics. The effects were dire for Biafra; people, and children in particular, were dying in their hundreds and thousands. The hospitals did not have the capacity for the many war casualties, of which I was one. Surgical procedures were carried out in the open under insanitary conditions, without anesthetic and by untrained, unqualified and unorganized personnel. The Red Cross were late in coming in their full battle-readiness because the whole war was meant to be a mere foray into that "dark spot" called Biafra. The war was a gory event, an unconventional war fought by Nigeria against Biafra.

Racism has had fundamental consequences on the equilibrium of the world, and has fueled the most egregious atrocities of the world. As we have seen, colonization and slavery had their roots in racism—oppression of a racial group and the belief that one is superior to another based on biological characteristics, with White supremacy at the head. The inherent racism of the Nazi movement had its origins in Hitler's belief in a "master race," and Apartheid was based on racism and White supremacy. Recently, some African nations have called for reparations. At the 2023 United Nations General Assembly in New York, Ghana's President Nana Akufo-Addo demanded the payment of reparations to African countries for the slave trade (BBC World Service Africa, 2023).

The evolution of racism in the United States

There has been a long history of racial subordination of non-Whites that included the expropriation of Native Americans, Black slavery and Jim Crow, the annexation of Mexicans, Chinese exclusion, and the Japanese American internment camps during World War II (Mills, 2017). As discussed earlier, long before Black people and their families were brought over as slaves, they belonged to a rich legacy of tribes descended from the continent of Africa (Boyd-Franklin, 1989). Slave owners worked to dehumanize the Black people by depriving them of their traditions, family bonds, rituals, food and customs (Kinney, 1971). Efforts were made to destroy traditional concepts of the family as enslaved men and women were not legally allowed to be married, and families, including children, could be torn away from each other and sold in an instant (Boyd-Franklin, 1989). Thus, the ethos of the destruction of the Black family. Slavery set the tone for Black people to be treated as inferior to White people (Boyd-Franklin, 1989).

African Americans have a long history with racism in the United States, beginning from their first experiences of being brought over as slaves, to Jefferson's ownership of slaves, to the Civil War in America between North and South (due to the enslavement of Black people), to immigrants being compelled to assimilate and become "White" to avoid discrimination. Immigrants were often labeled "foreign" or a "threat." In the last decade, we have witnessed an African American president, the Trump era, the Black Lives Matter protest of 2020, the recent striking down of Affirmative Action by the 2023 Supreme Court (Sangal et al., 2023), and recent actions by several states to ban African American history and books and redact several facts concerning slavery in the United States. Racism is a permanent fixture in the United States, one of the core tenets of critical race theory (Bell, 1992; Delgado & Stefancic, 2001).

Here is a small example of U.S. laws, court decisions and other acts that helped pave the way for racism to flourish.

In 1787, the Constitution of the United States reinforced the inferior status of slaves by referring to them as "three-fifths of all other persons" (Kozol, 2005). In 1857, the Supreme Court, in the Dred Scott case, confirmed that slaves were property and belonged to their owners. After the Civil War, slaves were freed. However, the newly freed slaves were seen as social outcasts and African Americans were generally segregated from social, educational, employment and mainstream White society and confined to poor neighborhoods (Kozol, 2005). In 1896, the Supreme Court case of Plessy v. Ferguson upheld the policy of segregation (Kluger, 1975). With little to no money, property or civil rights, African Americans were kept unequal and separate in American society due to fearful Whites who classified them as violent and second-class citizens (Kozol, 2005).

In 1935, Congress passed the Social Security Act, which excluded agricultural workers and domestic servants (mostly African American, Mexican and Asian). In addition, the Wagner Act protected American White workers by allowing unions to discriminate against workers for benefits or higher wages based on race.

In 1947, the GI Bill gave opportunities such as loans, college education and housing for White veterans and their families returning from World War II but did not challenge the discriminatory policies embedded for non-Whites.

With the 1954 landmark case of Brown v. Board of Education, however, racial segregation in schools was abolished (Kluger, 1975). By desegregating education, African American students could be educated alongside White students. The intention of desegregation was to provide access to social and economic mobility for African Americans (Henfield, 2011; Kluger, 1975). However, many African Americans continued to be viewed as second-class citizens by their White counterparts, as educational, social and economic opportunities were unobtainable (Dovidio & Gaertner, 2000).

The Civil Rights Act of 1964 was a pivotal moment in the efforts of closing the racial divisions created by the legacy of slavery (Pearson *et al.*, 2009). It brought about fundamental changes for African Americans, including eliminating most forms of open discrimination based on race (Foster, 2005). Discrimination is defined as the behavioral acts of prejudice and social comparisons manifested in negative attitudes towards an individual or a group (Jones, 1997). Efforts were made during this time to reduce racial workplace inequality by implementing enforceable Equal Employment Opportunity (EEO) laws, which legally protected the rights of many African Americans in requiring federal contractors to take Affirmative Action in the hiring and promotion of African Americans (Stainback, Robinson & Tomaskovic-Devey, 2005). In addition, African Americans were guaranteed legal protection to be treated equally, in the workplace, schools and other areas of American society (Dovidio & Gaertner, 2000). In 1965, the Voting Rights Act was passed, giving African Americans the right to vote. The Voting Rights Act further decreed that jurisdictions with histories of discrimination were required to obtain the approval of the Department of Justice to change any voting rules (Kozol, 2005). Although the Civil Rights Movement effectively changed some racial dynamics, racism continued to exist in U.S. society (Thompson & Neville, 1999). During this time, employment opportunities for African American men were scarce and the only employment opportunities for educated African Americans were low paying, or teaching jobs in segregated schools (Cross & Slater, 2000).

In 1967, the National Advisory Commission on Civil Disorders—the Kerner Commission—reported that racism by White people was the cause of Black civil disorder, and made recommendations that included improving police and community relationships (U.S. Department of Justice, Office of Justice Programs).

In 1980, the Reagan administration expanded on President Nixon's "War on Drugs," sending over 400,000 people, disproportionally minoritized, to jail for non-violent crimes by 1997. In the mid-1980s, the Reagan-Bush administration publicly denounced the Civil Rights Act of 1964, stating it was a "bad piece of legislation." The Voting Rights Act of 1965 was additionally criticized by the Reagan-Bush administration, which deemed it an unnecessary additional piece of legislation because it gave control of voting to local governments (Omi & Winant, 1994). According to the Reagan-Bush administration, the additional legislation of the Voting Rights Act was unnecessary because the Constitution already had sufficient protections for African Americans (Omi & Winant, 1994). The 2012 elections may be among the best arguments for the Voting Rights Act of 1965 because the act protected the rights of many African Americans from reported controversy of voter suppression and discrimination in many states.

When President Clinton entered office in 1992, his administration was supportive of the racial equality debate. In 1998, President Clinton's Race Advisory Board concluded that racism existed and was a divisive factor in American society; and those racial inequalities were very much a part of the American fabric, so much so that they were almost invisible (President's Initiative on Race, 1998). They also reported that the legacy of slavery continued to influence current policies and practices that create unfair disparities between Whites and African Americans. Most Whites were unaware of their advantages and had no idea how their actions and attitudes unintentionally discriminate against African Americans (President's Initiative on Race, 1998).

In 2005, Hurricane Katrina hit New Orleans. The damages were so bad that nobody could leave the city. Thousands of mostly Black residents had to wait outside the Superdome for sanctuary, often with no food and sleeping on the floors.

In 2012, Trayvon Martin, a 17-year-old African American male, was fatally shot by George Zimmerman, who was subsequently acquitted. The verdict led to massive protests nationwide, and birthed the Black Lives Matter movement. On August 9, 2014, Michael Brown, an 18-year-old, was murdered by police officer Darren Wilson (Halpern, 2015).

In 2013, the Supreme Court gutted the Voting Rights Act. The ruling struck down the system that blocked discriminatory voting policies before they harmed voters. Ironically, Justice Thomas, the only Black justice at the time, played a decisive role in this ruling.

In March 2020, the beginning of the COVID-19 global pandemic highlighted the health disparities between African Americans and other minoritized populations and their White counterparts.

On May 25, 2020, George Floyd was murdered by a police officer, which sparked national and global protests and a racial reckoning for the United States.

In July 2022, the Florida Education Association enacted the "Stop Woke Act" which stated that race must be taught in an "objective manner" and not used to indoctrinate students or persuade them into a certain point of view. It also banned workplace training about racism.

On May 28, 2022, Florida's governor, Ron DeSantis, signed the "Don't Say Gay" Bill, banning or limiting discussions in schools about gender identity.

In 2023, the Supreme Court struck down Affirmative Action.

In 2023, spearheaded by Governor Ron DeSantis, Florida's Board of Education approved new guidelines for its Black history public school curriculum. It characterized enslaved people as learning skills that were potentially beneficial to them.

SELF-REFLECTION FOR ART THERAPISTS, DISCUSSION QUESTIONS, ART THERAPY EXERCISES

Materials: Paper, scissors, glue, magazines, markers, paints, brushes.

Directives: On a piece of paper, reflect on these questions while creating art:

- When and where were you the first time you were aware of race and racism? Who said it, what did they say and what did you learn? Create a piece of artwork depicting what you remember about that time.

- What did you learn about the history of racism?

- What is your understanding of the historical, political and social experiences of Africans?

- What did you learn about people from the African diaspora?

- Was there anything you learned that was shocking to you?

- Reflect on your thoughts about colonialism in Africa. Does this affect how you work with Black people in therapy? If yes, in what ways?

Toni Morrison stated:

The function, the very serious function, of racism is distraction. It keeps you from doing your work. It keeps you explaining, over and over again, your reason for being. Somebody says you have no language, and you spend 20 years proving that you do. Somebody says your head isn't shaped properly, so you have scientists working on the fact that it is. Somebody says you have no art, so you dredge that up. Somebody says you have no kingdom, so you dredge that up. None of this is necessary. There will always be one more thing. (Morrison, 1975)

If I take your race away, and there you are, all strung out. And all you got is your little self, and what is that? What are you without racism? Are you any good? Are you still strong? Are you still smart? Do you still like yourself? I mean, these are questions... If you can only be tall because somebody is on their knees, then you have a serious problem. And my feeling is: White people have a very, very serious problem, and they should start thinking about what they can do about it. Take me out of it. (Morrison, 1993)

Reflect on writer, poet and civil rights advocate Toni Morrison's statements about racism and White supremacy and create a piece of artwork of your understanding of the two narratives.

Denial, minimization and distortions of the existence of racism

The experiences of Black Americans and the harmful effects of racism are sometimes downplayed or ignored in several White spaces. *Color-blindness* and an inability to "see color" negates Black people's experiences and ascribes to the notion that recognizing color differences is bad, and that denying or pretending away the existence of race is more palatable (Sue *et al.*, 2007b). This is harmful because it tends to silence necessary discussions about racial bias and inequality (Sue, 2015). Denial and minimization of racism often suggests that racism and discrimination are no longer the central factors affecting minoritized lives (Bonilla-Silva, 2017). When there is a minimization of the existence of racism, it gives leeway to policies and legal rulings that negate the experiences of minoritized people; one such example is Affirmative Action. On June 29, 2023, with a ruling of 6–3, the Supreme Court ruled that race-conscious Affirmative Action admissions in North Carolina and Harvard universities were unlawful (New York Times, 2023). Conservative Chief Justice Roberts, in his decision, stated that universities for far too long have "concluded, wrongly, that the touchstone of an individual's identity is not challenges bested, skills built, or lessons learned but the color of their skills. Our constitutional history does not tolerate that choice." He failed to offer a "measurable" objective to justify the use of race. In essence, minoritized people should stop playing the "race card" and work towards meritocracy—based on ability and skill, not racism. In her dissent,

Justice Sotomayor wrote that the decision "rolls back decades of precedent and momentous progress." Justice Ketanji Brown Jackson called the decision "truly a tragedy for us all" (CNN, 2023).

According to anti-racist activists James Baldwin and Ida B. Wells-Barnett, dismantling and eradicating racism is contingent on first recognizing and naming the realities of its existence. This is important for art therapists to remember when working with their culturally diverse clients. We cannot change racial oppression and racism if we do not name it when incidents occur. When racist acts are committed, many White people are more comfortable explaining away racism, saying it "might" be or could "possibly" be, anything but racism (Harper, 2012). On August 26, 2023, in Jacksonville, Florida, a White supremacist, using a gun with swastikas on it and fueled by hatred for Black people, killed three Black people. Media and news outlets branded the killings "racially motivated" rather than a racist act. Words matter. The killings were a racist act. When you downplay the harm of the violence and killing, you deny Black people their reality and experiences of racism. We must tell the truth in a meaningful way to eradicate the problem of racism.

The eradication of American history—slavery—2023 and beyond

Enslavers defended slavery from abolitionists by arguing that enslaved Black people benefited from American slavery and were better off than peasants in Africa and Europe because they were "civilized" by American enslavers. On July 19, 2023, Florida's Board of Education approved new Black history standards that noted that enslaved Black people developed skills that "could be applied for their personal benefit." This is a dishonest and inaccurate telling of the history of slavery. Here are some headlines, YouTube videos and a story about the eradication of the teaching of slavery in American history education:

> DeSantis doubles down on claim that some Blacks benefited from slavery. (Sullivan & Rozsa, 2023. *The Washington Post*)

> WTH?!? Arkansas governor Sarah Huckabee Sanders CLAIMS Black History Course SPREADS "HATE." (Martin, 2023. YouTube video)

> Arkansas officials require teachers to turn over AP African American Studies lessons and course materials for inspection. They're looking for evidence of critical race theory and indoctrination, banned by new state law. This is not a drill. (August 21, 2023, X Post. https://arktimes.com)

The following passage reveals the frustration and surprise a high school teacher in Florida felt about the replacement of wording surrounding slavery.

> I am a high school teacher and I teach U.S. history in Jacksonville, Florida. I am also a White woman. In orientation for the Fall semester, we were instructed that we were no longer allowed to use the word "slavery" when teaching about African American history. Instead, we've been asked to replace the word slavery with "involuntary employment." My jaw has not yet come off the floor. I need to be creative about this because slavery was SLAVERY! (Jillian (pseudonym), high school teacher, August 20, 2023)

REFLECTIONS, DISCUSSION QUESTIONS, ART THERAPY EXERCISE

- What are your thoughts on the banning of books that teach us about slavery?

- What are your thoughts about the 2023 headlines? Do you think slaves benefited from slavery? What do you make of words like "involuntary employment" to describe slavery?

- What are your thoughts on Governor Ron DeSantis' policy on new teachings about slavery?

- Reflect on the idea of racial healing as it relates to racism. What does that look like? Create a piece of artwork that illustrates your thoughts.

Summary

The aims by Florida Governor Ron DeSantis to eradicate American history that included slavery, and Governor Sarah Huckabee Sanders' to ban books about slavery in her state of Arkansas, are attempts to whitewash/water down history; this is state-sanctioned White supremacy and projects anti-Black resolutions. Recently, to counteract this, Black churches in Florida are now picking up the baton and teaching the unfiltered version of Black history in Sunday church. It is important that art therapists and other clinicians learn, understand and remember the horrors of colonialism, slavery and Jim Crow, and how they were a violation of human rights, as they address the psychological consequences and racial trauma caused by these factors and how it influences the lives of their Black and other marginalized clients today. The impact of racial differences on the therapeutic process cannot be denied, and ongoing broaching within the therapeutic relationship remains

THE HISTORY, ORIGINS AND EVOLUTION OF RACISM

essential. The denial and minimization of racism, and portrayal of the illusions of color-blindness, hurts the therapeutic relationship and process.

The eradication of the history of racism appears to be an attempt for White supremacy to ensure its continued dominance over minoritized people and maintain the racial hierarchy, which continues to be detrimental to Black lives. Those that remain silent and go along with racism and the systemic eradication of it from American history are choosing inaction against the culture of White supremacy. To overcome racial inequality, we must confront our history.

> A people without the knowledge of their past history, origin and culture is like a tree without roots.

Chapter 3

Microaggressions

What are microaggressions?

FIGURE 3.1: "RACIAL MICROAGGRESSIONS" BY CHIOMA ANAH,
© 2015 (MIXED MEDIA, ON PAPER, 14" X 11")

Prior to the campaigning and subsequent election of Donald Trump in 2016, public acts of overt racism, publicized hate speech and racist violence and policies were seemingly less visible in the United States (Beutler, 2017; Center for American Progress, 2017). Rather, it was in the private interactions that subtle racism seemed to present themselves (Solorzano, 1997). American psychiatrist Chester Middlebrook Pierce first coined the term "microaggressions" in the 1970s to refer to automatic and often subtle put-downs directed towards African Americans (Pierce *et al.*, 1978). Microaggressions have also been described as "subtle insults (verbal, nonverbal, and/or visual) directed towards people of color, often automatically or unconsciously" (Solorzano, Ceja & Yosso, 2000, p.60). They can also be conscious and direct, and the intent is to send denigrating messages to people of Color, women and the LGBTQIA+ community (Sue & Spanierman, 2020). Microaggressions can be linked to racism, sexism, genderism, classism, heterosexism and ableism, and can be expressed towards any marginalized group in our society (Sue *et al.*, 2008a). In this book, I focus primarily on research-supported forms of *racial microaggressions*, that are both direct and covert, and I touch on *gender-based microaggressions* and *sexual-orientation microaggressions*.

Racial microaggressions

Pierce *et al.* (1978) conducted an experiment to investigate the role of television commercials in reinforcing racist attitudes and behavior. The study proposed that television commercials, as innocuous as they may seem, served as a common and frequent source of microaggressions, mostly offensive to African Americans. Pierce *et al.* stated that the rationale and data presented in the study would heighten awareness of television content and how it marginalizes various groups, thus leading to more sensitive, positive media portrayals. The results of this study further revealed that to a disproportionate extent those African American actors in the commercials were shown to be more subservient (Pierce *et al.*, 1978). African American men were never placed in a familial context and portrayed with a stable family. White women, on the other hand, were portrayed as the pinnacle of ideal beauty, with a stable family (Pierce *et al.*, 1978). These results illustrated the excessive ways in which African Americans were negatively represented in television commercials and within the subconscious of American society in general (Pierce *et al.*, 1978; Sue, 2010).

Sue *et al.* (2007b) expanded on the work of Pierce and colleagues (1978) and proposed a conceptual framework of how racial microaggressions manifest in the everyday lives of people of Color. Sue *et al.* defined racial microaggressions as "brief and commonplace daily verbal, behavioral, and environmental indignities, whether intentional or unintentional, that communicate hostile, derogatory, or negative racial slights and insults to the target person or group" (Sue *et al.*, 2007b, p.273). Racial microaggressions are also subtle, insensitive, automatic and sometimes unconscious verbal, non-verbal and/or visual insults and indignities directed towards African American people or people of Color (Solorzano *et al.*, 2000). Simply stated, these are quick, everyday interactions that send denigrating messages to people of Color (Sue *et al.*, 2007b). Although racial microaggressions can be conscious and direct, research has primarily focused on unconscious, subtle and indirect exchanges of those who hold power over those less powerful (Sue *et al.*, 2007b).

Perpetrators of racial microaggressions are often unaware of the highly charged racial situations, which could be challenging for all involved (Solorzano *et al.*, 2000). Racial microaggressions could be conveyed verbally, non-verbally and through different environments. Verbal racial microaggressions include any negative forms of expressions about African Americans (Sue *et al.*, 2008a). An example of this is the implication that an African American is "lazy," "angry" or "loud," perpetuating the stereotype of African American people. Non-verbally, racial microaggressions can be conveyed by minimizing a racial assault by ignoring it, and not confronting the situation (Solorazano *et al.*, 2000), or, for example, a White woman clutching her purse tightly as she passes an African American man. This act non-verbally conveys fear that there is potential for harm (Sue & Sue, 2008).

Taxonomy of racial microaggressions

Derald Wing Sue is recognized as one of the most influential scholars focusing on the study of racial microaggressions. The racial microaggression taxonomy (Sue *et al.*, 2007b) posits that well-intentioned Whites in American society still harbor racial biases and display discriminatory behaviors towards African Americans (Sue *et al.*, 2019). The taxonomy of racial microaggression outlines the central components of subtle and overt racism, as well as the repercussions of these assaults. Racial microaggression theory outlines three major forms: microassaults, microinsults and microinvalidations. Microassaults are deliberate and are known as overt "old-fashioned" racism, while microinsults and microinvalidations are subtle, unconscious and ambiguous. Microinsults and microinvalidations have been categorized into nine themes (Sue *et al.*, 2007b): (1) Alien in own land, (2) Ascription of intelligence, (3) Color-blindness, (4) Criminality/assumption of criminal status, (5) Denial of individual racism, (6) Myth of meritocracy, (7) Pathologizing cultural values/communication styles, (8) Second-class citizen and (9) environmental microaggressions.

Microassaults

Microassaults are frequently overt, racially charged, intentional discriminatory attacks or avoidant behaviors (Sue *et al.*, 2007b). They are defined as "an explicit racial derogation characterized primarily by a verbal or nonverbal attack meant to hurt the intended victim through name-calling, avoidant behavior, or purposeful discriminatory actions" (Sue *et al.*, 2007b, p.274). Microassults are often premeditated and deeply entrenched in the hatred of African Americans, and they are deliberate and conscious acts by the perpetrator (Dovidio & Gaertner, 2000). An example of a microassaultive encounter would be an African American person being called a racial epithet, like "monkey" and "N-word," while walking down the street.

Microassaults are often conscious, easy to detect, and the intention of the perpetrator is to directly and deliberately inflict harm on the recipient (Sue *et al.*, 2007b). Other examples include racist jokes between groups of White people; the hatred of African Americans by the Ku Klux Klan and White supremacist groups; and public displays of racist symbols such as the Confederate flag in the workplace. Former President Donald Trump has had his fair share of hate speech and assaultive racism towards Black Americans. Trump called for the execution of the "Central Park five" in New York. In 1989, five teenage boys were convicted of the rape and assault of a White female jogger. This case sparked outrage due to the unjust ways the boys were subjected to police coercion (Harris, 2019). The boys maintained their innocence but were imprisoned for 6–13 years. They were finally exonerated after DNA evidence and were awarded 41 million dollars in 2014 from the state of New York, but Trump remained unapologetic. He also declared Black people "lazy." Trump stated that 80 percent of all shootings in New York City were by Black people. He also labeled COVID-19 as the "China virus" and advocated a Nixon-like "law and order" approach to dealing with protesters against racism.

Microinsults

Microinsults are described as "communications that convey rudeness and insensitivity and demean a person's racial heritage or identity" (Sue *et al.*, 2007b, p.274). The perpetrators do not always intend these as messages of rudeness to African Americans.

The four themes that are subcategories of microinsults are (1) Ascription of intelligence, (2) Second-class citizens, (3) Pathologizing cultural values/communication styles and (4) Assumption of criminal status (Sue *et al.*, 2007b). Ascription of intelligence refers to assigning a particular level of intelligence to a person based on their race (Sue *et al.*, 2007b). For instance, seeing African Americans as intellectually inferior is a common microinsult (Sue, 2010). The theme of second-class citizens includes treating an African American person as less than a White person (Sue *et al.*, 2007b). Pathologizing cultural values/communication styles are characterized by White people's assumption that the values and communication styles of African Americans are defective and displeasing (Sue *et al.*, 2007b).

The last theme, assumption of criminal status, is defined by the assumption that all African Americans are presumed dangerous and criminal (Sue *et al.*, 2007b). This is the theme that has been most dangerous to African

American men, often resulting in deadly consequences. The creation of images of criminals as primarily belonging to the African American group has not helped the perceived stereotypical relationship between African American men, dangerousness and crime, even with people who consciously believe the contrary (Correll *et al.*, 2011). Perceptions of criminality, violence and deviance continue to be the underlined message given about African American men, which can lead to policies like racial profiling, and, even more devastating, can result in deaths, as in the cases of Trayvon Martin, Michael Brown and Philando Castile, and many more (Anah, 2016a), such as George Floyd and Tyre Nichols.

This microinsult is a theme African American men complain most about (Sue, 2010). President Obama on July 19, 2013, in a landmark moment, following the acquittal of Zimmerman for the killing of Trayvon Martin, stated:

> Very few African American men have not had the experience of being followed when they were shopping in the department store. That includes me. In addition, there are very few African American men who have not had the experience of walking across the street and hearing the locks click on the doors of cars. It happens to me, at least before I was a senator. There are very few African Americans who haven't had the experience of getting on the elevator and a woman clutching her purse nervously and holding her breath until she had a chance to get off. That happens often. (Obama, 2013)

Similarly, in the case of 18-year-old Michael Brown, 29-year-old White officer Darren Wilson highlighted the reasons he shot and killed Brown on August 9, 2014. This is what Officer Wilson stated he saw on that day:

> I felt like a five-year-old holding onto Hulk Hogan... Hulk Hogan, that's just how big he felt and how small I felt just from grasping his arm... The only way I can describe it, it looks like a demon, that's how angry he looked. He comes back towards me again with his hands up... At this point it looked like he was almost bulking up to run through the shots, like it was making him mad that I'm shooting at him. And then when it [the bullet] went into him, the demeanor on his face went blank, the aggression was gone, it was gone, I mean I knew he stopped, the threat was stopped. (Anah, 2016a; Halpern, 2015)

Officer Wilson described manifestations of microaggressive behaviors directed towards African American men: they are subhuman, "Hulk Hogan," "demon"-like, bad and dangerous, angry, aggressive and ultimately criminal; they need to be stopped for the threat to be gone (Anah, 2016a). Officer Wilson's dehumanization and "demon"-like assumption of Michael Brown cost Michael his life (Anah, 2016a). As with Philando Castile, the officer involved in his shooting also saw him as an implicit criminal threat. Officer

Yanez, who killed Castile, stated that "a million things started going through my head. And I thought I was gonna die" (Park, 2017).

Microinvalidations

Microinvalidations are defined as "communications that exclude, negate, or nullify the psychological thoughts, feelings, or experiential reality of a Person of Color" (Sue *et al.*, 2007b, p.274). Examples of microinvalidations include African Americans accused of being too sensitive or paranoid when complaining about experiences of subtle racism, which gives the message that racism does not exist.

The following four themes are subcategories of microinvalidations: (1) Alien in own land, (2) Color-blindness, (3) Myth of meritocracy and (4) Denial of individual racism (Sue *et al.*, 2007b). The first theme assumes that all African Americans do not belong and are outsiders in their own country (Sue *et al.*, 2007b). For example, a White person assuming that all African Americans would like to visit their homeland in Africa someday. The constant questioning and the citizenship conspiracy of President Obama's birthplace by Donald Trump and other "birthers," despite very clear evidence that he was born in Hawaii, shows the microinvalidation that he is not a natural-born citizen, not an American and an alien in own land.

FIGURE 3.2: "WE ARE NOT ALL THE SAME" BY CHIOMA ANAH, © 2015 (MIXED MEDIA ON PAPER, 14" X 11")

Color-blindness is the idea that recognizing color differences is bad, and that denying or pretending away the existence of race is more palatable (Sue *et al.*, 2007b). It is the most common microinvalidation directed towards African Americans (Sue, 2010). Color-blindness is harmful because it tends to silence necessary discussions about racial bias and inequality (Sue, 2015). For instance, White individuals, as a way of highlighting to African Americans that they are not racist, state that they "do not see color" and that they treat everyone the same. A similar theme of microinvalidation—denial of individual racism—refers to the denial of the existence of racism or the role of the perpetrator (Sue *et al.*, 2007b). This suggests that there is no such thing as White superiority, and Blacks and people of Color have no right to feel inferior, nor is there any racism because everyone is treated the same (Sue *et al.*, 2008a).

Myth of meritocracy refers to individuals making statements that communicate that a person's race has no role in their life success (Sue *et al.*, 2007b). This microinvalidation suggests that everyone is on an equal playing field, and that success or failure is due only to how hard one works, and not race (Sue *et al.*, 2008a). There is little attention given to the higher unemployment rates among African Americans as opposed to their White counterparts. African Americans, in general, are hesitant to seek therapy, and those who seek out counseling usually report a negative experience with the process because they feel their counselor does not understand them and minimizes their experiences (Constantine, 2007). In their study on African American supervisees in cross-racial dyads, Constantine and Sue (2007) found that, most often, White supervisors blamed their African American clients for their problems, particularly when it involved issues of racism.

For African American men, the following microaggression themes are particularly common (Sue *et al.*, 2008a): ascription of intellectual inferiority; second-class citizenship; assumption of criminality; assumption of inferior status; assumed universality of the African American experience; and assumed superiority of White cultural values/communication styles. In the workplace, microaggressions create inequalities for African Americans and send messages of exclusion and expectation of failure (Miller & Travers, 2005). Many African Americans complain that their ideas or opinions are often overlooked in meetings with their White peers (Alleyne, 2004). Talking "Black" is an accusation that many White Americans have of African Americans, which is associated with intellectual inferiority and superiority of White communication styles (Sue, 2010).

FIGURE 3.3: "MYTH OF MERITOCRACY" BY CHIOMA ANAH,
© 2016 (ACRYLIC ON PAPER, 11" X 14")

Environmental microaggressions

Environmental microaggressions are microassaults, microinsults and microinvalidations that occur on a larger environmental and systemic level. Sue (2010) states that "environmental microaggressions refer to the numerous demeaning and threatening social, educational, political, or economic cues that are communicated individually, institutionally or societally to marginalized groups" (p.25). Environmental microaggressions can be conveyed visually or verbally (Pierce *et al.*, 1978). African Americans encounter microaggressions in various environments, including school, work and the community (Sue, 2010). For example, African American men on a college campus experiencing *hyper-surveillance* from campus police sends the message that they do not belong there and are out of place, which causes high levels of psychological stress (Smith *et al.*, 2007). Another example of environmental microaggressions occurs in the workplace, when African Americans note that their ideas are being ignored or devalued while their White co-workers' ideas are put into practice (Alleyne, 2004). This conveys the message that African American ideas are not respected or welcomed (Sue, 2010). Workplace inequity and subtle discrimination against marginalized populations has been called "microinequality" (Rowe, 1990). Another common example of an environmental microaggression in a professional work environment for African American men is when most of the decision makers within that institution—managers, top-ranging employees—are White men, making it difficult for them to trust or feel comfortable in that setting. Environmental workplace conditions where African Americans are underrepresented, where they are not valued or are ignored, lead to feelings of mistrust and perceived threat (Sue, 2010). Other examples of environmental microaggressions include the deplorable state of some of the city school buildings in Baltimore, and the many liquor stores in African American communities.

All these messages imply that African Americans do not belong; they would not succeed, as there is only so far that they can go, they are deviant, and they do not value education (Sue *et al.*, 2007b). Harwood *et al.* (2012) reported that students of color identified environmental racial microaggression themes on campus that communicated to them that they did not belong. Students noted that many of the residential halls appeared to be segregated by race, there were racial slurs written in the shared spaces on campus, and racial jokes and comments seemed to be acceptable on campus (Harwood *et al.*, 2012).

Psychological dilemmas of racial microaggressions

Art therapists should recognize the psychological dilemmas associated with racial microaggression. Solorzano *et al.* (2000) and Sue *et al.* (2008a) suggested that because microinsults and microinvalidations include uncertain and subtle discriminatory situations, they often contribute to the recipients experiencing psychological problems. In addition to the themes and categories of racial microaggression discussed above, racial microaggression theory also reveals four psychological dilemmas and dynamics that are created when African Americans experience racial microaggression (Sue *et al.*, 2007b):

- Dilemma 1: Clash of racial realities.

- Dilemma 2: The invisibility of unintentional expressions of bias.

- Dilemma 3: Perceived minimal harm of microaggressions.

- Dilemma 4: The catch-22 of responding to microaggressions.

In his new book *Disillusioned: Five Families and the Unraveling of America's Suburbs*, Benjamin Herold (2024) discusses how racial injustices created the American suburbs, using zoning codes and low access to loans to exclude Black people and make housing only available to White people. He also examines the devastating effect that "White flight" had when Blacks and other people of Color started moving into the suburbs. As the upwardly mobile White families moved out, this left the Black families with the bills for maintenance and repair. Schools are now in deplorable condition and there is an aging infrastructure.

The clash of racial realities suggests that Black and White people struggle to connect with each other and that the American suburbs are changing and eroding. For many White families, racism is invisible and unimportant when discussing how the suburbs were originally created, while Black people experience these racist issues as part of their racial reality.

The invisibility of unintentional expression of bias suggests that acts of racial microaggression are often unknown to the perpetrator, and often go unnoticed, invisible and unchecked by those involved (Sue, 2010). Art therapists should be aware of this within the client-therapist relationship. These invisible unintentional expressions of bias exist because of cultural conditioning that may be connected neurologically with the processing of emotions that surround discrimination (Sue, 2010). For example, a White manager who compliments an African American employee about how well spoken he was during a presentation genuinely thinks that he is giving a compliment; however, the underlying message is that African Americans typically are not well spoken (Sue, 2010). Another example is when White employees seem to be extra cautious regarding security in the workplace around African American employees. In all these cases, the perpetrator has no conscious awareness that they have acted differently on the basis of race.

Perceived minimal harm of racial microaggression suggests that when African Americans experience racial microaggression and confront their aggressors, they are typically dismissed as being too sensitive and overactive, and they are encouraged to let the incident go (Sue *et al.*, 2007b). Similarly, in the psychological dilemma of racial microaggression, victims do not know how to respond (Sue, 2010). In a catch-22 situation, African Americans question whether the incident occurred, whether harm was intended, and whether or not to respond (Sue *et al.*, 2007b). In addition, an African American man responding angrily to a racial microaggression may give credence to the stereotype of the "angry Black man" for the White perpetrator (Jones, 1997). Because these microaggressions are usually done unconsciously by the perpetrator, they are unaware of the extent of the harm they have inflicted on the victim. Therefore, usually, after considering and weighing all these consequences for responding, most victims choose to remain silent (Sue, 2010). African Americans feel that you are "damned if you do, and damned if you don't" (Sue *et al.*, 2007b).

Psychological effects of racial microaggressions

Racism has a powerful and systemic effect in the lives of African Americans, and the energy lost dedicated to coping with this issue is draining (Smith *et al.*, 2007). Although the research is limited, the psychological repercussions of racial microaggressions are documented in some research studies (Pierce, 1978; Solorzano *et al.*, 2000; Sue *et al.*, 2008a; Thompson & Neville, 1999). There are studies indicating that exposure to discrimination and racism has a devastating impact on the psychological health of African Americans and poses a public health threat to African American men (Alleyne, 2004; Constantine & Sue, 2007; Harrell, 2000; Smith *et al.*, 2011; Solorzano *et al.*, 2000; Sue *et al.*, 2007b). The build-up of racial microaggressions over time is detrimental to the health and overall quality of life for African American men (Smith *et al.*, 2007). Literature suggests that racial microaggression, due to its subtle and sometimes unintentional nature, is often overlooked by the perpetrators, but has a devastating impact on the targeted group, who are most often African Americans (Foster, 2005; Sue *et al.*, 2008a). African Americans who encounter racial microaggression report it as being disappointing, frustrating and painful (Constantine & Sue, 2007). Feelings of invisibility, powerlessness, loss of integrity due to forced compliance and pressure to positively represent the African American community all add to the emotional and psychological effects of racial microaggression (Sue *et al.*, 2008a).

According to Pierce (1978), African Americans have the added psychological stressor of identifying when, where and how to resist racism, and when, where and how to adapt to the assaults. The stress associated with dealing with the unique characteristics of the invisibility of unintentional bias and the catch-22 of racial microaggression adds to the turmoil reported by African Americans (Sue *et al.*, 2008a). Further, African American men have reported feeling powerless when faced with subtle discrimination, for fear of being labeled as "angry and aggressive." These poor mental health outcomes experienced by African Americans can also be passed on to family and friends, even across generations (Smith *et al.*, 2007).

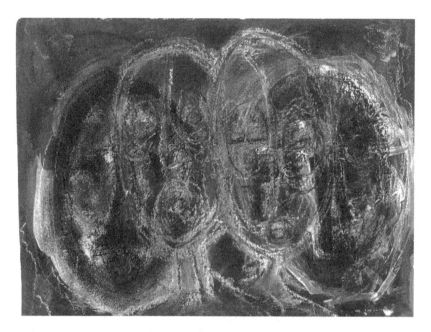

FIGURE 3.4: "INVISIBILITY" BY CHIOMA ANAH, © 2015
(PASTEL/CHALK ON PAPER, 14" X 11")

African Americans have a higher incident of mental health disorders as compared to their White American counterparts, and there is a connection between discrimination and negative mental health outcomes for African Americans (Smith *et al.*, 2011; Sue, 2004; Williams, Neighbors & Jackson, 2003).

Smith *et al.* (2011) suggested a strong relationship between the health and well-being of African American men with higher levels of education and racial microaggressions. How African American men coped with and responded to racial microaggressions also contributed to their psychological health. Furthermore, microaggressions are related to the self-esteem, quality of life and identity of African Americans (Brondolo *et al.*, 2003; Smith *et al.*, 2007; Sue, 2004; Thompson & Neville, 1999; Utsey *et al.*, 2002). Alleyne (2004) suggested that African Americans who experienced racial microaggressions in the workplace also experienced mental health problems such as PTSD and depression. Other mental health disorders affecting African Americans included anxiety disorder and stress-related problems (Smith *et al.*, 2007).

Physical effects of racial microaggressions

Racism has been shown to have detrimental effects on the overall physical well-being of African American men, for example various stressors such as discrimination, inequality, harassment and victimization account for physical health problems for African Americans (Utsey & Hook, 2007; Williams *et al.*, 2003). Inequality and discrimination are unique stressors that may contribute to poor physical health outcomes in African Americans, particularly in cases of cardiovascular health (Williams *et al.*, 2003). Further, the physiological consequences of racial microaggressions for African American men are numerous (Smith *et al.*, 2007). African American men are generally in poorer health than their White counterparts are and are susceptible to alcohol consumption and poorer health status (Utsey & Hook, 2007). High social and health risk factors among African American men have been equated to their experiences of discrimination (Williams *et al.*, 2003). Thirty percent of African American men are involved in the judicial system and they have shorter life expectancies than other ethnic groups in the United States. This shorter life expectancy is due in part to physiological issues (Butterfield, 1995; Hammond & Young, 1993).

African American men are susceptible to health risk factors such as diabetes, hypertension or high blood pressure, and cardiovascular disorders (Dolezsar *et al.*, 2014; Wyatt *et al.*, 2014). In 2010, it was found that 38 percent of African American men have high blood pressure, compared to 16 percent of White men having high blood pressure (U.S. Department of Health and Human Services, 2010). African Americans also have a higher incidence of HIV and certain cancers (e.g. prostate cancer). According to the U.S. Department of Health and Human Services (2010), diabetes is a chronic condition and a leading cause of death and disability for African Americans.

Results from a study conducted by Din-Dzietham *et al.* (2004) showed that hypertension and cardiovascular disease were closely linked to exposure to racism and experiences with discrimination in the workplace. The study participants were 356 African American men and women aged 21 years and older. The findings from the study suggested that race-based discrimination had a negative effect on cardiovascular health and the overall health of African Americans (Din-Dzietham *et al.*, 2004). Similarly, Brondolo *et al.* (2003) linked heart disease and hypertension with racism.

The psychological and physiological consequences for African Americans are well documented in research (Constantine *et al.* 2008; Pittman, 2012; Solorazano *et al.*, 2000; Sue *et al.*, 2008a, 2008b). Due to the double messages they carry, particularly microinvalidations, racial microaggressions are viewed as the most harmful and insidious because they deny African Americans their racial experiences and reality (Sue, 2010) and undermine and limit their rights and opportunities that are crucial for advancement in several areas of society (Sue & Sue, 2008). Racial microaggressions negatively impact the well-being of African American men (Solorazano *et al.*, 2000) and play a crucial role in the increased risk of depressive and somatic symptoms (Alleyne, 2004).

The realities of racial microaggressions

For art therapists, it is important to understand that effective therapy with Black clients has to accept the realities of microaggressions. Due to the invisible and subtle nature of racial microaggression, it continues to oppress African Americans in all areas of American society. Within the context of racial microaggression, most White Americans believe that, in the present time, considerations of race are no longer relevant in people's lives in the United States. This was clearly illustrated on June 25, 2013, when the Supreme Court struck down a core provision of the Voting Rights Act of 1965 that helped to secure the right to vote for millions of Americans, mostly African Americans. The 5–4 ruling, authored by Chief Justice John Roberts, stated that "things have changed dramatically" in the South, and the law that previously protected mostly African Americans from discriminatory practices, including blocking a voter ID law in Texas and South Carolina, was no longer needed. The fact that the majority of the justices indicated in their ruling that such protections and provisions for mostly African Americans, such as the Voting Rights Act's preclearance provision, were no longer needed, because America was different, is, in essence, a microaggression. Similarly, on June 29, 2023, the Supreme Court struck down Affirmative Action in college admissions, declaring that race could no longer be a factor, and that colleges should look at new ways to achieve diversity.

When President of the United States, Barack Obama was not immune to racial microaggressions. During his presidency, he was saddled with questions about his place of birth, suggesting that he is an "alien in his own land." President Obama was also questioned about whether he was qualified to attend Columbia University and Harvard Law School, suggesting that he was too intellectually inferior to be in an elite school (Sue, 2010). Racial microaggression is present today in the United States and should not be undermined or minimized (Solorazano *et al.*, 2000).

SELF-REFLECT AND RESPOND TO THESE QUESTIONS USING ART MAKING

Materials: Paper, magazine, scissors, glue, paints, brushes, markers, pencils, colored pencils.

Purpose: Self-awareness: understanding racial microaggressions.

1. What are some of your assumptions, biases and stereotypes about Black people, White people, Indigenous people, Latinx people and Asian people?

2. Have you ever committed racial microaggressions? What type and category? What motivated you to act this way? What do you think was the impact of your actions? What have you learned here about that offense?

3. Have you experienced racial microaggression or have you witnessed anyone experience it? What was the assault? How did you respond?

4. Could you have responded better to the same incident?

5. How can you be a better ally to those experiencing racial micro-aggressions?

6. As a White art therapist with racial privilege, how can you support and assist your clients in processing their experiences of racial micro-aggression during their art therapy session?

7. As a Black art therapist or art therapist of Color, how do you work with culturally diverse clients who have experienced racial microaggression?

Using art materials, create a piece of artwork that illustrates the type of racial microaggressions you committed, your internal dialogue at the time, and ways you would do things differently today. Use three separate pieces of paper for each situation.

Gender-based microaggressions

There are about twice as many women as men in the United States (U.S. Census Bureau, 2014), but because of the autocratic nature of society, they have had disadvantaged status, historically subjected to discrimination and prejudice. Women continue to face both gender-based discrimination and sexism in professional and social settings.

Gender inequality can result from microaggressions towards women and from judicial decision-making. In 2022, the Supreme Court, with a 6–3 conservative majority, overturned the landmark Roe v. Wade decision that ensured a constitutional right to abortion. Women today face oppression and high levels of psychological and economic stressors (Sue *et al.*, 2019). Like racial microaggressions, sexism can operate in subtle and overt ways (Swim & Cohen, 1997). Here are some examples:

- A female doctor being mistaken for a nurse.

- Gender role stereotyping—questioning why a woman aged over 40 is not married; assuming that a woman who is not married at a certain age must be a lesbian.

- Sexually objectifying a woman.

A large number of women have reported countless interactions where they have been sexually harassed and disrespected due to their gender (Lord, 2010). Women report that gender microaggressions frequently occur in a way that depersonalizes them as objects of desire and devalues and dismisses their worth and contributions in many professional spaces (Banaji & Greenwald, 1995). It is estimated that, during their lifetime, 19.3 percent of women are raped and 43.9 percent suffer from sexual violence of another kind; 21.2 percent of Black women have been raped at some point in their lifetime (Breiding *et al.*, 2014). In 2017, the #MeToo movement brought to light just how much women were subjected to unwanted male sexual advances and sexual violence.

Gender-based microaggressions occur in therapy and can disrupt the therapeutic alliance and client growth. Bias can also occur in the diagnosis of female clients. In working with female clients, art therapists must be aware that the problems their clients identify should be viewed and treated within a social context in which discrimination and deprecation of women is a common occurrence (Sue *et al.*, 2019). Women tend to internalize their feelings, and may become anxious and/or depressed. Look for those mental health problems when treating women. Further, effective clinical treatment with female clients requires an understanding of gender-based social and professional pressures, harassment, sexual objectification, victimization and ageism (Sue, 2010). Feminist therapy has been effective in addressing the inequalities and discriminations faced by women in society.

QUESTIONS: IMPLICATIONS FOR ART THERAPY CLINICAL PRACTICE

1. What are some of your assumptions and biases about women?

2. What are some of the biases in the diagnosis and treatment of women clients, and how do you as an art therapist combat this?

3. What are some art therapy techniques you can use to improve your female clients' self-esteem, sense of worth and self-growth outside of traditional roles?

REFLECT AND RESPOND USING ART MAKING TO THESE QUESTIONS

1. Have you experienced gender microaggressions? What were the circumstances? What did you do?

2. What are some of your coping strategies when you encounter gender microaggressions?

3. Reflect and respond to ways you can encourage your clients' growth and choice of life path without influencing your biases about directing them towards traditional gender roles.

4. Reflect on women with multiple identities; for example, Black women, lesbian Black women or LGBTQIA+ women. How do you encompass all these identities in treatment?

Sexual-orientation microaggressions

Very much like racism and sexism, heterosexism can operate in covert and overt ways. Sexual-orientation microaggressions are brief, everyday insults and invalidations that communicate heterosexist and homophobic slights towards gay, lesbian, bisexual, questioning, pansexual, polysexual, asexual and queer individuals (Nadal *et al.*, 2016). As with racial microaggressions, there has been a dearth of literature in art therapy in anything pertaining to sexual-orientation microaggressions or even healthy sexuality. I was pleasantly surprised to see Volume 40, Number 4 of *Art Therapy*, the Journal of the American Art Therapy Association (2023), dedicated to the special issue of *Sex Positive Art Therapy* (Potash, 2023). Many thanks to Editor in Chief

Jordan S. Potash for putting this all together and filling the sparseness of this very important topic in art therapy literature.

Sue *et al.* (2019) state that:

> The acronym LGBTQ refers to individuals who have an affectional and/ or sexual attraction to persons of the same sex (gay men and lesbians) or to members of both sexes (bisexual), individuals whose gender identity is inconsistent with their assigned gender (transgender), and individuals who self-identify as queer. (p.454)

Although the American Art Therapy Association has not published any specific guidelines for working with LGBTQIA+ clients within its ethical documentation (2013), the special issue on *Sex Positive Art Therapy* provides a wealth of knowledge for working with this population. For instance, Galinsky (2023) discusses using a *diorama* for working with the LGBTQIA+ population and using boxes and vessels to explore sensitive material in a secure environment where the container acts like a metaphor for sexuality:

> Diorama, a three-dimensional scene created within a box or vessel...used in art therapy to explore aspects of sexual self, including: sexual identity, fantasy, and desire, as well as issues pertaining to self-image, gender identity, and sexual empowerment. (Galinsky, 2023, p.197)

Fielding (2021) states that sexuality is fluid and suggests that art therapists working with LGBTQIA+ clients should approach a client's sexuality with the knowledge that sexual identity, desire and practice will inevitably evolve over the course of time. "To this end, the therapist should strive to support the client in what is true for them in the here and now while also encouraging ongoing exploration and self-discovery during treatment and beyond" (Galinsky, 2023, p.202).

In addition, there is an addendum on the American Art Therapy Association website written by Michael Galarraga regarding the LGBTQIA+ population. Galarraga (2022), in the piece "Creating an inclusive and equitable space for LGBTQIA+ clients," set out American Art Therapy Association guidelines for art therapists working with LGBTQIA+ clients within its ethical document. Those guidelines included creating an inclusive and equitable space for working with LGBTQIA+ clients, building inclusivity and fostering trust with individuals in the LGBTQIA+ community. The guidelines reminded art therapists to consider the importance of being culturally responsive, having non-judgmental attitudes towards the client, focusing on their needs, keeping informed of political actions that affect the LGBTQIA+ community, and the importance of referring to another art therapist who is an expert in working with this community (Galarraga, 2022).

In my practice as a clinician and art therapist, I have used art making, specifically collage making, with LGBTQIA+ clients to explore sexual identity, homophobia, sexual trauma and abuse, bigotry and coming out. Art therapists must be aware of how discrimination and social stigma and other microaggressive acts threaten the emotional and physical health of LGBTQIA+ clients. Art making utilized in the treatment of LGBTQIA+ clients should be explored more, as research has shown that the art therapy process facilitates the self-discovery process (Chambala, 2008; Ganim, 1999; Liebmann, 1990; McNiff, 2004).

SELF-REFLECT AND RESPOND USING ART MAKING TO THESE QUESTIONS

1. Have you ever worked with a client in the LGBTQIA+ community? What was your experience? What interventions did you use?

2. Reflect on and examine your own views about heterosexuality and how it might impact your work with LGBTQIA+ clients. What do you understand about heterosexual and cisgender privilege? How would you handle having an LGBTQIA+ member of your family?

3. If you are part of the LGBTQIA+ community, how might your work be impacted by LGBTQIA+ clients? How would your understanding of heterosexual and cisgender privilege affect your work with LGBTQIA+ clients and other clients? As an LGBTQIA+ member of your family, how has your family supported or not supported you (if they know about it)? How can family, friends, the community and systems support you more?

4. What are the LGBTQIA+ resources around you, should you have a client as a member of that community?

5. What more do you need to learn about the LGBTQIA+ community and how best do you think you could go about learning?

Chapter 4

Special Study: Results and Findings

Experiences of racial microaggressions and coping skills among African American Professional Men.

—ANAH, 2014

Until the lion learns to speak, the tales of hunting will only be heard from the viewpoint of the hunter.

—AFRICAN PROVERB

Introduction

The purpose of this study was to examine the experiences of racial microaggressions in the workplace and coping mechanisms among high-achieving African American professional men. Semi-structured interviews and art-based focus groups using collages were conducted with six African American professional men, between the ages of 35 and 45 years old. They were from the District of Columbia (DC), Maryland and the Virginia region of the United States, and they acknowledged that subtle and overt racism exists in contemporary U.S. society and had personal experiences in the workplace. All were born and raised in the United States, self-identified as African American and were willing to share their experiences and coping mechanisms with other African American professional men in a focus group.

A phenomenological methodology and art-based research with the use of collage was used to uncover the lived experiences of these professional African American men as well as their coping habits. Results of the analysis uncovered eight themes that described experiences of racial microaggressions, seven themes that described the reaction/responses, ten themes that described the impact and consequences of racial microaggressions, and twelve themes that described the coping mechanisms. The themes of racial microaggression included ascription of intelligence, criminality/ assumption of criminality/the shadowy boogeyman, angry/aggressive Black man, second-class status, sexual objectification, always being watched/ assessed, sameness/all Black men look alike, and the Obama effect. Coping strategies included family and social support, prayer, armoring, mentoring, humor, music, food, self-care, being a "chameleon" numbing feelings, and documentations. The study also revealed significant visual metaphors from the collages.

Instrumentation

The purpose of this study was to listen to the voices of African American professional men, their experiences and coping responses for racial micro-aggressions in their workplace. Each participant was interviewed once for approximately 60–90 minutes. The questions were aimed at generating examples of microaggressions in the workplace, how these incidents affected the participants, and their coping responses. Questions inquired about the following: (a) types of subtle and covert racism and racial microaggressions experienced, (b) responses to the microaggressions, (c) the impact and consequences of the experiences of racial microaggressions in the workplace, and (d) types of coping mechanism. Follow-up probing questions were used to clarify responses.

The art-based focus group served as one of the sources for data collection, with the interviews and collages serving a secondary function. The art-based focus groups were conducted for approximately 120 minutes. Within those 120 minutes, 100 minutes were used to produce the two collages, one focusing on participants' experiences and the other on coping mechanisms. The last 20 minutes were used to debrief and discuss the process and the results of their collages. Participants then provided an explanation of their collages, answered questions posed by the researcher and reflected on their artwork with the other focus group members, for better understanding.

Tables: Results and findings of the study

Table 4.1 provides a description of the participants. A summary of experiences of racial microaggression themes, reaction, impact and consequences is presented in Table 4.2. A summary of the coping themes and clusters of racial microaggression is presented in Table 4.3.

The art-based focus groups revealed further themes and representational imagery that supported the interviews. Metaphors were revealed in the collages regarding experiences and coping mechanisms as they related to racial microaggressions. A summary of the collages is presented in Table 4.4. Many of the metaphors reinforced the messages of oppression, isolation, self-doubt, as well as functional coping methods and hope for the future. Some of the visual images also provide food for thought for the viewer to derive their own interpretations or conclusions about the visual metaphors.

Table 4.5 provides examples of visual metaphors of experiences of microaggressions and coping mechanisms. Under criminality/assumption of criminality, for example, most participants featured the image of police presence prominently in their collages (Figures 4.2, 4.3 and 4.4), and one participant had the image of an African American man being frisked by a White man (Figure 4.3), stressing the level of racial microaggression experiences. In addition, the concept of always being watched as a racial microaggression experience was presented by images of cameras and watchful eyes by participants in their collages (Figures 4.2–4.6), and this also contributed to the feelings of uneasiness and paranoia they felt in the workplace.

What follows are the results of the study, a series of reflections by study participants on their experiences of racism, the impact, their responses and their coping strategies. It includes verbatim the participants' encounters and experiences, and it invites self-reflection. It also works to create future inquiry as it relates to clinical practice, and ongoing consciousness regarding the issues around covert and overt racism. It is important to note that, during the time of this study, *12 Years a Slave* was a current movie at the box office, and President Barack Obama, the first Black president of the United States, was in office—and both factors feature significantly as references for the participants.

Table 4.1: Description of participants

Participants	Age	Race	Gender	Occupation/Years	Experienced racial microaggressions (RM)
Randolph	35	AA	Male	Department of Education/10yrs	Yes
Jackson	36	AA	Male	Anesthesiologist/4yrs	Yes
Dwayne	35	AA	Male	States attorney/10yrs	Yes
Lewis	40	AA	Male	Defense lawyer/10yrs	Yes
Phillip	37	AA	Male	Therapist/5yrs	Yes
James	42	AA	Male	Therapist/5yrs	Yes

Note: Phillip and James are the only two participants affiliated with a fraternity organization. Years refer to the number of years in occupation. RM: racial microaggressions.

In addition to the eight primary themes that emerged from the accounts of the experiences of six African American professional men in the workplace and twelve coping mechanisms, seven themes of their reactions/responses to racial microaggressions and ten themes about the impact and consequences of racial microaggressions were also revealed. The data analysis also resulted in the identification of three underdeveloped themes that emerged from the accounts of the experiences of these African American professional men in the workplace, and two underdeveloped negative coping themes.

Table 4.2: Experiences of racial microaggressions,
responses/reactions and impact/consequences

Categories	Themes	Meaning
Experiences of racial microaggressions in the workplace	RM: Ascription of intelligence	Viewed as incompetent and lazy, based on stereotypes
		Mistrust of expertise in the workplace
		Constantly being questioned about credentials and work skills
		Psychologically damaging and crippling to psyche
	RM: Criminality, assumption of criminality, the shadowy boogeyman	Being viewed and presumed to be dangerous, criminal and deviant, based on stereotypes
		Black men seen as the "shadowy boogeyman"
		Black men as sexual predators who rape White women
	RM: Angry/ Aggressive Black man	Based on stereotype, seen as threatening which creates fear in Whites and is detrimental to career path
		Having to play Sambo the clown, so as not to appear a threat at work

RM: Second-class status	Inferiority of Black men—viewed as being lesser human beings than Whites based on legacy of slavery and stereotypes
	Assumption of lower position in the workplace, e.g. assumed to be a nurse when you are a doctor
	Mental bondages that keep Black men under duress
	White privilege
	"Microinequities"—pattern of being ignored, dismissed, devalued, not respected in the workplace
	Creates environment of isolation and exclusion in the workplace
	Not made to feel welcome in the work environment
RM: Sexual objectification	Seen as sexual objects by White women in the workplace
	Creates a fear of sexual harassment
	Based on stereotype of Black men's sexual prowess
	Threatened by White men as seen as competition for White women
RM: Always being watched/ assessed	Under constant surveillance in the workplace
	Creates an atmosphere of paranoia
	Always being careful/extra cautious
	Pressure to always put on a smiley face, be the jester and be non-threatening
	Not being oneself—being an imposter at work
	To play Sambo the Happy Slave
	Pressure to abandon racial identity and culture, and conform to White norms to be successful in the workplace
RM: Sameness/ All Black men look alike	Negates individuality of Black men—seen as the same
	Assumed universality of the Black experience
	Deemed the spokesperson for their race

Categories	Themes	Meaning
	RM: The Obama effect/syndrome	Racism no longer exists Denial of individual racism Perceived minimal harm of racial microaggressions Color-blindness Being the exception to the rule/tokenization
Experiences of microaggressions: underdeveloped themes	Microaggressions from other African Americans in the workplace Ageism microaggressions Microaggressions based on being divorced	
Reactions/ Responses to racial microaggressions	Confront directly and assertively	Cognitive response Increases awareness for the perpetrators
	Confront with humor	Cognitive response Limits perception of the aggressive and angry Black man Makes co-workers more comfortable
	Ask questions for clarification/ conversation	Cognitive response To bring awareness to the perpetrator
	Do nothing, let it go and become the invisible, silent Black man	Cognitive response Rationalize that it would not help anyway Trying to be nonaggressive and not feed into the stereotypes of Black men being aggressive Avoiding disciplinary actions like write-ups and complaints
	Rescue or protect the perpetrator	Cognitive response To justify in their minds that people are not racist
	Anger, frustration and resentment	Emotional response

	Actively shattering preconceptions	Behavioral response Proving how great you are by doing a great job at work to shatter stereotypes
Impact/ Consequences of racial microaggressions	Self-doubt/ Self-inferiority complex	Imposter syndrome Low confidence Questioning if they belong Questioning if the American Dream is attainable for Black men
	Pressure and burden to represent the whole African American race/ group	Constantly under pressure not to disappoint anyone Representing an entire community and race Pressure of the weight of the world on their shoulders daily Fear of spoiling the chances of other Black professionals in the field based on how successful they are
	Burden to fight negative stereotypes	Creates psychological stressors
	Constant pressure not to offend anyone at work or make mistakes	Being overly careful Feeling uncomfortable at work Looking for approval from supervisors and co-workers
	Burden to make White co-workers and clients comfortable	Overcompensation Sometimes take on the persona of Sambo the Happy Slave, at work
	Develop fake persona and being a "chameleon"	Being inauthentic—feeling psychologically exhausted/feeling that they are not themselves
	The Sambo the Happy Slave Effect/Loss of integrity	Having to play a clown, smile and pretend that everything is okay Compromised integrity
	Paranoia within the work environment	Not comfortable Mistrust of the nurturing of the work environment Tend to leave job quicker and not interact with co-workers Isolation in job environment

Categories	Themes	Meaning
	Sadness, depression and pain and the futility of it all	Hard and sometimes impossible to be a Black man on a daily basis Futility of the struggle to be successful Fear of the burden of success Feeling trapped—no way out Not sure of the direction to freedom
	Not thinking about the daily assaults	Numb feelings at work, which can be psychologically damaging

Table 4.3: Coping theme clusters of racial microaggressions

Themes: Coping mechanisms	Meaning
Family/Social support network	Stress reliever Seeking advice and/or processing experiences of microaggression The entire Black race is seen as a community—sharing stories, collective consciousness from the Black community Healing Helps you process when you are getting the RM Helps you compose yourself and successfully navigate around them Support from organizations and fraternity
Prayer/Spirituality	Functions as support network Healing Empowering Uplifting Gaining strength to deal with the assaults and as a means of protection from daily assaults
Armoring	Pride in culture and historically black colleges and universities (HBCUs) Excelling in job/personal excellence The Obama effect/turning it to pride Not the exception to the rule Shattering preconceptions and stereotypes Advertising excellence in a professional capacity
Mentoring/ Mentorship	Sharing strategies to help buffer assaults for those being mentored

Humor	Less threatening Sambo the Happy Slave/clown
Music	Automatically helps elevate mood Stress reliever Healing qualities Helps to deal with the world Helps decompress from daily stressors of work
Food	A social event of sharing/love expression Connections/bring people together Relieves stress/helps with coping Spiritual and mental nourishment
Alcohol	Used as a stress reliever Metaphor for celebration/reward Sign of maturity and being an adult Used as a reward/privilege for hard work
Self-care	Reading, writing poetry Taking vacations with family Physical exercise Good nutrition Self-reward—shopping for expensive clothes, cars and goods Possibly counseling Living in the present Stress reliever
Being a "chameleon"	Changing persona and "code switching" at work to cope with a variety of different situations Seen as gift to be able to have this skill The Sambo Effect—having to play a clown sometimes so as not to be seen as a threat or aggressive
Numbing feelings and not thinking	Too painful to think about it
Documentation	"Covering my ass" through emails, and other correspondence Although tedious, a necessity for protection
Underdeveloped themes: Negative coping	Smoking cigarettes (only one participant) as a stress reliever/time-out Past use of marijuana (only one participant) as a coping mechanism

Table 4.4: Collages of participants' experiences and
coping mechanisms of racial microaggressions

Participants	Experiences	Coping
Randolph		
Jackson		
Dwayne		

Lewis		
Phillip		
James		

Table 4.5: Visual metaphors and images of experiences of racial microaggressions, and coping mechanisms

Visual representations/ metaphors	Themes
	Experiences
Images from the movie *12 Years a Slave*	"Are you an engineer or a nigger?" The double standards put on African American men about who they are and where they fit in American society The history and legacy of slavery and mental bondage they still feel today
The Black shadowy figure	Fear/Criminality Aggressive Black male
Black man being frisked by a White man	Suppression/Oppression Assumption of criminality Second-class status
Police presence (cars, policemen)	Criminality/Assumption of criminality
Camera/lenses and watching eyes/ binoculars	Criminality—always under the lens at all times/always being watched Promotes paranoia in work environment
Being put in a box	Not being seen as an individual Assumed universality of Black Experience Denial of individual racism
Little boy in big suit	Imposter syndrome Unable to be true self at work
Sports/tackling/ basketball game	The struggle, the hurt and anger from the legacy of slavery and second-class status The impact and burdens of racial microaggressions Psychological damaging impact of racial microaggressions
Man in wheelchair	Crippling/Psychological damage of racial microaggressions—ascription of intelligence
Exploding Mucinex bottle	Stress/Psychological damage of the experiences of racial microaggressions Anger and frustration Other emotional reactions to racism
Attractive White woman White woman smiling/ looking seductive	Reminder of the dangers that can come with interactions with White females at work—mixed messages/sexual harassment Sexual objectification of African American men

Half-naked muscular African American man	Sexual objectification of Black men
Clean-cut shaven Black man Bryant Gumbel Well-dressed man with glasses and bow-tie	Non-aggressive, not angry, tamed and more professional The standard of a non-threatening Black professional man classically/traditionally non-threatening
Naked White man freely running around	White privilege/negligent ignorance of Whites
Stacked iPhones	Having to be the best/armoring/not making mistakes
Painting *The Last Supper*	Feeling betrayed and sacrificed like Jesus Legacy of slavery/legacy of the sacrifice of Jesus
Coping mechanisms	
Images of intact family	The importance of family members as comfort and stress relievers Children couples (the joy of having children as part of their family dynamics)
Praying	Spirituality/Prayer Buffer evil and negative energy
Playing sports/bicycle/ lifting weights	Self-care exercise Relieve stress Release negative energy
Vacation	Metaphor for self-care/relieve stress Plane
HBCUs	Metaphors for armoring/pride
Former Mayor Kurt Schmoke Morgan State University Dean Nelson Mandela	Pride Cultural pride Pride/Freedom
Music/Jazz/Classical	Soothing power to uplift Relieve stress
Food	Metaphor for socialization/love expression
Romance—cologne/ perfume	Metaphor for family/being married Metaphor for romance with wife
Bottles of champagne and alcohol Bottle of Moet	Metaphor for celebrating/having a good time Reward for hard work in the office Having a good time

Visual representations/ metaphors	Themes
Man holding a camera	Metaphor for capturing images in the present/living in the present/less stressful
Chameleon	Metaphor for changing persona at work
Sprig of leaf/pregnant woman	Metaphor for sign of hope/new life/better days
Man jumping out of the box	Metaphor for survivor/resiliency/be brave
Cigarettes/Marijuana	Metaphor for escape from reality/relief Stress reliever/time-out

Section I: Experiences of racial microaggression themes

The data analysis identified eight primary themes from the accounts of the experiences of six African American professional men in the workplace. Table 4.2 provides a list of emergent themes, which include: (1) Ascription of intelligence; (2) Criminality/Assumption of criminality/The shadowy boogeyman; (3) Angry/Aggressive Black man; (4) Second-class status; (5) Sexual objectification; (6) Always being watched/assessed; (7) Sameness/All Black men look alike; and (8) The Obama effect/syndrome. Several of the themes are interconnected to some degree. This section features prominently the racial microaggression themes found from the study. Each theme is described accompanied by specific examples of participants' experiences of racial microaggressions using direct quotes from the interview transcripts and visual metaphors and images to support those quotes.

Theme 1: Ascription of intelligence

Ascription of intelligence was a major racial microaggression theme revealed in this study. This theme emerged from both the interviews and the art-based focus groups. Ascription of intelligence refers to, and can be described as, racial microaggression that assumes and assigns a degree of intelligence to an African American based on his race (Sue, 2010). All six participants discussed having interactions with supervisors, managers, colleagues and clients who questioned their ability to do their jobs, and that conveyed the belief that the African American man is intellectually inferior based on his race. Participants used words like *incompetent* and *reliability* to describe their experiences of the way they were treated by White colleagues and some clients in the workplace. Some participants felt susceptible for blame if something that was not their fault went wrong in the workplace. One participant described how his professionalism and reliability elicited surprise in others in his work environment.

> My reliability is always in question no matter how consistent I am profes-
> sionally. It's always a surprise, as if it's unnatural for me as a Black man to
> be reliable or competent, to be prompt and on time, to be proficient in any
> way. If there is a complication, they are more apt to believe that it was due
> to negligence and incompetence on my part than they would be for my
> colleagues. (Jackson)

All participants indicated that they had experienced feelings of being stereotyped as not being good enough, deemed unqualified, being frequently underestimated when called on to do a task, and having their competency frequently questioned. Participants highlighted instances where they felt that their competency was being questioned due to the perception that African American men are not as intelligent and capable in their abilities to perform their jobs.

They referenced the concept of White privilege when describing their experiences of being questioned about their competency and expertise in the workplace. One participant noted:

> The Black man is so unique. We have a unique set of circumstances where we
> must fit into the stereotypes unless we are met with microaggressions. I see it
> daily. If a White attorney walks into a courtroom, there's just a presumption
> by most people that he is competent. Whereas with a Black attorney, it's
> going to be wait and see. If you are a White man, we are good. Everyone
> else has to prove themselves. The only time you can walk in and your word
> is gospel is if you are a White man. (Dwayne)

Other participants noted many examples of how they were constantly questioned about their qualifications and skill to perform the job. They discussed the impact of the ascription of intelligence microaggression theme on education and training, particularly with African American men who have been educated in historically black colleges or universities (HBCUs). They discussed that there was the perception that African Americans educated in an HBCU were not as intelligent as others educated in other colleges or universities:

> I went to an HBCU for my undergraduate degree, which I'm very proud
> about, but many Whites in my profession are not impressed with that, and
> then I went to a very prestigious law school. When I come into the court-
> room, the first thing that people see is my color, and with that, they ascribe

a certain degree of intelligence to my Black male presence. But then you see their faces change when I start speaking and defending my client; all of a sudden, you see them pay better attention to me. The White prosecutors who don't know my reputation, when they hear me work, realize that they have to come with their A game if they want to battle with me in the courtroom. (Lewis)

Images in the collages supported the impact of the ascription of intelligence microaggression theme on African American professional men. One participant shared how the constant questioning of his skill and competence made him feel some self-doubt in his collage (Figure 4.2A).

Here in big quotes, it says, "I'm a phony." That also coincides here with some of the Affirmative Action words because, again, I'm not made to feel welcome professionally in my workplace; it's always "How did you get here, are you really qualified, are you equal with your non-Black colleagues and counterparts?" (Jackson)

(Figure 4.2A) I have a well-dressed Black man but I cut his head off and above it says, "You are an idiot." What this means is that no matter how well put together I seem to be or even appear to be, the face of it is less than that. That is how it's perceived by my colleagues, that I'm not on par in some manner, so every day that I am, and demonstrate that I am, they inquire about my training, and they are terribly surprised that I was able to accomplish those things and be successful. (Jackson)

One participant in his collage had an image of an African American man in a wheelchair with the word "Crippled" to support the impact the ascription of intelligence microaggression theme had on his mental health (Figure 4.4A).

On the top left you'll see a figure of a Black man in a wheelchair with the word "Crippled!" in big letters. I can't tell you how much damage the constant questioning of your intelligence does to your psyche. The stress to constantly have to be on guard or prepared to fight for the right for them to see you as an intelligent human being gets to be crippling at times. Once I've proven myself, then things are okay, but to constantly—daily, hourly—have to explain, to prove my worth, is exhausting and damaging. (Lewis)

Theme 2: Criminality/Assumption of criminality/the shadowy boogeyman
All participants in this study shared their experiences of the assumption of criminality racial microaggression. This theme emerged from the interviews and the art-based focus groups in this study. The shadowy boogeyman was a prominent metaphor and theme for some participants in the study. One

participant illustrated his experiences with the following vignette about how Black men are perceived as the shadowy boogeyman and many Whites are fearful of them.

> The boogeyman has always been the Black man, no matter what it is... Trayvon Martin...everything. Whatever the threat is, the threat is a Black shadowy figure. (Jackson)

Another participant shared an example in history of how the Black man was seen as a sexual perpetrator whose primary desire was to rape White women. He added that Black men have been thought of as aggressors for many years and this was ingrained in the culture and history of the United States.

> There are so many instances where stereotypes have been perpetuated in mainstream culture...there is a story about Coca Cola and part of the reason for them taking the cocaine out. Coca Cola was made available in vending machines as opposed to the soda shop, which meant that anyone with the coins could get the Coca Cola, which also meant that Black people who couldn't go to the soda shop could now get this soda, which had cocaine in it. So part of the campaigns to get rid of this was that this cocaine turned these Blacks into these savage violent offenders, who want to rape White women, as it's been ingrained in society that the primitive primal desire of Black men is to rape and sleep with White women. When you go through the history of lynching and abuses, almost every one that you hear of, the main factors and accusation is of coveting, looking at, whistling at, a White woman, which has been justification for arrests, abuse, murders, lynching; it was retribution for it. (Jackson)

Jackson also talked about Black men being used as scapegoats when people want to get away with a crime, and how easy it is for society to accept these stories of the Black man who did it.

> Even the woman down in North Carolina who drove her kids into the lake, who's the boogeyman? Oh, some Black guy carjacked us! This woman made this story up about being kidnapped and raped by a Black man. She was out in the fields, I mean, there was no Black person around for miles and there was another woman who called to report that she saw the man walking through her yard. It turned out that the whole thing was all made up, and the real story was that this White woman was simply having an affair and got home late, and she didn't know how else to explain to her husband why she got home late, and so she made up this story. (Jackson)

Many participants discussed examples of the impact of their experiences with the criminality theme of racial microaggressions in the art-based focus groups. In the collage (Figure 4.3A), one participant highlighted the impact of the criminality/assumption of criminality microaggression theme. There was a perception that even the life of a convicted White male criminal was worth more than that of a professional African American man.

> The man in the orange jumpsuit (Figure 4.3A), what stood out for me, was that I recognized him—that's the golfer, John Daly. And when White men are depicted in this way, it's always from a *fall from grace* circumstance. Whereas it's the norm when it's a Black face depicted in this kind of criminal imagery. And so, the dialogue about that particular individual has been such like, "Oh, he's an alcoholic, he's had a fall from grace." But not only does his life have more value and is worth more than mine will ever be as a Black male, but his consequences will be more favorable, even though he's in a jumpsuit. So that's something that I noticed about that. You don't see images of Whites depicted in these wrong-doing images, and if they are they are often disowned and shunned by the greater White community. Whereas it's embraced and accepted if it's a Black face. (Dwayne)

Theme 3: Angry/Aggressive Black man

Participants discussed the double standard of being perceived as too aggressive in the workplace. They expressed that they were considered aggressive and angry, just by their mere presence in the company of their White counterparts at work. This theme emerged from the interviews and the art-based focus groups. They were seen as threatening and intimidating when they were being assertive and passionate, which, ironically, are the same behaviors that their White counterparts exhibited. These attributes, the participants added, were detrimental to their career path and work environment.

> Being Black has an imposing stereotype to it—that even the smallest, meekest Black man is a danger. It's just the way things are and it's ingrained in our history, which has given reason for cause, the same reason that says, if I raise my voice, I am angry and aggressive, whereas if my White counterpart raises their voice they are seen as passionate or stressing their point. I'm seen as a threat. (Jackson)

In the discussions during the art-based focus groups, the image of a clean-shaven African American man was depicted as a metaphor for a non-aggressive, tamed, professional Black man (Figure 4.1A). One participant shared that the perception is that clean-shaven Black men are less aggressive looking, and less feared by White people.

> In the imagery of this clean-cut man (Figure 4.1A), there's something to not

having facial hair. There's an aggressiveness to a man, all men, but exceedingly so a Black man; having any facial hair is perceived as aggressive. It's seen to be a scary thing, it's untamed. I've had facial hair for the last 18 years, I guess, but I know that it's a part of the initial impression, and I've frequently wondered out loud with some colleagues of mine what White people see when they see Black people. (Randolph)

President Obama doesn't have a beard or a goatee or anything and I feel that he never could because if you have a mustache or a beard, you are considered a rogue, or you have something to hide, which paradoxically is funny in the world of politics, because they are all clean-cut to try to show that they have nothing to hide. But with a clean-cut Black man, maybe they can see that they can trust him, that he's acceptable, he's someone who they can be cool with or who they can relate to. But when they see the man with the beard, they don't see the same thing. There is a photo of a well-dressed Black man in my collage. He has glasses and a bow-tie which classically have been the traditional views and imagery of an educated, non-threatening Black man. (Jackson)

One participant placed an image of Bryant Gumbel in his art-based collage (Figure 4.3A) and talked about how this image of an African American man was more acceptable and non-threatening to White people in the work environment.

To the right of that is Bryant Gumbel (Figure 4.3A) who is typically seen—which is deserved or not, and I don't have any idea as I don't know him to say—as the figurehead for what an acceptable, non-threatening Black person is or should look like or should be, which is not what I am or appear to be. It's typically offensive to most Black folks who know better. So being a professional Black person, someone like this, is offensive and repulsive. He is somebody who represents what he is supposed to represent, and I by no means try to attempt to fit into that mold—that is not a goal of mine—but some people do and so I recognize that for what it is. (Dwayne)

One participant had an image of a clown in his collage (Figure 4.2A) and explained that this represented having to appear clown-like so as not to seem aggressive and threatening in the workplace.

This is a clown, and that's what it feels like at work. That you are a clown, that you are some way a Sambo of some sorts because the most common way to disarm situations and appear that you are not a threat is to be a prankster of sorts, and to deflect, like a radio clown, deflect the danger around you in that way. (Jackson)

Theme 4: Second-class status

Many participants reported experiencing the second-class status theme of racial microaggression in the workplace. This theme emerged from both the interviews and the art-based focus groups in this study. It refers to the African American professional man being treated as a lesser person in their workplace. All participants acknowledged that they had experienced microinequities and patterns of being ignored and dismissed, disrespected, being invisible sometimes and being excluded and feeling isolated. They cited instances where their experiences disclosed a blatant disregard for valuing African American men, and the privilege White men have in this country. Many of the participants directly related this second-class status to the legacy and consequences of slavery, inferiority of African American men based on stereotypes, and White privilege. One participant noted:

> But it's not uncommon for a White person to go all the way through high school, all the way through undergrad, even through grad school, and never have had a long-term meaningful relationship with a person who is not White. The stereotypes of the inferiority of Black people are still ingrained in them. That's just the way it is in this country, it is very common, and I don't think people realize that until they get into the workforce and they are around people who are not White and they have to work in an intimate and close environment. It's the first time in their lives they've ever had to do that and they might be 25, 30, 35 years old at that time. That is something I recognize, so when things like that happen in settings where I feel like I've been slighted or disregarded or shunned, it's not always because they know who I am or that they don't like me, it's because I'm not White, and I'm somehow inferior. And I also recognize that that could be subconscious on their part, as people don't always recognize when they are doing that. (Lewis)

The concept of second-class status/citizen was related to one participant's description of a racial microaggression that involved not fitting people's expectations at work. Some participants noted that Whites are positioned in top professional careers and do not expect African Americans to hold those positions.

> I know that I don't fit the part, I know that I don't fit people's expectations. I'm 36 and I look about that age or younger, anywhere between 30 and 40 I guess, and I'm a Black male. I know that people don't expect me to be their attending physician, especially for anesthesia, which people have various understanding of, but many people know that it is a highly specialized field, whereas they are used to seeing you as a nurse, a secretary, maybe

a physician's assistant or something like that. I know I don't fit the part. (Jackson)

The concept of White privilege and the inferiority of African American men was related to this participant's description of a racial microaggression that involved being perceived as a second-class citizen and assumed to be inferior based purely on the color of his skin, and the disadvantage this created for him in the courtroom.

> In my profession, if you are a White person and you walk into a courtroom and you have a case against a defense attorney, as a prosecutor you automatically have the benefit of the assumption that you are competent and you are good. Whereas I feel that by the way I'm treated by other defense attorneys, until they actually have a trial with me, I don't get that same respect, I don't have the benefit of that same amount of competency, which works to my detriment because I'm not feared. The attorneys who go to trial with me, they don't want to go to trial with me again, but I have to get to that point, which could mean that a case that otherwise could have pled out will go to trial because they are looking across the table at a Black man who couldn't possibly be that good. And that's powerful, that's a powerful advantage that I do not have, but there is nothing I can do about it except continue to be great and better than all my counterparts every time. (Dwayne)

Another participant described an incident where the color of his skin and his perceived second-class status were clearly factors in prohibiting him from performing his professional duties.

> There have been instances where we've had patients whom you speak to and get the full medical, everything is set, and then they'll make a comment or request that they prefer that there be no brown people in their surgery. I've had that happen. (Jackson)

One participant in his collage depicted a White male dancing naked with the word *smile* on his body (Figure 4.3A). This participant related this image to the privilege and freedom White people have and African Americans do not have as second-class citizens.

> He has written on his chest "smile," his arms are raised in the air, he is smiling and he is just happy and free, and to me that is representative of the privilege that White people, especially White men, have in this country of being able to just be free and essentially do what the hell they want to do. Such as being on the stage with a bunch of people butt naked and smiling and having a good old time, and that is something a Black person could never do—not that I would want to do that, but it's just representative of

privilege that I don't have but that I recognize is there, whether other people recognize it or not. Others looking at this image don't see or think race at all, but I see race in a lot of things—in most things. (Dwayne)

Another participant used an image from the movie *12 Years a Slave* (Figure 4.2A) to depict the mental bondage that continues to enslave many African American professional men, because he felt that White people kept reminding them, with many microaggressions, not to overstep their place, and to keep them in their second-class status.

This is another scene from *12 Years a Slave* (Figure 4.2A). This is a scene where Solomon Northup had crafted a raft to go through a canal, and in a lot of ways he did not realize his place, as now being a slave he was overstepping his bounds by showing his engineering experience and thoughts and ingenuity. They actually asked him, "Are you a nigger or are you an engineer?"—to which he had no answer. And I often feel this way—that there is a part that I'm supposed to play and I'm frequently straddling being in and out of bounds of that part. And if ever asked if I'm a nigger or an engineer, I'd also struggle to find an appropriate answer. (Jackson)

In his collage (Figure 4.2A), one participant wrote "medical assistant" as he shared with the group that he was often mistaken for any service worker position in the hospital, but not for the doctor that he was.

Here it says medical assistant, which is another way again to degrade me and what my position is. That is frequently used; I am a nurse, an assistant, an orderly, a janitor, anything except what I am—a doctor. I'm not always made to feel welcome professionally in my workplace. (Jackson)

Theme 5: Sexual objectification of African American men/exoticism of Black men

The fifth theme found in both the interviews and the art-based focus groups was the sexualization and exoticism of Black men in the workplace. Many of the participants reported the sexualization of African American men as a major racial microaggression that they experienced in the workplace. One participant stated:

White men and women really believe in that stereotype about how big a Black man's penis is, and they tend to treat you according to their fears. White men always want to challenge you, and White women are always curious. (James)

Other participants discussed how the continual subjugation of African American men to roles of sexual objects affected them in the workplace.

This happens to me all the time now. Women, particularly White women, will look me up, it's not hard to find people these days with Google and the internet, and they will set up an appointment because they want an attorney. But then when they come in, yes, sometimes it's legit and they need a lawyer for one thing or the other, but more often than not, they just come to meet me, and try to flirt with me because they've seen my picture on the internet. It makes me feel a little uneasy, because some of these women are really aggressive with it; it's really bad. (Lewis)

In the art-based collages, the participants portrayed images of half-naked and shirtless muscular African American men (Figures 4.2A and 4.3A) as a metaphor for the sexual objectification and exoticism of African American men that they experienced in the workplace.

In the art-based focus group, all participants expressed their caution about their interactions with White female co-workers. The central figure of a White female expressed one participant's metaphor of this behavior (Figure 4.3A).

I also chose an "attractive" White woman here. I have to be conscious of how I interact with White women, at work and in professional settings, because, generally speaking, White women love me. People love me in general, but White women love me too. I have to be conscious of how I interact with them because I know that I'm being watched, and how I talk to them in front of people, how I touch them, you know, physical contact, how I speak to them, and things of that nature, in a way that I know that other people don't have to. And you know, not all Black males are conscious of that, but I'm glad that I am. There are a lot of pitfalls that can come to Black men for not being conscious of that. (Dwayne)

Other participants expressed the objectification of African American men by White women in their workplace, and the caution and uneasiness they felt when working with them (Figures 4.5A and 4.6A).

To the right of my collage, you see a White woman and she is smiling, with the word "Look" to her left (Figure 4.5A). I just feel that this is a metaphor for the dangers of getting close to a White female co-worker at work. The woman smiles enticingly and invitingly, I mean, she's flirting with you, but you are only to look at her, and not touch or get too close. You know? Really tricky; and I never fall for it. (Phillip)

Theme 6: Always being watched/assessed

This theme of always being watched or assessed emerged in both the interviews and the art-based focus groups of this study. Many of the participants felt that their presence and contributions were deemed less valuable than their White counterparts, and felt that they were always being watched to catch any wrongdoings at work. This created feelings of uneasiness and paranoia and made them feel like an imposter, and as if they were being inauthentic in the workplace. Participants also noted a required sense of self-sacrifice and superficiality in order to conform to the White standards in the workplace. In addition, participants felt tremendous pressure and burden from this close surveillance. Dwayne stated, "I know I'm being assessed constantly, even by people I'm not speaking to. You are being assessed by your race, your clothes, by the way you walk, and by the way you speak." Many of the participants noted that always being watched and always being under surveillance in the workplace resulted in an atmosphere of paranoia, which sometimes led to unhappiness in the workplace, and early departure from that employment. Phillip shared, "Paranoia in the workplace does not exactly help make you become a productive employee. I was so unhappy at a job once because of the constant surveillance that I only stayed for five months." Another participant shared a similar experience about the racial microaggression of being always watched at his place of employment.

> It seems like you really are paranoid for thinking that you are being watched in the workplace; sometimes it's hard to figure out if you became paranoid because of the surveillance or if you came into the workplace paranoid already and the paranoia from being watched made you more paranoid. You know? It's just another thing you have to think about in the workplace and figure out if the environment you are in is too watchful or if you can deal with it. If you can't then you start looking for another place of employment, or better still, start your own business, your own thing. I left a job after four months because it was just getting too crazy. (James)

All of the participants in their collages had an image of a camera, watchful eyes and the police, as visual metaphors depicting that they were always being watched with everything that they did in the workplace (Figures 4.1A–4.6A).

Dwayne stated, "There is a camera…which is symbolic for me of typically being always under the lens at all times."

> Cameras are constantly present in your daily existence. Everybody is watching you, to see what you are up to, all the time. I know for a fact that White people don't feel this burden. That is why I put the big sign "Can't Walk" in my collage (Figure 4.6A), because that's how you sometimes feel with all the watchful eyes around you. It makes you feel cautious about everything that you do, more careful. (James)

There is a long telephoto lens and above it, and it says "now you say cheese" (Figure 4.2A) because it always feels like not only am I being watched but that I have to put on a smiley face and be a jester to a degree, in order to be non-threatening—to be the Bryant Gumbel, if you will, of where I am in the workplace. (Jackson)

You are always being watched. You are being watched to see how aggressive you are going to be; you are being watched to see how acceptable you are; we are being watched to see how we handle our past, and to see how free we are really going to be. (Randolph)

Not being able to be one's self at work and feeling like an imposter, not authentic and unable to properly fill those expectations of the watchful eyes was a feeling that participants felt was related to the racial microaggression of being always watched in the workplace. One participant depicted this feeling in his collage with an image of a little African American child in a suit that was too big for him (Figure 4.1A).

The child is in an oversized suit. You can't really be yourself; you must constantly fit in other people's shoes; you must be better than and wiser than White people, as well as pave the way for those who follow you. And in my opinion, that's such an insurmountable task, because you'll never really fit. So, you mean to tell me that I have to be better than the person who designed this suit, and I should also be better than the people who follow me? That's a huge task. So that child represents trying to fill in those shoes but still being yourself and trying to attain something that you probably will never fit into. (Randolph)

Theme 7: Sameness/All Black men look alike

Many of the participants in this study shared about their experiences regarding the racial microaggression of sameness, which conveys that all African Americans are the same, look alike and there is no distinction between one African American and the other. This theme emerged from both the interviews and the art-based focus groups. One participant shared an experience he had in the workplace that highlighted this theme.

As an intern, I remember a circumstance when I was there with another doctor and friend of mine, and we were the only two, but they would always get our names wrong and call us the other's name all the time. And aside from being Black and both between 150 and 350 pounds and both being somewhere between 5-foot 5 inches and 6-foot 5 inches, we basically looked nothing alike. And it was funny because in that building, we had different colored uniforms, and I had a white coat and he had a blue coat, so there was no reason not to know it, but even our co-workers always got us mixed up. One day we stood together and we told them that there was a difference between the two of us and they should not just see a Black doctor but that they needed to see the individual doctor. (Jackson)

One participant in his collage used an image of a White woman in a box (Figure 4.3A) as a metaphor for being placed in a box by White people for their comfort while he was in fact a unique individual.

To the left of that, a White female in a box (Figure 4.3A). A lot of times I feel like I'm being trapped in a box, with a bunch of people trying to trap me and make me more acceptable to them or more easily understandable to them. So there is always a constant struggle because I don't really fit in a box at all, I'm pretty unique, I'm an individual person, and I've done things my own way for the most part as far as my courtroom style goes. It's what works for me, and in terms of my personality, I'm not like anyone. I think that life is constantly a struggle not to be kept in a box that typically people want Black men to be in, so that they can be comfortable around them. We are not all the same. (Dwayne)

All participants noted that the consequences of the sameness theme of racial microaggression in the workplace was that White colleagues seemed compelled to have one African American represent and speak for all the African Americans in that work environment or even outside that environment. Two participants also talked about experiencing being deemed the spokesperson for the entire African American race, particularly with topics relating to race. Phillip stated, "It's really offensive to me that every Black topic that they talk about, they always want my opinion, like I'm the expert for all things Black. My Black is not always the same as another person's Black."

James added, "I love it when every Black topic or decisions involving race is directed towards you because they think that you are the authority, particularly when it concerns another Black colleague, student or client."

Theme 8: The Obama effect/syndrome

The Obama effect or syndrome in this study represented many factors that the participants highlighted, that affected them as African American professionals since President Obama had been in office (since 2008). This theme emerged in both the interviews and the art-based focus groups. One of the overarching findings was participants' descriptions of subtle techniques and comments used by co-workers and supervisors to infer that now that Obama was in office, there were no excuses for African American men to feel discriminated over, and that racism was over. One participant shared how other White colleagues in his office engaged him about how racism no longer existed, post President Obama.

> I can't tell you how many White folks I've spoken to believe that we are living in a post-racial era. They start with, "Since Obama is in office, I know you guys are happy and have nothing to complain about." I mean, they don't even bother to say President Obama, and give our president his respect, it's Obama, Obama; so disrespectful. But I really can't get over them feeling that just because a Black man is in office, racism is over. I mean, it's a new form of racism now; they've blocked every possible thing he has tried to do in office, and I think the same frustration he feels is the same frustration we Black professional men feel every day at work. Undermined and very much patronized. (Phillip)

> A colleague also told me once that now that President Obama was in office it was time to get rid of dedicating an entire month to Blacks, "Black history month is no longer necessary, don't you think?" And I smiled and said that while we were at it, that we should also get rid of breast cancer awareness month, heart disease awareness month, and all the other months that bring awareness to causes. She avoided me for two weeks after that conversation. (Randolph)

In one collage (Figure 4.2A), a participant portrayed the disrespect that many African American professional men are subjected to despite their prominence as leaders in their fields, just like President Obama.

> Here is the word, "Obama." I chose that because it doesn't say President Obama, it just says Obama, and what that represents to me is the disrespect of a successful Black man, the president of our country, who is somehow other, he's exotic, he's detached and he doesn't warrant the respect given to his office, his position or his accomplishments. I relate to that in a lot of ways. (Jackson)

Many of the participants reported the negative effects of having President Obama as the president—the perception of reality shattered because presidents do not come as Black, and this threatens all the perceptions of White people.

> We have a Black president, and opposition to him is so hyper-racialized and hyper-polarized, strictly because he is Black, and again, the perception, the anticipation, that some White people have, they cannot process that he is their president, because presidents don't look like that. So, it has shattered

their whole perception of reality and it has threatened their whole perception of self. What does this mean? So, when they say, things like, "This is the demise of America." They are absolutely right, if America means to them their way of life of being superior and dominant and unchallenged in every way—if that's the America they mean, then yes, that way of life is going by the wayside. But they have a hard time articulating that in ways of any substance. And we see how the President has coped with that; he does not cope with that in an aggressive manner, or by falling into the stereotype of being that angry Black man. So, they find other things wrong with him: he's a Marxist, he's a dictator, he's secretive, and everything about his description is of a shadowy boogeyman, something is mysterious about him, he's from an exotic foreign land, he secretly wants these things. It's all boogeyman stuff, and it's all because he's Black. So, it's very similar for the rest of us, while having this President is an advancement in so many ways, and may in fact help in a positive way with people's perceptions, it also highlights the perceptions that linger and remain, and that's the same, whether you are president, or a doctor, or you work in an office building—you still have those same perceptions. (Lewis)

Many of the participants reported how now that President Obama's approval rate had gone down, his lack of success somehow reflected on the entire race of African American men. Phillip noted, "It's so ignorant that everyone thinks that President Obama's approval rate is a reflection of how I do at work. But it is. This healthcare thing is killing my approval rate here at work." Jackson added:

The idea that people think that we are all going to be in this non-racial society is crazy. We need to be aware of all our differences, learn from them, and perhaps the world could be in balance—I mean, truly.

It's interesting. For some reason White folks seem to equate how President Obama is doing in the approval ratings to how I'm doing. Ever since he came into power, if he's popular, somehow my professional life is easier, but when he's not, it's not always so good for me. It's like we are judged based on what he does in office. We are kinda at his mercy, well, sort of. It really is interesting how that works. (James)

The concept of denial of individual racism in this study was equated with the microaggression caused by the Obama effect/syndrome. Many of the participants cited examples of colleagues minimizing the importance of their racial identity, since Barack Obama became the President of the United States of America.

Being the exception to the rule and feeling tokenized was another concept that participants highlighted based on President Obama coming into office. One participant shared an experience where his colleagues viewed him as not being a typical African American man, and being like Obama, not sharing in the stereotypical behavior that is perceived as unacceptable to White people.

> Prior to President Obama being in the White House, it just seemed to me that people didn't think that people like us existed. One of my supervisors, a great woman, and a White woman, was showing a potential new hire around our building. It was right at the time that President Obama was re-elected in 2012, and they both came to my office, and I'm this Black guy, and maybe intimidating looking to them. I think maybe to help ease their minds, my supervisor actually said, "Oh, this is [name deleted], he's like Obama, one of the good guys." And I know she meant that as a compliment, but it was stunning for me to hear. (Phillip)

Another participant shared his experiences of his White colleagues sometimes talking politics to him and talking about the African American struggle, and they asked him why it was possible for him to escape the struggle because he was the exception to the rule, like President Obama.

> Politics usually brings out the worst in people. During the election cycles, it's about entitlement programs, and how these marginalized folks need to take care of themselves, and they pull out these streams of conservative consciousness. I don't think that they often realize what they are saying. And it's really funny how that works because they'll speak to how these welfare states are abusing the system. But the perception and the expectation are that because I'm there with them, I share their view, I'm also a conservative who looks down on these other people. It's like you're not like the rest of them, you are somehow different because you are among us, to a degree. (Jackson)

Color-blindness was another racial microaggression attributed to the presidency of President Obama. Supervisors and co-workers delivered microaggressions in perceived conscious and unconscious ways that directly or indirectly demonstrated color-blindness and a need to aspire to the White culture. Many statements the participants voiced indicated that their White co-workers did not feel that they were equal to them. One participant shared an experience he had with his supervisor within the supervisor-supervisee context.

> My supervisor was notorious for saying things like, "When I see you, I just see another human being." Obviously, this was unacceptable to me as it clearly

denied me my racial experiences and my individuality. I remember doing supervision with her and asking advice on how to work with a particular African American boy with issues, and she said, "Kids are kids. What would any other 16-year-old boy need at this time? All Obama needed at that time got him to the presidency." Oh, the ignorance! (Phillip)

Experiences of racial microaggressions: Underdeveloped themes
The interviews and the focus groups mentioned a number of incidents that could not readily be classified into any of the eight major themes, because all the participants did not mention them, and the incidents were not probed further. However, there were underdeveloped themes that emerged in the experiences of microaggression for some participants in the workplace that included *microaggressions from other African Americans, ageism microaggression* and *microaggressions based on being divorced.*

Section II: Reactions/Responses to racial microaggressions
As revealed in this study, there was no question that the recipients recognized that a microaggression had occurred, and they did not require a process of pondering whether a situation had occurred that was a microaggression or not. However, the question and the dilemma were sometimes how or whether to respond and deal with it. Each participant indicated that they always knew that it had happened. One participant described this process.

> It's not like I don't know when it happens. I know immediately. But the funny part is that sometimes they don't know that they've said something really dumb. I'd like to confront it in a manner that directly teaches them something, and I can be patronizing at times, but they need to get the message. I don't feel like I overreact or that I'm hypersensitive, I just feel that they need to be told in a manner that is meaningful to them that they've said something really offensive. (Phillip)

The reactions of African Americans involved cognitive, emotive and behavioral expressions (Sue *et al.*, 2008a). Other themes regarding the reaction of African Americans to racial microaggressions revealed in this study included: healthy paranoia, sanity check, empowering and validating self and rescuing offenders (Sue *et al.*, 2008a). Reactions were sometimes emotional or cognitive. Reactions in the study were mainly cognitive: (1) Confronting directly and assertively, (2) Using humor, (3) Asking questions for clarification, (4) Doing nothing and (5) Letting it go to become the invisible, silent African American man. There was one emotional theme, (6) Anger, frustration and resentment, and one behavioral theme, (7) Actively shattering perceptions. Altogether, seven reactive themes and responses emerged from both the interviews and the art-based focus groups in this study.

Confronting with humor

Some participants noted the use of humor to confront a microaggressive act and situation. One participant shared blatant examples of how he used humor and comedy to tell his colleagues what to do gently, by presenting it in a way that non-aggressively let them know what the right thing to do in a job situation was. This tended to limit perception of the aggressive and angry Black man. One participant discussed ways he used humor to his advantage in his workplace.

> I don't intend to embarrass my colleagues, saying to them, "Well you should know this, or you should know that." It's not that, you give people the dignity to say whatever, and you respond in a comical way where 70 percent of the comment is joke and the other 30 percent is directed in intelligent discussion, so it's a way to be disarming for everyone, and it's also in some ways—if you use a slave mentality—me demonstrating that I'm in my place and that I'm not trying to overstep my boundary to you and usurp any authority to you. I'm going to defer to you in this comical way even though I'm giving you information, even if you don't know it or that you need to know it. So, if it's night time and there is a moon out and the master says, "What's that light in the sky?" And I say, "Well I don't know, Boss, could it maybe possibly be the moon?" So that's a way I am not telling him what it is. And then he can pretend that it's his idea, that yes, it's the moon...run along now... So, that's very much a large part of how it goes. So, for me, humor is the easiest way for me to do it, and I'm hysterical. (Dwayne)

Another participant discussed how he had handled patients in the past, with humor.

> Sometimes it's comical. For example, I had a fellow, and he was getting off to sleep and everything was fine, but he had these old swastika tattoos and things like that and I made no comment about it because it just is what it is and he was a middle-aged guy in his early 40s or so. Before we were getting ready to go to sleep he just started babbling about, "Hey, I used to have these feelings and then I went to college," and then he told me about his encounter with this one lone Black friend, who played on the baseball team with him and how he was a good guy. It was like he was trying to make atonement, and in a way, he was more uncomfortable than I was, and I think it was because of the tattoos and there was no way for him to hide what type of

feelings they might have represented. So, he went on to tell me how he'd had encounters with good Black people and that he'd had a different viewpoint and perspective about them. I've had similar encounters to this with people with similar tattoos like this and I play with them. With patients, I try to play with it and to work in the word "brother" at some point in the conversation, like, "I'm a take good care of you, brother." (Jackson)

Confronting with humor, according to one participant, limits the perception White people have of the aggressive and angry Black man, and makes all their colleagues feel comfortable.

Humor is a way because I know when I speak about things, if I'm in a meeting, like I was recently, and I feel a certain way about something, I know that I'd better make jokes about it while I speak because if I don't, and I'm just hammering home a point, the room is going to get tense, and there is going to be a perception that I'm aggressive and angry. So you have to lighten it up and be the Eddie Murphy of the room, so to speak, to make others comfortable about what you are saying. You have to speak articulately, you have to play the role and everything about you has to be non-threatening, because at the end of the day, that's what will happen. (Randolph)

Jackson further added, "I try to do these things in a non-confrontational way and a humorous way."

Section III: Impact and consequences of racial microaggressions

Racial microaggressions create an invalidating climate for African Americans that results in anger, frustration, rage, depression, anxiety and loss of self-esteem (Sue, 2010). All participants noted in both their interviews and the art-based focus groups that the impact and consequences of racial microaggressions affected their psychological well-being, behavioral patterns and attitudes towards work and the working environment. Ten themes regarding the impact and consequences of having to deal with racial microaggressive events on a daily basis emerged out of the interviews and the art-based focus groups of this study. Themes included: (1) Self-doubt/self-inferiority complex; (2) Pressure and burden to represent the whole African American race; (3) Burden to fight negative stereotypes; (4) Constant pressure not to offend anyone at work or make a mistake; (5) Burden to make White co-workers and clients comfortable; (6) Develop fake persona and be a "chameleon;" (7) The Sambo the Happy Slave effect; (8) Paranoia within the work environment; (9) Sadness, depression, pain and the futility of it all; and (10) Not thinking about the daily assaults.

James noted how racial microaggressions impaired his work performance because of the way the inequities he experienced at work sapped his energy. He stated, "Having to constantly defend who you are as a valuable human being to people who really don't give a shit about how you feel or think that you are blowing things out of proportion is psychologically damaging."

In this session, the following themes are highlighted: Self-doubt/inferiority complex, Pressure and burden to represent the whole African American race/group, Burden to fight negative stereotypes, Develop and fake a persona/not themselves at work, and The Sambo the Happy Slave effect/loss of integrity.

Self-doubt/inferiority complex

All participants noted that they experienced self-doubt because of their daily experiences with racial microaggressions in the workplace. One participant highlighted the origin of the inferiority complex for African Americans, and related it to the legacy and consequences of slavery.

> Well, it comes from slavery and colonization, and it never went away and that's just one of the lingering effects of that. And things that are white are perceived to be superior whether we are talking about dolls or schools or skin. Some people know that it's not true and some don't. (Dwayne)

One participant wrote the word self-doubt on his collage (Figure 4.2A) and discussed how his feelings of self-doubt in his professional experiences were directly linked to his daily experiences of racial microaggressions in his workplace.

> I put self-doubt in here (Figure 4.2A) because all these things collectively have instilled a level of self-doubt. I bristle at what I feel that these aggressions are telling me—that I am less than. Sometimes I frequently question whether I am all that I think that I am. (Jackson)

Pressure and burden to represent the whole African American race/group

Many of the participants reported, in both the interviews and art-based focus groups, feeling increased pressure to do excellent work and represent their race well in the workplace, because of the cumulative microaggressive experiences, and as an attempt to negate those stereotypes their White colleagues had at work. This theme was the most prevalent in terms of impact and consequences of racial microaggressions in this study. This strategy to represent the entire African American race can result in race-related fatigue (Sue, 2010).

If I mess up, I mess it up for all the other Black lawyers that have gone before me and those that are coming after me. And collectively there is more pressure because, like it or not, you still collectively represent a race, and that's how people see you, and there is no way around that; they see you as a Black lawyer or doctor, not a lawyer or doctor. It's a great task and burden to carry the weight of an entire group of Black lawyers on your shoulders, and I think it's the same with other Black professionals in their various fields. (Lewis)

One participant discussed how he tried to represent the African American race to limit the stereotypes and elevate the perceptions White people have of African Americans in his profession.

If it's a patient that seems to have concerns or issues, I simply help them by reassuring them, because I know that there is a boogeyman in their minds, and my job is to let them know that I'm not that boogeyman. The sad part is that I'm not able to go a step further to say that there may not be a boogeyman at all, but I can't do that—all I can tell them is that right here, right now, there's no boogeyman here. And you just have to deal with it on a case-by-case basis. All I can do is be the best that I can, reassure people, listen to them, and take into account these things. And there have been circumstances when the feedback comes in and they feel compelled to write a letter saying how wonderful you were, even above and beyond your White colleagues, saying, 'He's the best I've ever had." Or they send gifts and things to you because you've shattered a preconception that they had and anticipation that things would not be done well, and they are so beside themselves that they compensate for it tremendously. And the next thing you know they go around, and they tell you, "I had this wonderful Black doctor, who took such good care of me the last time and you remind me of him so much." And it's like, "Great ma'am; I hope I don't disappoint you." And if they mention someone, and I know who it is, I say, "You are right, he is an excellent doctor, I'm glad you had that opportunity, I have a lot to live up to, but I'm going to do everything I can to make sure that you have a good experience." So collectively, that's how we help one another. But yes, I take it on as an individual, this is all I can do, but if we are all doing that then, collectively, we've moved it forward. (Jackson)

One participant equated this pressure to represent one's group to White privilege and how Whites do not have the added burden of representing their entire race.

I think you would be hard pressed to find a White person who views them-selves as representatives of their community, their race, their church, their family, their extended family. I think you would be hard pressed to find White folks who feel that their aunts', cousins', uncles' and grandparents' hopes, dreams and aspirations are riding on them. Whereas those pressures are extremely common for Black folks. In addition to the everyday pressures of being a responsible adult, that is all added weight on our shoulders. We are for the most part blazing a trail with the people behind us. For me, I feel like I have that responsibility to be the best, I feel like my other counterparts don't really have to. (Dwayne)

Another participant felt this burden to represent a whole race, or be a trail-blazer, as a huge responsibility, particularly when the road to success was not so clear and he did not know which direction to take.

Let me give you an analogy of the fear of this burden, because it is a burden when you become successful and you are not turning your back, you are trying to help and guide. But the analogy is this: I'm a slave running from freedom at night, but I can't see the North Star, and people are following behind me, and we are hauling ass, hopefully to freedom, but we don't know which direction we are going. So, when the sun comes up, I might have run us all further into the south. That's how it feels to me. Because I don't have the answers, I don't know which way to go, but I'm hauling ass in this direction. So, it's almost a thing like, don't follow me, don't follow me because I don't know where I'm going. (Jackson)

Many of the participants in their art-based collages used the images of tackles and physical contact in sports to illustrate the daily impact, pressures and burdens that came from their experiences of racial microaggressions (Figures 4.3A–4.6A). In the art-based focus group discussions, participants discussed the burden that African American professional athletes have to represent their entire community.

This basketball image is effective (Figure 4.3A). There is a foul going on in this picture, but my inclination and my tendency is to assume that the foul is being called on the Black player and I have no context for that picture and no knowledge of what has happened there but my gut immediately says that they called a foul on this Black kid. Talking about Robert Griffin III, there was discussion about his success and failure as a Black quarterback. But if you are a White quarterback, you fail and it's just simply that; you've disappointed yourself, you've embarrassed yourself. But as a Black quarterback, you represent an entire community and race. And if you are unsuccessful, it somehow reflects on the entire race of people. (Dwayne)

In the discussion, Dwayne shared that the Black player with his head bowed down on the lower right side of his collage is a metaphor for the burden that African American professional men have to carry with them, which Whites do not have to.

> The Black college quarterback also reflects on every other Black college quarterback who is coming, who might not get drafted, or who is going to get a lower draft spot, which is dependent on a handful of other Black quarterbacks. It is not that way for Whites. He represents his family, his community, everyone who has had hopes and dreams for what he has accomplished and what he hopes to accomplish. The White player is kinda looking up and he looks like he really doesn't have any burden there, but just an observer of what is going on, with no idea of what is really going on, that is my interpretation of that. (Dwayne)

> This guy right here (Figure 4.3A) is an athlete and he just looks like he has the weight of the world on his shoulders, and I feel like that on a regular basis. I don't get the impression from my White counterparts that they ever feel that way. I feel that I am constantly under pressure, professionally, in my household, to be a husband, a father, to support the household, keep my spouse happy, keep my children happy, not feel that at work, the stakes are really high, and not to disappoint a lot of people. (Dwayne)

Burden to fight negative stereotypes

All participants noted that one of the consequences of racial microaggressions in the workplace was that they had to constantly fight the negative stereotypes of the Black man, which many White colleagues, supervisors and clients had in the workplace. This burden of fighting negative stereotypes emerged both in the interviews and the art-based focus groups of this study. One participant in this study stated:

> I think that Black men are portrayed in the media, whether it is print, television or the internet, as aggressors, sexual aggressors, uneducated, and the majority of African American males are in jail. For some reason, the media picks the most inarticulate Black person they can find to speak about an incident that has just occurred, and you see popular culture holding on to those images. All these stereotypes definitely affect our society, and whether it is spoken or not, I feel like, every day once I walk out of my house, as a professional Black male, there is a lot of pressure on me to have to fight those stereotypes so that people will know that not all Black men fit those particular stereotypes. So, when it comes to interacting in a professional manner, not just with my co-workers, but also in my job, I definitely have to

act in a more professional way and more over the top than my non-African American counterparts. (Phillip)

Develop and fake a persona/not themselves at work

All participants in this study shared how they had to be different people in the work environment in order to be received well, from how they really were with their families and friends. Participants reported having to constantly juggle two worlds: one persona at work and one at home. This consequence of the experiences of racial microaggressions emerged in both the interviews and the art-based focus groups in this study. One participant shared:

> In the workplace, if you come in and you are the way you are outside, you are not received well. I tend to code switch. If you are a little bit cooler and you kinda have swag, you're not really received as well. In the office setting, you have to be more welcoming and polite in order to be accepted. Everyone is kinda scared of the angry Black man, so to speak. So, I totally don't feel like I'm myself in the work environment. I constantly have to be a little bit more on guard and not offensive or too aggressive, not ask for things too harshly, so I have to watch my words sometimes, to make sure that everyone is receiving what I'm trying to say. (Lewis)

Jackson added, "At work, I'm not the real me, because I'm busy being everything to everyone because I have to hit the calculations. The real me is only revealed in very short doses in very private moments." In his art-based collage, Randolph depicted an African American professional man, with a White male peering behind him (Figure 4.1A), showing the many ways that African American professionals have to change their persona, and the burden and consequences of changing one's persona and being a chameleon.

> I'm starting the collage from the middle, and it looks like what appears to be a well-dressed Black man that's clean cut, trying to appear professional, and the only way that he can be professional is to have the image or the persona of a White person that peeks out at him. So it brings a lot of mental conflict where you sometimes have to choose who you are going to be, when you are going to be and what you are going to be or when you are going to be it. It's a burden. (Randolph)

The Sambo the Happy Slave effect/loss of integrity

Some of the participants shared that based on the burden and pressure to conform to White cultural values and standards they felt that they had to change their persona and act like "Sambo the Happy Slave" at work. This act in the workplace created feelings of disingenuousness and tended to compromise the integrity of that participant. James described the consequences of dealing with racial microaggressions in the workplace: "There has to be a daily and conscious shifting of self-sacrifice that has to go along with surviving in a predominantly White workplace. You definitely cannot be your true self, and you have to appear happy, at least happy-go-lucky, all the time." In addition, this change of persona was to negate the negative stereotypes of the African American male. The consequences of the experiences of these racial microaggressions emerged in both the interviews and art-based focus groups and were represented in some of the collages.

Section IV: Collages—experiences of racial microaggressions and visual metaphors

The art-based focus groups revealed further themes and representational imagery that supported the interviews. Metaphors were revealed in the six collages that focused on the experiences of racial microaggressions. Many of the metaphors reinforce the messages of oppression, isolation and self-doubt, and leave little doubt about their intended meaning. There were some participants who juxtaposed an image with another image, suggesting other meanings to their visual metaphors. Some of the images also provided food for thought for the viewer to draw their own interpretations or conclusions about the visual metaphor. It is important to note that some of the verbatim statements from the focus groups have been also placed in relevant sections of the results of the interviews, to enrich the study.

Major visual metaphors and representations that emerged in this study regarding experiences of racial microaggressions included: Visual images from the movie *12 Years a Slave*; the black shadowy figure; a Black man being frisked by a White man; police presence (cars, policemen), camera/lenses and watching eyes; being put in a box; a little boy in big suit; sports/tackling/basketball game; a man in wheelchair; an exploding Mucinex bottle; an attractive White woman looking seductively; a half-naked muscular African American man; a clean-cut shaven African American man/Bryant Gumbel; a naked White man freely running around; and a picture of *The Last Supper.*

FIGURE 4.1A: RANDOLPH: EXPERIENCES OF RACIAL
MICROAGGRESSIONS IN THE WORKPLACE (11" X 14")

Themes in Randolph's collage included anger and having to be an imposter (a kid with a suit that is too big for him) in the workplace. The only way to be professional is to be clean-shaven. The word "Obama" symbolized a lack of respect for the highest workplace in the country because his full title was not used, and this symbolized the general feelings of the Black professional men in the workplace who participated in this study. The themes in Randolph's collages about his experiences centered around anger, about being treated as less than a person, which leads to not always being yourself and having to be an imposter at work, constantly fitting into others' shoes, and wearing a suit that does not fit. In the art-based focus group, Randolph said that the child in the oversized suit in his collage (Figure 4.1A) was a prominent image for him in his experiences of racial microaggressions at work. The image was a metaphor for the pressures of not quite fitting in at work, having to develop a fake persona to negate his cultural background, and the burden that comes with being an African American professional man in the workplace.

Although there were a lot of images of anger, Randolph shared that this anger had to be suppressed in order to be professional in the workplace (Figure 4.1A). He also stated that the theme of his overall collage was the daily conflict he felt dealing with racial microaggressions in his workplace.

> So, the collage as a whole is just about the conflict that we constantly feel in the workplace when we are trying to balance ourselves, versus the White person that they want us to be, in order for us to succeed and get acceptance in this White world and become an executive and move forward in society. (Randolph)

Randolph discussed the image on his collage of what appeared to be the entertainer Dick Clark gesturing an "okay" sign, with the words "Hot or Cold" (Figure 4.1A). This represents the constant surveillance that African American men have to go through with the added pressure of trying not to make any mistakes at work, always seeking approval and acceptance from the White supervisor, and, at the same time, making sure that he does not appear threatening in the workplace.

> On the corporate side, I have a picture of the acceptance of the White man, is he hot or cold? There's no in-between for you as a Black man, and so you have the okay sign, and for you to be okay, you have to be completely hot. There's no in between where you can be free and make mistakes, so you have to be on or off. (Randolph)

Randolph also shared that the stacked-up iPhones in his picture (Figure 4.1A) was a metaphor for always having to be the best, and as an African American, he wanted to compete or "stack-up" against his White co-workers. Randolph stated, "I have the iPhones stacking up with the sign 'future' showing that you have to be the best, the best of the best stacking up, and you can't make mistakes and you have to be precise." Being the best and not making mistakes was another prominent theme of Randolph's collage.

Randolph discussed receiving negative messages about how a successful professional African American man was to be presented in the workplace. The image of the clean-shaven African American professional man presented by Randolph in his collage was shared as the only way African American men would be successful in the workplace. Any facial hair on the features of an African American professional man was seen as menacing, and appeared threatening to White co-workers. Randolph added, "A clean-shaven man is more trustworthy and acceptable to them than a man with facial hair."

FIGURE 4.2A: JACKSON: EXPERIENCES OF RACIAL
MICROAGGRESSIONS IN THE WORKPLACE (11" X 14")

The major themes of Jackson's collage centered on self-doubt and feeling like an imposter, and having to play or portray the character of Sambo in the workplace to fit in to the cultural stereotypes and be less threatening. In addition, the racial microaggression of being watched was illustrated by the metaphor of the camera lens (Figure 4.2A). Jackson shared that the words "You're an idiot," "I'm a phony," "Affirmative Action," "Self-doubt" and "The Rookie" were all residual feelings from his experiences of the microaggressions of ascription of intelligence in the workplace.

An image from the movie 12 Years a Slave was another visual metaphor in Jackson's collage to illustrate that the legacy of slavery continues to permeate the lives of African American professional men today.

Another visual metaphor was the prominent presence of police officers in Jackson's collage (Figure 4.2A). He discussed how police presence was a menacing experience for him: "There's martial law, and in my interpretation, they are all menacing; the police officer is just menacing to me from my experiences." The image of the half-naked African American boxer symbolized sexual objectification for Jackson, but also, with the addition of the text around that image, the experience of being the spokesperson for every African American, as well as the denial of unique experiences as an African American man.

> There's a picture of a boxer... (Figure 4.2A) It represents the viral Black buck, the over-sexed athlete, non-thinking man, and surrounding these pictures, I have the words "marijuana" with a question mark, there is a Viagra advertisement, and HIV syphilis testing. No matter what I do...the jokes and the comments that always come out are always about pop culture or athletics, or those are the connections, the common ground that I'm forced to make with my White colleagues and counterparts. I'm not seen as a professional, I'm not seen as a physician, I'm not seen as a scholar or an academic; I'm still seen as a shirtless boxer at the weigh-in, with all the negative stereotypes that go along with that. Are your experiences with drugs outside ours? What's your experience? What's your community like? What do you think? Should we be doing syphilis and HIV testing with all these patients? What the hell are you asking me for? (Jackson)

Jackson also discussed his experiences of microaggressions at work since he got divorced.

> I have the word divorce...and it seems to come up quite a bit in my professional workplace, and it always comes up as a bit of a slight or a "less than," as if you are unsuccessful or are a failure. (Jackson)

There were several major metaphors and themes depicted in Dwayne's collage (Figure 4.3A), including a shadowy figure; a Black man being frisked by a White man; a camera metaphor for always being watched; a basketball scene, as a metaphor for the daily racial conflict; a scene from the movie *12 Years a Slave*, as a metaphor for the legacy and consequences of slavery that still haunt us all today; Bryant Gumbel, as a metaphor and universal symbol for the ideal acceptable African American man in a White professional environment; and a White woman in a box, as a metaphor for the assumed universality of the Black experience and the sexual objectification of African American men.

> The shadowy figure/upper left (Figure 4.3A) looks like a person of color being frisked by a White person against the wall and the White person is smiling. That is an image that depicts suppression and oppression in my mind—not being taken seriously by someone who doesn't take us seriously because of what he's doing and doesn't appreciate the effects of what he is doing. (Dwayne)

FIGURE 4.3A: DWAYNE: EXPERIENCES OF RACIAL
MICROAGGRESSIONS IN THE WORKPLACE (11" X 14")

During the art-based focus group, Dwayne stated that the images on his collage (Figure 4.3A) of the White and Black basketball players were a metaphor for racial microaggressions and the daily struggles that African American professional men are subjected to. The daily struggle that African American men go through at work was visually represented in his collage with a scene from the movie *12 Years a Slave*:

> Upper right is a scene from *12 Years a Slave* and that is significant to me because we are still feeling the effects and our communities are still ravaged, and our country is still ravaged by the effects of slavery, and so I feel like it is fitting to see slavery addressed and talked about and discussed and not swept under the rug because it is still a part of our history that hasn't been dealt with appropriately and it affects me every day as a Black person. (Dwayne)

Other visual metaphors discussed by Dwayne included a White female in a box (Figure 4.3A) illustrating the sameness/assumed universality of the

African American experience. Dwayne added, "I don't really fit in a box at all times, I'm pretty unique, and I'm an individual person." Bryant Gumbel is shown as a metaphor and universal symbol of the acceptable standard and non-aggressive African American professional man.

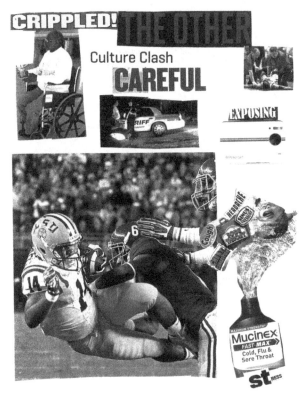

FIGURE 4.4A: LEWIS: EXPERIENCES OF RACIAL
MICROAGGRESSIONS IN THE WORKPLACE (11" X 14")

Major visual metaphors and themes in Figure 4.4A include the impact of ascription of intelligence in the workplace; criminality; the impact of daily racial microaggressions; always being watched; and emotional reactions to racial microaggressions. Lewis featured an image of an African American man in a wheelchair with the word "Crippled!" (Figure 4.4A) as a visual metaphor to support the impact ascription of intelligence had on his mental health. The image of the police car and police presence in the collage metaphorically illustrated the criminality/assumption of criminality theme of racial microaggression. Lewis stated:

Obviously, I don't trust the police; that is why that image is in the middle of my piece here. They symbolize unrest and unfairness for me, so I always have to be careful around them, even if you're doing the right things.

The concept of emotional reactions and psychological stressors was related to the daily exposure to racial microaggressions in the workplace, and was visually represented by an exploding bottle of Mucinex. Lewis added, "There really is that much daily pressure for me in my professional life, and exploding, much as I would love sometimes just to get it out, is not an option."

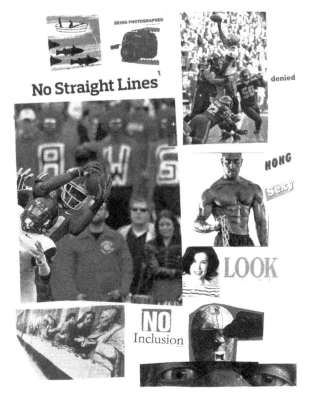

FIGURE 4.5A: PHILLIP: EXPERIENCES OF RACIAL
MICROAGGRESSIONS IN THE WORKPLACE (11" X 14")

Phillip cited many visual metaphors in his collage regarding his experiences of racial microaggressions in the workplace. The sports tackle pictures in the collage represented the daily psychological impact and conflict from racial microaggressions. Phillip stated, "The legacy of slavery is alive and well today, at least in my daily experiences at work." Other visual metaphors included watchful eyes and a camera, described by Phillip as examples of the racial microaggressions of dealing with criminality and always being watched. The sexual objectification of African American men in the workplace was visually represented by a half-naked muscular African American man, juxtaposed with a White woman with the word "look" in bold letters. Phillip pointed out, "It's a double standard. The Black male physique is admired and very much lusted after by White women, but at the same time we evoke fear and danger in them. Which one is it?" Phillip also discussed the danger element of being too close to White women in his work environment, "I really don't get into hanging out with White women at work. I just think it's dangerous. I don't flirt, and I always make sure I'm professional."

In the art-based focus group, Phillip shared that the painting of *The Last Supper*, featured at the bottom left of the collage (Figure 4.5A), was a visual metaphor for betrayal, and the legacy of betrayal, which was akin to the betrayal and death of Jesus Christ. He further discussed that, like the legacy of slavery, which African American men are being affected by in the workplace today, Christians are also living the consequences of the death of Jesus Christ today.

> At the bottom left of my collage I have the image of the painting *The Last Supper*. I forget whom it's by, but it struck me that Jesus probably dealt with a lot of microaggressions. My Catholic faith always reminded me of how Jesus was mistreated, devalued, considered a second-class citizen by the Romans, just like we are now, after slavery. I just thought this picture and metaphor spoke to me. (Phillip)

In his collage from the art-based focus group, James discussed the image of a White man on a fishing boat, with his binoculars presenting the visual metaphor for the racial microaggression of always being watched.

The sports and tackle games metaphorically represented the daily struggle, conflict and battles African American professional men have to go through in their daily work experiences. James stated that the daily struggle was something that he did not share or unloaded with everyone: "These daily battles can be so incredibly painful that I don't always share it with my wife because they would be way too overwhelming for her. But I do find solace in sharing with my fraternity brothers and God." James noted that the image of the White woman looking seductively was a visual metaphor for the danger and the sexual objectification of African American professional men in the workplace.

> You see the face of a White woman looking at you seductively, and at the top, the words "Read her Signals" to remind you not to fall for this trap, because it is a trap which could involve the police—I put "Baltimore Police" at the

bottom of her image. It's a very tricky thing this business of working with White female co-workers. A lot of them flirt with you, shamelessly, but that danger sign always comes up for me every time. (James)

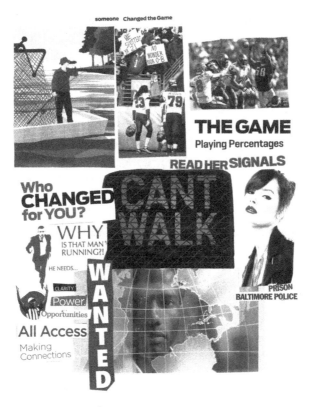

FIGURE 4.6A: JAMES: EXPERIENCES OF RACIAL MICROAGGRESSIONS IN THE WORKPLACE (11" X 14")

Again, the word "wanted," according to James, represented the racial micro-aggression of the assumption of criminality, as well as the sexual objectification of African American men. James went on to state, "The word 'wanted' is another prominent word here because it depicts the stereotypes of all Black men in this country; we are wanted criminally, and we are sexually wanted by White women." James explained how the feeling of always being watched had in the past contributed to his sense of paranoia in his workplace and dissatisfaction with his workplace, and had impacted on his current ability to be authentic as an African American professional man. The words "can't walk" symbolized being careful because of "watchful eyes around you."

Section V: Coping with racial microaggressions in the workplace

In this study, 12 themes of coping with the experiences of racial microaggressions emerged from both the interviews and the art-based focus groups. Coping themes included: (1) Family/friends and social support; (2) Prayer and religion; (3) Armoring; (4) Mentoring; (5) Humor; (6) Music; (7) Food; (8) Alcohol; (9) Self-care; (10) Being a "chameleon"/changing persona; (11) Numbing feelings; and (12) Documentation. There were healing themes that emerged out of the strategies used to cope with racial microaggressions from the participants, and these included using food, music and alcohol to feel good, and sharing social spaces with their families and friends, which seemed validating, cathartic and healing for the participants. Prayer, the form of God, gave participants protection from the *evils* of racism, and a pathway to healing. Armoring and mentoring gave the participants a sense of pride of self and validation. In addition, one participant mentioned his past use of marijuana and his smoking habits. These themes are undeveloped because only one participant mentioned them and there was no consensus with other participants that this was a utilized coping strategy. This section discusses the coping themes that emerged in this study.

Theme 1: Family/friends and social support

The participants found family, friends and social support to be prominent in their coping mechanisms for dealing with racial microaggressions in the workplace. This theme emerged in both the interviews and the art-based focus groups. The importance of being with family, including wife and children, was highlighted in one participant's collage. Visual metaphors to illustrate this theme included images of couples hanging out together, a couple with a child, Christmas stockings, and cologne (to symbolize romance).

For most of the participants, being part of a community and social network was noted as a key resource for social support. All participants shared about the importance of a community network of social support from family, friends, colleagues and the Black community.

> But you have your coping community and that community is from every Black person. And it's not just in medicine, and it's not even just professionals, it's grandparents, people's parents, your friends and everyone, because we all have stories to tell, we've all told instances or shared them, and also shared how we deal with them, how it made us feel, how we got through it, can you believe that this happened, so that kind of spoken word collective consciousness from the community is part of your mechanism. The Black community has affirmed and lifted me up, when I have been made to feel devalued and insignificant by a particular situation at work. (Jackson)

Participants talked about the value of a fraternity support network in coping with racial microaggression in the workplace. This network served as a source of brotherhood, guidance and advice. Other participants discussed the importance of support networks in Black alumni organizations. Lewis stated, "The support I get from the HBCU Alumni Organization is amazing. It just provides a comforting feeling to know that you are not so isolated in the professional world. It's powerful."

Theme 2: Prayer and religion

Prayer and spirituality were found to be another core coping mechanism for the participants. This theme emerged in both the interviews and the art-based focus groups. Prayer was noted as a key practice for most of the participants for protection, guidance, strength, assurance and validation. Prayer was part of healing for some participants.

> God is a coping mechanism for me because I just feel like we are surrounded by evil, surrounded by evil people with evil intentions. But in the midst of all of that there are a lot of times that I have to remind myself that none of those people or none of those forces are greater than God. And none of these people who want to harm me, or who are wishing to do me harm or who are plotting my demise, are greater than God or greater than the plans God has in store for me. Through prayer, I've been able to see hope and heal amid racial devastation. I am comforted by prayer. (Dwayne)

Theme 3: Armoring

Participants noted, in both the interviews and the art-based focus groups, that armoring in the form of personal excellence, and pride in self and cultural background, was a core coping strategy for buffering against the daily assault of racial microaggressions in the workplace. One participant highlighted, "I must be better than the best of them. You really must be the sharpest knife and it shows because my supervisor does recognize me for my great work." Excelling at his craft was one of his coping skills.

Other participants in the study shared about how excelling in this field was an avenue for validation.

> One of my coping mechanisms is excelling, trying to use it in a positive way, because I think if I didn't have that burden it would be easier to be mediocre. Thinking about it from a competitive perspective helps as well, because I am naturally competitive. I like to look at things sometimes without racial lines but in terms of competition, so if I'm against an adversary in court, I want to be the best lawyer in court, and not just the best Black lawyer in court,

and I apply that to everything I do, so that makes the racial component of it take a back seat in my mind. (Dwayne)

Most participants spoke about the importance of being excellent in order to gain the respect of White co-workers and to counter negative stereotypes they have about Blacks, and to some extent accept the burden and responsibility of representing the African American race in a positive light. Lewis stated, "The moment I come into the courtroom and excel at what I do, that usually shuts everyone up in that room that doubted me based on their preconceptions and stereotypes."

Many of the participants noted that they used armoring through pride in having an HBCU education as a strategy for dealing with racial microaggressions. Some of the participants credited their Black education for instilling pride in self and culture, and the importance of hard work, and for preparing them to know how best to deal with racial microaggressions when they occurred.

Theme 4: Mentoring

Many participants in this study talked about the importance and value of having mentors, as well as being a mentor to other African American men, as an effective way of dealing with racial microaggressions in the workplace. This theme emerged in both the interviews and the art-based focus groups. Two participants talked about feeling validated and empowered by their mentors. James stated, "In my training as a psychologist, I had a very supportive Black male supervisor who provided crucial mentoring that was instrumental in my growth and identity as a Black male psychologist—that was important to me." Lewis added:

> There is nothing more empowering and validating for an older, more experienced, gentleman in your field who has mentored you to be successful in your field dealing with all the crap that you have to face at work, just because you are Black.

Another participant talked about how important it was to provide mentorship to other upcoming African American professional men. He stated, "There is nothing better than shaping the young minds of African American men to be brave and understand that their experiences have meaning and significance."

Theme 5: Humor

Humor as a coping mechanism for some participants was seen as a way to lighten the heavy mood of racism, and a non-threatening, sometimes passive-aggressive way of confronting a situation. This theme emerged in both the interviews and the art-based focus groups. One participant, for example, was considered non-aggressive and less intimidating because of his frequent use of humor for his coping mechanism to buffer against racial microaggressions.

> Humor is a large part of how I deal with things. First of all, that's my personality, and since my childhood, confrontations have been dealt with disarmament, frequently through humor. And as a result, my first or natural response to things is humor, even if I'm not giving it out to you to disarm it, I just find it amusing. I have, on multiple occasions, said to someone directly, "Is this because I'm Black?" And when you do that, it's comical, it's overt, it's playful, but they have to respond. And sometimes their response is humor as well, and it may be like, "You got it!" Or we just move into something else. Or sometimes when you say that they get all flustered, like, "No! Jeez, come on!" and it's one of those things. But you can diffuse a whole energy with humor. (Phillip)

Another participant shared an incident that occurred in his workplace and how he used humor to cope with the racial microaggression he received.

> I had an older gentleman, he was in his 90s, and we were going into the room, and I asked him, like I ask many patients, what kind of music he likes because we often have music there so I'll play music for patients as they go to sleep to try to calm them down. And his response was so comical to me, because I said, "What kind of music do you like?" and he said, "Well, not jazz." And I just chuckled because it was funny to me, he meant so much more than what he was really saying. He was too old to say "not hip-hop or rap" or something else, instead he said, "Not the Black music of my lifetime and whatever you like young man, I don't like that!" And that's the way I interpreted it. And I said, "That's fine; I don't think we are playing jazz." (Jackson)

Theme 6: Music

Many of the participants highlighted music as a core coping mechanism for dealing with the daily onslaught of racial microaggressions. This theme emerged both in the interviews and art-based focus groups. Music for the participants was a way to escape, recharge and make sense of their experiences of racial microaggressions. Many of the participants featured music prominently on their coping with racial microaggression collages. Dwayne stated, "Music helps me deal with the world and it is very important to me, that's why I made it a part of my collage." He also stated in the art-based focus group about his collage (Figure 4.3B):

Music is what the musician represents. Music is very important to me. I think it's the universal language, just automatically it can change your mood, make you feel good. It's just a great celebration of expressions of all kinds of emotions and I've always loved music. (Dwayne)

One participant, in his art-based collage, had the word "music" prominently displayed on the upper right corner (Figure 4.2B). Jackson shared that music was seen as a coping skill, and a way to connect to the past but also reach out to others:

It's a way not only to connect back to historic times in my own life and experiences, but also to be broadened about new experiences to share. It's another one of those languages where you can just have experiences with people very different from you, and that's important to me and that's a way that I cope with things.

Theme 7: Food

All participants identified food as a highly valuable coping mechanism in dealing with racial microaggressions in the workplace, both in the interviews and the art-based focus groups. Jackson stated, "Food is one of my love expressions; it's how I express my love to my friends, my family, to myself." Food as a coping mechanism is visually represented in most of the collages from the art-based focus groups (Figures 4.2B–4.6B). Food was noted as a valuable avenue for social connections and healing, as well as a metaphor for spiritual and mental nourishment and healing. Lewis stated:

There's nothing like getting together with your friends and family and eating and connecting. Sunday dinners are when my family gets together; after church, we all get together and share what's going on in our lives that week. And you know what they say about a burden shared…it's like a relief. It really is an exercise in healing. In those moments, I am validated as a human being, a father and member of the family, and a member of my community; I am listened to, respected and honored for my wisdom. And in turn, I get to be that person for one of my family members.

Theme 8: Alcohol

Most participants identified alcohol as an important coping resource. In their art-based collages, most participants included the image of an alcoholic beverage as a coping mechanism and as a symbol of celebration and a metaphor for maturity and privilege. For example, one participant discussed the symbolic metaphor of alcohol in their collage (Figure 4.2B).

There is alcohol here because that is a coping mechanism for me. It symbolizes so many things to me; it symbolizes maturity and being an adult, it symbolizes socialization and celebration, happiness, friendship and all of those things. I don't look at it so much as a coping mechanism to bury your sorrows in; it's more of a privilege and a true celebration of things. (Jackson)

Theme 9: Self-care

All participants shared that they utilized a number of self-care activities to deal with the daily racial microaggressions they experienced in their jobs. Many of the participants talked about engaging in physical exercise, which included lifting weights, playing basketball, cycling, and generally being in the gym. Lewis stated, "I play basketball with my boys every Wednesday evening. It's a routine for us. Gives us a chance to reconnect and blow off a bit of steam." James said, "I lift weights twice a week at the gym, just to stay fit and relieve some stress from work. It's very helpful in releasing all that negative energy." Phillip stated, "I try to work out in the gym on Saturdays. It helps. But I realize that I need to do something every day just to get out the daily assaults I receive at work."

Many of the participants reported that they were cognizant of the need to take care of themselves by taking vacations and getting away. For example, Phillip explained during his art-based focus group: "The plane is a symbol of getting away, and I tend to go away every chance I get, and now that my daughter is older now, I tend to take her whenever I can." Lewis also shared that going on vacation with his family was an important way of regaining his balance after stressful daily events at work.

Many of the participants discussed how they rewarded themselves with expensive things because no one else in their work environment rewarded them. In his art-based collage, one participant had a symbol of the Mercedes Benz logo (Figure 4.2B): "Here's a Mercedes Benz symbol and that just represents kind of a self-reward. I have one that I got as a reward to myself because life itself wasn't providing many rewards to me" (Jackson).

Theme 10: Being a "chameleon" at work/changing persona

Some of the participants reported being mindful about changing their persona at work in order to fit in to the White cultural environment of their workplace. For example, one participant had the word "Chameleon" on his collage (Figure 4.2B). Jackson stated the following about being a chameleon:

> It says chameleon because that's the only way to survive as I must be whatever the circumstances require me to be. I can be a different person at various moments. And if that means that I am an academic, a professional, if it means that I'm more of an aggressive hip-hop type of talking person at

that moment, then that's what it is. And at the end of the day, I leave, and I go back to my life at home and with my friends and then I show back up tomorrow and chameleon my way through the work day all over again.

Theme 11: Numbing feelings

Many of the participants reported not dealing with the assaults. Others cited the fact that racial microaggressions are too painful and one of the ways they deal with them is not to think about them. This theme emerged in both the interviews and the art-based focus groups in this study. Participants shared that, for truly painful situations, they tended to block them out. Jackson stated, "I don't take it personally, at least I don't remember. I guess truly painful things you block out." He added, "It's not paramount in my thoughts because I just go about the way that I am and maybe that's just the result of all the years of dealing with it." Dwayne stated:

> Not thinking about it is a coping skill; you could drive yourself crazy thinking about it and stress yourself out—although, subconsciously, it's there. And with other people, it affects them negatively and turns them into bad people or into inauthentic people because they think about it too much and the way they chose to respond to it is different from the way I chose to respond to it.

Theme 12: Documentation

Four out of six participants discussed being mindful about using documentation to cover themselves at work. One participant shared that he always documented every correspondence with his superiors and co-workers, just to "cover my ass" (Randolph).

Another participant spoke about the importance that documentation had in his workplace. He noted that although it was time consuming and tedious, it was a necessary evil that he did in the workplace in order to keep a paper trail that protected him.

Section VI: Collages—coping with racial microaggressions in the workplace, visual metaphors

In Figure 4.1B, the prevalent visual representations were the bicycle and the motorcycle. Randolph discussed that bicycling and being on his motorcycle were both his hobbies and self-care rituals to buffer against the daily assaults of racial microaggressions: "The bicycles and the motorcycles are really just the hobbies you do to get yourself out of that space of despair and powerlessness."

Randolph shared several themes and visual metaphors during the art-based focus group regarding his coping strategies to buffer racial microaggressions in the workplace. He shared that his coping mechanism was based on hope. The visual metaphor of this hope was depicted in his collage with a sprig of leaf in the middle of his collage with the word "hope" underneath the image (Figure 4.1B).

> My coping is based on hope. I started from the middle and kind of bled out from there. And hope, with the plant growing, means that there is a possibility for the future. The only way that I can deal with everything that I do is with the expectation that one day it will be a little different just for me. And that is why it's just one plant growing and not a whole group of bushes or a whole group of flowers. (Randolph)

FIGURE 4.1B: RANDOLPH: COPING WITH RACIAL MICROAGGRESSIONS IN THE WORKPLACE (11" X 14")

Another coping mechanism for him was armoring and pride in his accomplishments, but also a sense of responsibility to carry on that feeling of pride. He stated that the phrase "Be the first" had significant meaning for him.

> To be the first, I am the first. The first one to go to college, the first one in my family to have a successful marriage, I'm the first one in my family to have a financial goal, I'm the first one in my family to break the mold. So, understanding that I am the first means that I also have to have that responsibility. And so, having that responsibility now means that I have to deal with all of the things that are on the other side. So, in order for me to really cope with that, I have to mentally prepare myself every single day and think to myself. (Randolph)

Randolph shared that family support and support from friends was also one of his coping mechanisms. The visual metaphor was represented by the image of President Obama kissing his wife, Michelle Obama. Mentorship was another coping mechanism for Randolph. He stated, "The ways that I deal with it is to really seize the moments for vacations and with opportunities with friends, opportunities with mentorship, with family, wife." The visual metaphor of the drink, and the word "party" were discussed by Randolph as another way of letting loose and relaxing with his wife and friends.

> The cocktail is being able to let loose and work hard and play hard as well, and being able to commune with friends and to vent these things with my wife. I think that being able to do that and have fun in your day-to-day, in between all of this, is really something that you have to do to be able to cope with it. (Randolph)

Randolph discussed the meaning of the words "Bring the heat" in his collage and a figure coming out of a box. He shared that preparation and always being prepared for whatever anyone may throw at you, and being resilient and a survivor, and being brave in facing challenges, were some of his coping mechanisms.

> Bring the heat—do whatever you need to do to get through your day. Jump out of the box and just do what you really have to do. You can't really have anyone else dictate to you what you have to do in order to be happy because we all have our own issues and we all have to deal with it on our own. That's why the man is jumping out of the box. (Randolph)

Randolph shared that the words "What have you got to lose?" in his collage was the most powerful statement and was about the importance of having courage, being brave enough to take on whatever daily assaults come your way, and not using racial microaggressions as a crutch not to succeed. He stated:

> What have you got to lose? In order to move forward, you really have to have that mentality, you have to move forward with a no-doubts and a what-have-you-got-to-lose mentality, and if you don't, all these things will now be your crutch because you can look going back. You can look at them not accepting you because you went to a Black school or see that people from Black schools don't get certain jobs. What do you have to lose is one of the most powerful statements in this collage because you have to go in and just do what you have to do without any qualms.

FIGURE 4.2B: JACKSON: COPING WITH RACIAL
MICROAGGRESSIONS IN THE WORKPLACE (11″ X 14″)

In Jackson's collage (Figure 4.2B), prominent visual metaphors and representations included music, sports, food and material possessions. The word "Sambo" was placed prominently in the middle of the collage. Words like "perfection," "passing the torch," "saving lives," "music" and "pride crafted with passion" were also prominently displayed. At the base of the collage, the participant wrote the word "chameleon." The Mercedes icon was a status symbol and a reward for the work that he put in for his profession.

Coping strategies included armoring, being the best at his craft and taking cultural pride, university pride and money as a reward. The Mercedes Benz symbol was a reward for hard work. The Obama family picture was a metaphor for family support and pride in families. Food was a metaphor for love, socialization and nourishment for the soul. "Sambo" was a metaphor for having to be a clown in the workplace so as to seem less threatening. "Chameleon" was a metaphor of having to change in the work environment depending on the work situation. Alcohol symbolized socializing, privilege, celebration and maturity.

FIGURE 4.3B: DWAYNE: COPING WITH RACIAL
MICROAGGRESSIONS IN THE WORKPLACE (11" X 14")

In Dwayne's collage, his major visual representations and metaphors for his coping mechanisms to deal with the daily experiences with racial microaggressions included armoring through self-pride and culture, and pride in attending an HBCU; family support and love; self-care; music; food; luxury items; and alcohol. Dwayne noted armoring as a particularly valuable coping mechanism:

> Upper left we have Earl Graves [Morgan State University Dean] who is representative of our alma mater...and I put his picture on there because just surrounding myself with and learning about and celebrating greatness that has come out of my school, which is an HBCU, gives me great pride and joy, and I just love it and I felt that it was important to put him up there.

Dwayne noted that staying in the moment and being present limited the stress that came from dealing with racial microaggressions. He used the visual metaphor of the camera in a different way to illustrate this.

> There is a man holding a camera, and to me, it's the flip side of the camera images that I used in the other collage, because it spoke to capturing images and living in the present, and that's something that helps me cope—living in the moment and allowing myself to appreciate the blessings of every day and not allowing myself to getting caught up in always looking ahead, because there's always a lot of pressure to do that. It's super stressful, so that's what that represents to me. (Dwayne)

Dwayne noted self-care in the form of exercise as an important coping strategy for dealing with his experiences of racial microaggressions. He visually represented this theme with the image of the sneakers in his collage. Dwayne stated, "Physical fitness, that's what the sneakers represent. It's very important to me just getting some exercise, relieving stress and taking care of my body the best I can." The importance of music and reading was highlighted by Dwayne in his collage, as a way of dealing with racial microaggressions.

> The picture of Miley Cyrus, Das Punk and Jay-Z are just again representative of music and hip-hop and pop culture. These are some artists that I love, especially Miley Cyrus who is my favorite—that was a joke, but Miley is cool. But this is just something that helps me deal with the world; music helps me deal with the world, and it is very important to me. That's why I made it a part of my collage. (Dwayne)

Food for Dwayne was also another important coping mechanism.

> I have the chef there, food. I just have a good appreciation for food, cooking and just enjoying fine cuisine. It's something that relieves stress for me and helps me cope with everyday life. I love cooking and I love eating, so that works. (Dwayne)

Dwayne shared that family support, hanging out with family and friends and romance with his wife were major coping mechanisms for him. His collage had visual examples of this, seen in the couple having "fun at the beach."

In the art-based focus group Dwayne shared that alcohol was a valuable coping mechanism that symbolized celebration and reward to him:

> The picture of the bottle of Moet symbolizes celebration and just having a good time. It's important to work hard, but it's also important to have fun. So as often as I can, I try to have a really good time.

FIGURE 4.4B: LEWIS: COPING WITH RACIAL MICROAGGRESSIONS
IN THE WORKPLACE (11" X 14")

Major visual metaphors for coping strategies in Lewis's collage included images of vacations, a man playing basketball and a man swimming to depict self-care as a coping skill; and the image of an alcohol bottle and the words "at last" and "party" to depict privilege and celebration.

Other visual metaphors and themes included the image of a family and a couple walking on a sandy beach to show family support; the image of people at the piano and the word "music" to depict the importance of music as a key coping skill; and the image of food to show connection with family and friends. The word "praying" and "Bible" symbolized another of Lewis's coping strategies, and "Give it up for HBCUs" showed his pride in going to an all-Black college. Mentorship was depicted in the image of the White coach with his arms around the African American player.

FIGURE 4.5B: PHILLIP: COPING WITH RACIAL
MICROAGGRESSIONS IN THE WORKPLACE (11" X 14")

Phillip shared many images and metaphors regarding his coping mechanisms with regard to racial microaggressions. Prayer was an important coping mechanism for Phillip as well as armoring and pride in cultural history. The image of Nelson Mandela in his collage, Phillip noted, was a visual representation of his cultural pride, and hope that as Nelson Mandela triumphed fighting against Apartheid in South Africa, so too will the African American people triumph against racism in the United States.

FIGURE 4.6B: JAMES: COPING WITH RACIAL MICROAGGRESSIONS
IN THE WORKPLACE (11" X 14")

James's visual representations and metaphors of coping with racial microaggressions in his collage included the support and love from family, visually represented by the family image; armoring and pride in his cultural background and mentorship, represented by the image of the former Mayor of Baltimore, Kurt Schmoke; the healing power and social support of food, represented by the image of food in the upper left corner; self-care and healthy activities, represented by the images of bicycling and lifting weights; the power of prayer, represented by the image in the top far right of the girl praying; vacationing, represented by the words "go places;" reading and music, represented by images of a book and a jazz poster; the love of a pet, represented by a picture of a dog; and the BMW symbol, as a metaphor for success and reward. James noted also that the image of the pregnant White woman symbolized hope for the future generation regarding human interactions that involve participants who differ in racial and cultural background.

SPECIAL STUDY: RESULTS AND FINDINGS

Section VII: How to combat racial microaggressions in the workplace

Some participants offered ways to combat racial microaggressions in the workplace. Many of the suggestions included training and awareness for the perpetrators. Examples included the following statement from Jackson:

> Collectively educating people, and a matter of good old fashioned race mixing, that's the only way it's ever going to happen. When you take the stereotypical racist redneck and his daughter brings home a Black man, and then he has a grandchild, more times than not, he's going to love his grandchild although that child is partially Black, and it becomes, "John here, the Black son-in-law, is different from the other Blacks." And I remember that being told to me so many times growing up, well, you are not like the rest. And it wasn't until I got out of high school and into a Black college that I would then respond with, "Actually, I am very typical, I can bring a busload of people just like me." It's just that their perception is different. But then, it's that story, when the redneck's grandchild comes out Black and he loves that child unconditionally it starts to change their perception, and then when he seeing the Black guy at the gas station he may see him in a softer light, more like John the son-in-law or the grandchild as opposed to that shadowy figure in the gas station, and this is the only way we are going to move forward.

> Education is the best way. I think that our schools do a very poor job at addressing race. Our schools try to act like race doesn't exist, which does everyone in society a huge disservice. Everyone should know, and it's the school's responsibility to teach people world history and U.S. history, which includes a lot of issues that are intertwined with race and that affect so much of what's going on today, whether it is politics or the economy, our criminal justice system, our educational system. So, people are entering the work-force in various fields—social work, criminal justice, education—having no concept of why the world is the way it is or why the children that they deal with are the way they are, why families are the way they are or why society is the way it is, because people really have no concept of what happened in America. I think that's what should be done on the front end, education, starting young with kids and going all the way up through high school and addressing race, and addressing it from a historical perspective so that people understand other people's experience and how that influences how various facets of society operate and why they are how they are. (Dwayne)

One of the major psychological dilemmas about racial microaggression is that the perpetrator has no awareness that they acted with racial bias. Sue (2007b, p.277) calls this "The invisibility of unintentional expressions of bias." Some participants talked about having the opportunity to bring both White and Black people together in order to better race relations.

> I think that everyone should have meaningful relationships with other people of different races and nationalities. I don't think that will ever happen in our country, but...at a minimum we have an obligation to educate our children so at least if we can do that, there'll be hope for the next generation or the one after that to be better prepared to deal with the racial dynamics of our society. (Lewis)

> I think what might help is along the lines of what you are doing now. Having African American people share their experiences. In the workplace, what would be helpful is to have co-workers share their experience because it personalizes their experiences with others that they work with on a daily basis. I think that when people work together, they've established some sort of relationship, and that relationship can be a catalyst to gain awareness about each other and about topics that are not typically popular. I don't see that happening often, but I do think that it would help. Although, I do think that political correctness has clouded the judgment and the ability for people to communicate effectively and candidly with other people, because I know that talking with my White friends, many of them have expressed that when they are in diversity trainings and so forth, they are afraid to say something for fear it might not be politically correct. But I try to tell people that, from a Black male perspective, the process of candid and honest dialogue between races is the key to better understanding. (Phillip)

> I wish that we could have these talks in our environment where our non-Black counterparts could hear about this, because we're not telling them about this, we are not telling them every encounter we have... And it would be great to have the discussion just to say, you can't say that you didn't know, and to see how they would respond, how it may affect their activities, actions and day-to-day encounters with Blacks. (Randolph)

Phillip added, "We need more Blacks in higher and more prominent positions, and once they get there, they must reach out to others to bring them up." Lewis stated, "Zero tolerance for racism in company policy seems to be the obvious deterrent for this type of stuff to take place in the work environment."

Some participants noted the importance of counseling to work out the impact and consequences of racial microaggressions in the workplace.

> It's an unfortunate truth that Blacks don't like counseling. Counseling would help a lot, definitely. There are a lot of people who do things and don't have

an idea why they do them or have certain attitudes or certain perceptions and have no idea that there is a reason for it. There is always a reason for it but usually it just doesn't get addressed—it gets repressed or suppressed and manifests in negative ways. So, I think that everybody should talk to a counselor or a therapist at some point. Just like I think that everybody should have to learn certain things pertaining to history. I think everyone should...there a lot of things that I think everyone should have to do...but it would be unrealistic. Counseling would be helpful in looking into ways my clients can deal with the burdens and consequences of racism in their daily lives. (Dwayne)

Section VIII: Participant thoughts about this study

Some participants offered some thoughts about participating in this study, the process, lessons learned, and racial microaggressions in the workplace.

This whole process was therapeutic for me, healing. Just putting thoughts in a lot of words which otherwise would have just been jumbled emotions and jumbled thoughts that we just live with and deal with pretty much as Black men, but never come out. Occasionally, it might come out to each other, it might come out to our loved ones, women in our lives. (Dwayne)

I feel encouraged that there was this opportunity to have these discussions, because when you have these discussions among yourselves at work, it almost feels like you are slaves talking about freedom, or talking about a reality that you can't have, or an equality that you shouldn't have and that it's wrong for you to even want to aspire to that. You even feel bad that you are complaining about equality. So, I feel good that there is an opportunity to talk about these things here today. (Jackson)

The project today wasn't difficult but the project of being Black itself is very difficult for me, and I was very eager to participate in it but it's a very difficult thing to discuss. And these are my brothers here, and we will occasionally get into things that are heavy but you don't want to burden yourselves during free time, to be wallowing about stuff. We've been here for hours, it's too much and we haven't even scratched the surface. I haven't even begun to figure out what all my feelings are. But what I realize though, for each of us, it is very different, but these coping mechanisms, while effective, what stands out to me is how scarce they are, and how much we need more of this, at least for our voices to be heard. (Lewis)

There hasn't been much acknowledgment for Black men who have gone through this process, and this resonates for me. It was important for me to see that I'm not going through this racial stuff alone. I think that a project like this where you can voice your daily experiences and explain them is powerful. I never thought that I would be able to do that, and I never thought that I would have so much anger and relief at the same time. So in closing, I think that understanding why it's been like this, understanding the situation and what it is we have to do to deal with it, being able to move forward and heal, and now being able to help other people and other young brothers that are going through this similar situation understand it, so that they can come to the game more prepared, is important. (Randolph)

I see race in almost everything in this life and it is overwhelming. Fortunately, we have communities of like-minded people that do support us, and there is a comfort in that, just like there was a comfort in being in a Black college. Being here today reminds me that there is an empowerment to understanding that I am not a zebra running around alone, that I'm not this anomaly running around, and that feels validating and empowering. That in of itself is the surrogate for getting those accolades that I'm not getting, by seeing other people like this, that's as good as it gets, to say, collectively, you guys are doing alright. (Phillip)

I hope there are more opportunities to do studies like this that involve hearing the voices of those who sometimes feel helpless and hopeless due to their circumstances. I hope what we've shared today goes beyond this study and out there where so many others can read about it. I think that this country has a long way to go in trying to right the wrongs of slavery. Awareness and exposure of some of these things are important, because some people are just not aware, and some wish not to know. The daily struggle of the Black man is real, but I'm glad I had this opportunity today. (James)

Summary and conclusion

The results of this study illustrated examples of the encounters of racial microaggressions African American professional men experience in the workplace, their responses, the impact and consequences of the assaults, and their coping strategies. The six participants experienced racial microaggressions and used several adaptive responses to cope. This study revealed the consequences of the assumptions of Black inferiority and White privilege based on stereotypes and a history of a country wrapped in the legacy of slavery. Thus, the key to understanding racial microaggressions and racism rests in addressing the legacy and consequences of slavery and White privilege, and most importantly, its abuse.

This study boldly and effectively added a strong dimension to the racial microaggression and racism literature through the addition of collages and visual images, which provided strong support that microaggressions pose devastating impacts and consequences, and highlighted the cost of racism and ways to heal for African American men.

There were healing themes that emerged from the study through coping skills, including music, food, prayer, family and social connections with family, allies and mentors. Other healing themes that emerged included a motivation for critical action and social justice advocacy to address racism. Also, healing themes emerged from the response of what the study meant to the participants, including motivation for doing healing racial trauma work through intergenerational psychoeducation and group work, as well as individual therapy to help build the tools for those in the throes of this trauma and to build knowledge and skills to pass down to the younger ones, to heal and to dismantle the cycle of racial trauma. Participants wanted to see more healing through sharing this study with others.

This study contributes to the social justice arena by addressing issues of inequality in practice and research with African American men in the workplace. It is clear that much more research is needed on racial micro-aggressions, and in the areas of how art therapists and other mental health professionals work with those on the margins of society who are the recipients. It is important for further research to gain more insights into the resiliency and empowerment of Black professional men and women when experiencing daily racial microaggression. In addition, conveying the realities of racial microaggressions to a wider U.S. community and building awareness and accountability for those who perpetrate the assault continue to be important. Further research should focus on learning about spaces that facilitate communal healing from racial trauma.

Chapter 5

Inequality, Social Justice and Advocacy

Do not get lost in a sea of despair. Be hopeful, be optimistic. Our struggle is not the struggle of a day, a week, or a year; it is the struggle of a lifetime. Never, ever be afraid to make some noise and get in good trouble, necessary trouble.

—FORMER CIVIL RIGHTS LEADER AND U.S. REPRESENTATIVE JOHN LEWIS, FOR THE STATE OF GEORGIA (TWITTER POST, JUNE 27, 2018)

What is social justice advocacy?

Social justice is defined as: "A process of acknowledging systemic societal inequities and oppression while acting responsibly to eliminate the systemic oppression in the forms of racism, sexism, heterosexism, classism, and other biases in clinical practice both on individual and distributive levels" (Odegard & Vereen, 2010, p.130). Chung and Bemak (2012) define social justice as the condition in which "society gives individuals and groups fair treatment and an equal share of benefits, resources, and opportunities" (p.27). Holcomb-McCoy (2007) define social justice as referring to:

> The idea of a just society, which gives individuals and groups their due. Social justice as a general concept is based on the idea of human rights. Thus, a broad definition of social justice would be the way in which human rights are manifested in the everyday lives of people at every level of society. Whereas equal opportunity and human rights are applicable to everyone, social justice targets the marginalized groups of people in society—it focuses on the disadvantaged. (p.17)

Fraser (2006) states that, in the pursuit of a just and fair society, these three social justice values should be considered:

- Minoritized groups have access to resources that are distributed so that everyone can live an adequately fair life.

- All human beings should all have equal human rights and should be recognized in all their diversity.

- Everyone should be represented and able to advocate on their own behalf.

Ratts and Hutchins (2009) state that the welfare of an egalitarian society depends on equal access and opportunity, fair distribution of resources and power, and working to empower individuals and groups with the right to determine their own lives.

Social justice is also an inclusive enterprise where people come together to work to change oppression, marginalization and other forms of power inequities within systems (Caldwell & Vera, 2010). The social justice counselor advocate is one who works with and/or on behalf of the client, to help mitigate oppressive and discriminatory practices that deny their clients equal treatment and access to services (Chang, Hays & Milliken, 2009). Social justice advocacy is defined as professional practice, research or scholarship focused on identifying and intervening in social policies and practices that have a negative impact on the mental health of clients who are oppressed and marginalized on the basis of their social status (Steele, 2008). Advocacy is the process of arguing or pleading for the case, cause or proposal of another. The concept of advocacy frames the social action context for social justice for art therapists. Advocates view art therapy from a systems perspective, and advocates attempt change in partnership with clients who often lack the knowledge or skill base to effect such change alone. Advocates must understand important system change principles, and have the skill to translate them into action.

Bell (1997) states the goal of social justice as:

> Full and equal participation of all groups in a society that is mutually shaped to meet their needs. Social justice includes a vision of society in which the distribution of resources is equitable, and all members are physically and psychologically safe and secure. (p.3)

Sue *et al.* (2019) define social justice counseling/therapy as:

> An active philosophy and approach aimed at producing conditions that allow for equal access and opportunity, reducing or eliminating disparities in education, health care, employment and other areas that lower the quality of life for affected populations, encouraging mental health professionals to consider micro, meso, and macro levels in the assessment, diagnosis and

treatment of client and client systems, and broadening the role of helping professionals to include not only counselor/therapist but advocate, consultant, psychoeducator, change agent, community workers... (p.90)

Fondacaro and Weinberg (2002) reflect that social justice values fairness and equity in rights, treatment and resources for marginalized groups and individuals, and groups with limited power in society due to their race, sexual orientation, age, socioeconomic status, physical ability, religious heritage and immigration status.

Given the many definitions of social justice, I propose that art therapists have the following targets for social justice advocacy:

- To recognize that systemic racism and oppression exist, and that the narrative that the attainment of success, power and equality is solely down to personal responsibility and not due to systemic and institutional failures is inaccurate.

- To facilitate conditions that create paths for equal access and opportunity.

- To work on art therapy interventions that validate voices and empower in favor of collective action ways to help increase the quality of life for marginalized communities.

- To encourage looking at clients not just individually but within their systems, to make accurate assessments and diagnoses and decide on treatment.

- To create more avenues for training, supervision and research to spread and facilitate goals of social justice.

- To broaden the role of the art therapist to include advocate, consultant, community worker and change agent.

- To facilitate conditions that create paths for healing and the value of the sanctity of human life.

- To work on forgiveness for those who have hurt us and empower hope to transform the pain into growth.

Thankfully, advocacy and social justice remain a central part of therapeutic practice (Corey, Corey & Callanan, 2015). Constantine *et al.* (2007), Bemak and Chung (2007), Ratts, Toporek and Lewis (2010) and Goodman *et al.* (2004) have all provided research that helps prepare counselors for work as social justice advocates. Frostig (2011) stated that taking a stance on social justice can be a powerful way to make visible the dynamics of privilege and abuse of power that ultimately lead to oppression and trauma. The conviction that counselors' roles must include social justice advocacy can be seen in the growing changes in ethical codes and standards of practice. For example, the American Counseling Association (2014) code of ethics calls for counselors to "advocate at individual, group, institutional, and societal levels to address potential barriers and obstacles that inhibit access and/or the growth and development of clients" (American Counseling Association, 2014, p.5). The Council for Accreditation of Counseling and Related Educational Programs (2016) has similar standards to inform counseling practitioners about providing services to diverse, marginalized and oppressed populations in multiculturally and socially competent ways. Similarly, the American Art Therapy Association's (2013) *Ethical Principles for Art Therapists* embody the values that safeguard the welfare of the clients art therapists serve. The Art Therapy Credential Board (2016) also holds art therapists to a specifically "developmentally and culturally sensitive" stance (p.4). The overwhelming realities we live with today make social activism even more relevant for us as members of a human family, as artists, as well as representatives of the art therapy and counseling profession. All responsible therapeutic practitioners should want the best for their clients, and a social justice outlook must be central to all human service endeavors.

REFLECTION AND DISCUSSION QUESTIONS

1. How would you define social justice and advocacy?

2. How can the art therapy field enhance its focus on social justice advocacy?

Art therapists' roles as agents of change

*To be just, it is not enough to refrain from injustice. One must go fur-
ther and refuse to play its game, substituting love for self-interest as the
driving force of society.*

—PEDRO ARRUPE

The current ethos of the world has significantly spiked the anxiety levels of many clients. Issues of social justice are important in art therapy because our clients inherently exist within social and cultural systems and contexts. The reports of human rights violations, the lack of care for other social and environmental conditions, the remnants of the Trump era and continued discrimination leading to everyday microaggressions and experiences of cultural trauma for those who live on the margins have been overwhelming, to say the least. Healthcare professionals, like art therapists, play an instrumental role in providing culturally specific and evidence-based care to marginalized and oppressed clients, and it is important to explore just what it means for art therapists to be advocates of social justice as well as how they integrate this work in their professional counseling. Are professional art therapists aware of the impact of oppression and disenfranchisement on mental health needs, and best practices for helping marginalized and culturally diverse clients? How far does their role as social justice advocates go? Do art therapists have a clear understanding of their role as social justice advocates, in the hopes of fostering conditions that lead to a healthy and more just society? It is important for art therapists and the counseling field to revisit, examine and explore their identity within a social justice advocacy context.

For art therapists and counselors to be "neutral" or "value-free" about their political views is inherently an endorsement of the status quo; being apolitical within the counseling process is not necessarily a view that is helpful to clients, particularly when that client is a member of a historically marginalized group (Anah, 2017). Art therapists are in positions of power and privilege to be the voice for those historically marginalized and must strive to work with their clients from a social justice advocacy and empowerment perspective in these times of uncertainty and high anxiety. It is also important to be aware that the most vulnerable members of society, and those who are disenfranchised, are subjected to the most social traumas, and therefore are those most afflicted with mental health issues. Art therapists who keep silent run the risk of perpetuating an inequitable society. To better meet the needs of our clients and create a healthier society, it is important for counselors to actively contemplate social issues and be better informed with domestic or local issues. They must become global citizens by expanding their knowledge base in order to challenge injustice, and ultimately empower and provide resources for their clients to challenge the inequality and injustices in their lives (Anah, 2017).

Social art therapy has the ability to challenge universal discourse on discrimination and provide the space to explore strategies of resistance and question microaggressions. It is able to explore the lived experiences of minoritized people. There is empowerment in encouraging clients to process the political and social influences on their lived experiences: "In our view, lifting the veil implies that art therapists become change agents for transcending our legacy of ethnocentric monoculturalism" (Talwar *et al.*, 2004, p.47). Section 7.0 of the 2013 revised version of the American Art

Therapy Association's *Ethical Principles for Art Therapists* included multicultural considerations on how art therapists must be aware of their own values, beliefs and biases, and how these impact the therapeutic relationship. Practicing art therapists are also required to be consciously aware of how their biases can affect their clients from different backgrounds. The guidelines go one further to state that practitioners are ethically responsible for gaining knowledge concerning how a client's cultural background influences their goals and values in therapy. This must be included in the client's treatment plan. At the 2023 American Art Therapy Association Conference in San Diego, the statement denouncing hate, discrimination and violence read:

> AATA denounces any form of discrimination against any group of people regardless of race; ethnicity; religious or spiritual beliefs; national origin; ancestry; age; abilities; sexual orientation; gender; gender identity, gender expression; socioeconomic, marital, immigration, or military status; political views; and new cultural identities as they emerge. (American Art Therapy Association, 2023)

Art therapy: A call to action for social justice and advocacy

Albert Einstein said it best when he stated, "Striving for social justice is the most valuable thing to do in life" (Anah, 2019a, p.20). Multicultural competence cannot be achieved without a commitment to social justice (Anah, 2020; Ratts, 2009). To this end, an important question to ask ourselves as art therapists is: "What does it mean to be an advocate for social change and justice? How do we fight for equality and dismantle inequality?" Goodman *et al.* (2004) have outlined six principles that define social justice work for mental health providers, which include the importance of self-examination; sharing power; giving voice to the oppressed; facilitating consciousness-raising around systemic oppression; building on clients' strengths; and arming clients with tools for social change. Goodman *et al.* also proposed three areas for social justice advocacy work for counselors: personal, professional and systemic work.

DISCUSSION QUESTIONS AND ART MAKING

Goal: What advocacy looks like for you.

Reflective artwork
Title: Advocacy

1. Reflect on your own personal advocacy. What does that look like for you?

2. Reflect on your own professional advocacy. What does that look like for you?

3. Reflect on systemic advocacy. What does that look like for you?

Create an art piece that reflects what you have learned about personal, professional and systemic advocacy, and how these are important in understanding your clients.

"SECOND-CLASS CITIZEN": THE CASE STUDY OF TRACY[1]

Tracy is a 46-year-old female who, although identifies as African American, has a mother who is Asian (Chinese American). She recently divorced Jim, her husband of ten years, and has primary custody of her two children. Jim is a 50-year-old White male who voted for Trump in the 2016 election but has since regretted his voting choice. Tracy is well educated, an alumna of Harvard Law School, and has worked very hard to be a senior member of her law firm.

Tracy is currently living with a number of stressors from her job and in her daily life. Although she is one of the senior members of the firm, she is still being treated as a "second-class citizen" and finds that she is still not taken very seriously by members of the firm. The other day, her brother was stopped by a White policeman and was almost put in jail, which upset Tracy. Tracy has experienced daily incidents of racial microaggressions. She feels formidable barriers in her efforts to gain equity and respect in her work environment. When she discusses these feelings with some of her White colleagues and supervisor, she is made to feel "ungrateful" for being "given" the opportunity to make it this far. Some have even called her "divisive" for bringing up issues of race and racism in the work environment.

In session, she talks about feeling "exhausted" most of the time from confronting these implicit racist acts. She shares with her therapist that some of her family members were among the many African Americans who faced difficulty accessing resources due to the inadequate response to the outbreak of the coronavirus. She says that many of the essential workers, such as bus drivers and other transportation workers, grocery store attendees, food and agriculture workers and factory workers, were

---

1   This case study and the one that follows are fictional, but reflect similar experiences of real clients.

Black and some were her relatives. She tells her therapist that COVID-19 sadly exposed inequality problems in the Black communities. She talks about how COVID-19 affected her family and killed one of her cousins and her grandmother. She has heard so much racist and xenophobic rhetoric from Donald Trump and she can't believe that he is going to be the Republican nominee again. She doesn't know if she can take another cycle of "racist policies and rants."

She is feeling a lot of pressure and stress from "me, work, my family and society." She is also extremely paranoid about the status of her position and over-compensates by working twice as hard as everyone else in the firm. Subsequently, she finds that she has little quality time for her two children, who are often asleep when she gets home. She feels depressed most of the time and is thinking about a career change. She isn't sure that law is a good fit for her anymore and feels that she now wants to teach. However, she doesn't think that teaching is a prestigious profession, as she has been told by her father (a well-known judge), and her many colleagues, that she might be looked down on for changing profession.

Tracy is a Baptist and attends church every Sunday, because she feels as if it grounds her, and it also makes her father happy.

"TRUMP IS GOING TO DEPORT ALL OF YOU": THE CASE STUDY OF JULIA

Julia is a 45-year-old woman, who identifies as Mexican American. She came to the United States illegally 20 years ago, but is currently working towards legal status, as she is married to Lisa, a 55-year-old White female from Indiana. They have two children. Julia worked in a factory for 11 years but suffered a severe back injury six months ago, resulting in her inability to continue working. She is currently on disability benefits and in severe pain most of the time. Lisa is a secretary at a doctor's office.

In session, Julia reports feeling anxious and sad. She has trouble sleeping and her appetite is poor. She says her wife is worried about her and feels guilty because she doesn't want her to worry. She still feels very unwelcome in the country, and lately the racist rhetoric has increased. The other day, her 14-year-old daughter came home crying saying that a classmate told her that "Trump is going to deport all of you." She has also experienced recent incidents of hate both as a Mexican and a lesbian. When she talks to Lisa about her experiences, Lisa immediately gets angry and has a hard time processing the situation in a calm manner. Julia knows that Lisa voted for Trump in 2016 and 2020 and plans to vote for him again if he's the Republican candidate in 2024. This has put a significant strain on their relationship. She has shared many articles and news media with Lisa regarding how she feels about Trump, and Lisa never takes Julia's worries about being an undocumented immigrant seriously.

Julia is worried about her 14-year-old daughter, who is exhibiting "maladaptive" behaviors at school due to the bullying. Julia only has a tenth-grade education and she wants her daughter to finish school and go to college. Julia is also thinking about finishing school and maybe getting an associate degree, but she's pretty uncertain about a particular vocational goal.

She is a non-practicing Catholic. She has been diagnosed with bipolar disorder by her psychiatrist.

QUESTIONS REGARDING BOTH CASE STUDIES

- What are the main issues in these case studies, and what is your understanding of the problems presented here? Does the locus of the problem lie in the individual or in the social system? Where would you focus your therapeutic energy on?

- What are the specific emotional issues experienced by the clients in these case studies? Are they both members of a marginalized group? What role do inequity and social justice play in these case studies? Why?

- What systemic and institutional problems are revealed in both case studies?

- How have the confluences of race, gender, class and ethnicity exerted powerful influences on the life of these women? Talk about inter-sectionality and social justice as it relates to these cases (age, race, ethnicity, disability, religion, geographic region, etc.). In what aspects are they privileged, and where are they oppressed?

- What are the systemic and institutional barriers that seem to be the root cause of some of the clients' mental health and social difficulties?

- How do the clients feel and think about their identity? What are the social conditionings—the messages the clients have/are receiving from society and those around them?

- Given the clients' ethnicity and backgrounds, what are some of the multicultural/social justice/global/political issues in these case studies? How would you incorporate them in your treatment approach?

- Has there been over-diagnosing going on? In Julia's case, is there evidence of bipolar disorder?

- What is Julia's perceived degree of personal control? Does she feel as if she has any control over her circumstances? In your role as an art therapist, how would you integrate any social justice advocacy?

- As an art therapist, how would you promote client empowerment and sociopolitical liberation?

- What information do you think is missing in these case studies, and how can that information help with counseling these clients?

- Identify any ethical and/or legal dilemmas introduced in these cases.

- As an art therapist, how do you *broach* with Tracy and Julia? How do you address inequality in therapy?

- As an undocumented immigrant, what difficulties is Julia facing regarding employment and healthcare? As an art therapist, how do you plan to work with her and advocate for her?

- What laws and policies in these cases influence the growth and development of the client?

- As an art therapist, how would you first approach this case as a social justice advocate, and what would be your plan to treat each client? What is your level of comfort in incorporating social justice advocacy in these cases?

DISCUSSION QUESTIONS AND ART MAKING

Political and social justice implications for art therapists: COVID-19/health inequality

The stories of discrimination and inequality experienced by marginalized groups in society continue to permeate our zeitgeist. Black and marginalized people suffered the most during the COVID-19 pandemic.

1. What are your thoughts regarding the health disparities African Americans faced when dealing with the coronavirus when considering the unequal economic and social conditions, which made it difficult to access resources and adequately respond to the outbreak of the virus?

2. How would you have worked with an Asian American going through incidents of hate sparked by the coronavirus?

3. How can you empower these marginalized clients to work towards ways to succeed in the United States?

Art therapists must be aware of continued client problems stemming from the experiences of COVID-19 and associated losses.

Self-reflection exercise regarding experiences during the COVID-19 pandemic

• What were your experiences during the COVID-19 pandemic? How do you think it might affect your work with clients?

Materials: Paper, collage images, decorative items, fabric, yarn, glitter, tissue paper, markers, pencils, crayons, colored paper, scissors, glue.

Create an art piece that reflects your experiences during the COVID-19 pandemic. What have you learned about your personal resilience? How has what you have learned about yourself improved your understanding of marginalized clients?

Summary

Providing best practices for helping the diverse, marginalized and oppressed is an important part of therapy for art therapists and other mental health therapists. Art therapists must be prepared to recognize and focus their therapeutic interventions not just on the individual but on the major societal and institutional failures that cause problems for their client. The client must be seen as existing within systems and culture that contribute to many factors in their lives. The use of art and culture, with the gatekeeping use of art therapy supervision, is a way of exploring, and understanding, inequalities. Equally important is providing social justice informed services. Since the controversial Trump administration, it is important for the field of counseling to recognize concerns in this area and increase the call for social justice advocacy for all counselors. I acknowledge the sensitive and complex borders between activism/social justice advocacy and therapy and how much more still needs to be done. If art therapists are concerned with improving the life circumstances of clients, and communities and society at large, then social justice advocacy must be the core tenet that guides the profession. Art therapists must continue to use their voices for actionable messages that help bend that "arc of moral universe" towards advocacy and justice.

Chapter 6

Intersectionality: Black Women in Art Therapy

What is intersectionality?

The concept of "intersectionality" was first posited in 1989 by American law professor Kimberlé Crenshaw, to expose how intersecting power relations affect social relations in individual everyday life experiences as well as across diverse societies (Crenshaw, 1989). As part of an analytic tool, intersectionality views categories of race, gender, class, sexuality, ethnicity, age and ability, among others, as mutually shaping one another. This concept works to explain the unique and complex intersectional experiences of Black women, the impact of racism and sexism on their lives, and their unique Black quality of being a woman (Crenshaw, 1990). Intersectionality is a way to help explain the oppression of Black women, understand how power operates, and interrupt the ways that power is consolidated in the hands of the dominant group, so that no one is left behind (Garza, 2020). Intersectionality is a central tenet of feminist thinking, and is defined as the convergence and interactions of the multiple dimensions that make up cultural identity, which influence an individual's personality and *worldview* (Crenshaw, 1989; McCall, 2005). It asks us to look at the world through a lens that is different from that of White people, so that we can see how power is distributed unevenly and on what basis, and how we can ensure that the world meets the needs of all those who have been marginalized (Garza, 2020). Crenshaw asserted that while racism and sexism intersected and impacted the lives of Black women, these occurrences were seldom examined together. Human lives cannot be explained by a single factor (e.g. gender)—minimizing an individual's personality or experiences to a singular factor risk and ignoring multiple factors of identity that may be essential in understanding the individual's overall reality (Crenshaw, 1989).

I am a Black, immigrant, cisgender, heterosexual woman who is able-bodied from an upper-middle socioeconomic status background. I am an educator and a practicing licensed counselor, artist and a registered art therapist, and intersectionality has been at the heart of my work, both in my personal artwork and with my work with clients. I have dedicated most of my personal and professional life to anti-racism and dismantling White supremacy. As a Black woman, my artwork responds to a multi-layered notion of *identity*. This means that the co-existence of privilege and marginality is a reality for me, and I have to embrace and integrate the two to avoid a fragmented existence. I have multiple social identities, systems of oppression and related privileges and oppression that intersect with my race, ethnicity and culture. I am a variety of things that form my whole identity. Areas of privilege in my social identities include being able-bodied, cisgender and heterosexual. My oppression status includes my race and my gender. As a member of a non-dominant group, I have experienced oppression in the form of racism, discrimination and inequality that overshadows any aspects of privilege in my social identities. The use of mixed media and collage in my art reflects the complex layers of my identity and my struggles (Figure 6.1). Core tenets of my work are social justice, human rights, equality and accessibility for all people. My view of intersectionality has helped in my own reflexivity and self-awareness about who I really am as a Black woman, immigrant, artist, art therapist, counselor and social justice advocate; there are many complex layers there. In my artwork, the use of mixed media and collage is a reflection of complex layers of my identity and the several struggles I call attention to in my art (Anah, 2018b). In essence, using an intersectional approach allows me to understand better my life experiences as well as the lives of my clients, particularly how they are perceived and treated in society in the United States. The majority of my clients face significant race-related oppression, discrimination and intersecting barriers.

As art therapists, it is important to consider additional dimensions and variables of a culturally diverse client, such as race/ethnicity, sexual orientation, gender and socioeconomic status, in order to develop custom-made treatment plans that effectively address their presenting problems in a culturally sensitive manner.

FIGURE 6.1: "NO SUCH THING AS A SINGLE-ISSUE STRUGGLE" BY CHIOMA
ANAH, © 2018 (MIXED MEDIA ON PAPER, ORIGINAL SIZE: 11" X 14")

This artwork was also part of a presentation given at the 49th American Art Therapy
Association Conference in Miami, Florida, on November 3, 2018, titled "Still I Rise: Reflections
of an Artist's Journey as Social Activist" (Chioma Anah).

Intersectionality: Black women in art therapy

In acknowledging the scarcity of Blackness in art therapy spaces, I wanted
to find out how other Black women art therapists navigate the complexities at the intersection of race and gender. I believe that intersectionality
is an important framework for understanding and effectively addressing
the deeply rooted societal and systemic problems of racism we face in

the United States today. The questions center around understanding the challenges they've faced in becoming an art therapist, how they've coped with those challenges and how those coping mechanisms could be used to improve the field of art therapy.

The interviews that follow provide an opportunity for us to learn from two art therapy legends, Gwendolyn Short and Charlotte Boston. We reflect on, and explore, how their own intersectional identities have influenced their journey as art therapists. These interviews also provide important information and techniques to use when working with culturally diverse clients and help them work towards healing.

Interview with Gwendolyn Short, MA, ATR-BC, LCPAT

What have been some of your challenges as a Black female in becoming an art therapist? How did you navigate intersectional invisibility? Did you have any mentors or support along the way?

I was first made aware of the field of art therapy by my advisor in undergraduate school. She had a friend who was an art therapist teaching at George Washington University (GWU) and said I could combine art and psychology in art therapy, rather than have to choose between the two. Once I decided to apply to the Art Therapy program at GWU, I spent all my efforts on that goal. A good friend had applied to the program and was denied at first, then accepted on her second try. She helped me select my pictures for my portfolio and assisted me in matting them. We also selected the ceramics I would present at my interview. Since I was living here in DC, I chose not to photograph my work but to carry it to my interview with Berny Levy, the Head of the Art Therapy program. So, armed with my portfolio and a grocery cart with my ceramics, I met with Dr. Levy, who laughed out loud at my grocery cart. I was accepted into the program, but whenever I saw Dr. Levy, he would always laugh about my grocery cart full of my ceramics. So, I always felt that grocery cart got me into GWU's Art Therapy program.

Intersectionality is a new term for me. When I began my career 40-plus years ago, keeping my eye on the prize was my goal. For three years (the length of time in the program), I was the only African American student in the program. I did what I had to do to succeed. I had to go part time because I worked full time. Initially, I had a practicum on Saturdays at a nursing home due to my schedule. Then to fulfill my internships, I had to quit my day job and find a night job (midnight to 8am) so that I could do my internships during the day and take classes in the evenings and on weekends.

I think I navigated intersectional invisibility by remaining present and not allowing myself to feel I wasn't good enough to be there. I must admit that, at first, I had some reservations—coming from a land-grant college and predominantly Black school, would my education measure up to my peers'? Would I be able to keep up with my peers? I had one deficiency of a class that was not offered before I graduated. After about two weeks, all of my worries subsided once I was in classes with my cohort. I could see I was well prepared for this journey and there were people who had three, four or five deficiencies. One person had eight, so I knew I could compete, and succeeding was up to me.

Mentors would come later, but support came from within my cohort. I was an older student and was able to develop friendships with some of the older students as well as many of the younger students. One student and I became very close as we interned at the same placement. We worked together, studied together, traveled to conferences together, met each other's families and supported each other in life, in general.

Kimberlé Crenshaw (1989) coined the term "intersectionality" to refer to the convergence and interactions of the multiple dimensions that make up cultural identity, which, in turn, influence an individual's personality and worldview. How can we apply intersectionality's intended principles in art therapy practice today?

I am a large, African American, Christian female, well over 60, with short, natural gray hair. I have been in the field of art therapy for over 40 years. I am who I am, and I am proud of what I bring to treatment sessions, to the organizations I am affiliated with and to the communities I serve and am a part of routinely. It is my history that brought me here and I cannot be any different. Have I always felt so strongly about my own identity? No, but when I look back and see those who helped me to become me, I wouldn't change a thing other than to be more of a voice for those who feel they cannot speak for themselves.

I take seriously engaging, supporting and encouraging others to get to know and be their best self. I do not pretend to be all-knowing and thus I work hard to learn the dynamics of why someone is here to work with me. In doing so, looking at how we can develop some coping skills, if necessary some "aha," I do have some strengths moments and use all of this to help someone see that they can push beyond where they are at this moment. Focusing on their positive, I find, is a more solid approach in the treatment session.

When I was getting my master's degree in art therapy in the mid-90s in our History of Art Therapy course, I learned about pioneers such as Margaret Naumburg and Edith Kramer. I didn't learn much about pioneers like Lucille Venture and

Georgette Seabrooke Powell until years later. Who are some of the important and inspirational Black female pioneers in the art therapy field? Is there enough known about them? If not, how can their contributions be more visible? What current voices of art therapists do you feel might be among us helping to shape an anti-racist vision of what is possible for the field of art therapy?

I studied art therapy in the late 70s and I took classes at GWU from the recognized pioneers in the field. I studied with Elinor Ulman, Edith Kramer, Hanna Kwiatkowska and others. So, my experiences of meeting Black female art therapists were at the American Art Therapy Association Conferences. I met and was taken care of by Lucille Venture, Georgette Seabrooke Powell and Sarah McGee. However, as a young student, at the time I was totally unaware of the value of these relationships. They did not tout their accomplishments, but all were strongly invested in seeing more Black art therapists. However, when I look back, I can say my tribute to them is my remaining in the field of art therapy and helping to make their histories known to all.

Is there enough known about them? Years ago, members of the Multicultural Committee of AATA decided we needed to make their contributions known, as well as some of the Black men who were also there. We saw the tremendous void and decided to compile a textbook about them. However, feeling that the task was a huge undertaking, we decided to make a video. Thus, we interviewed those who were still alive, or their close friends if they had passed away. This task was years in the making, but we did it: *Wheels of Diversity in Art Therapy: Pioneers of Color.* We have presented this at the AATA Conferences, including an opening plenary. We have written articles about these people to make the history of art therapy and AATA more complete. Many people have come together to make all of this happen, Black, White and others interested in completing a more inclusive history.

There is more known about them than before the efforts were made to bring them to the forefront. I can only suggest they be more a part of the art therapy programs and be taught as a complete history. Thus, while the original pioneers are presented in classes, it should be known that the pioneers of color were right there with Margaret Naumburg, as Lucille Venture had correspondence from her in her book, *The Black Beat in Art Therapy*, which was her dissertation for her doctorate. Yes, the first doctorate in art therapy was a Black female. Georgette Powell worked with Elinor Ulman, Cliff Joseph worked with Edith Kramer, Sarah McGee first presented art therapy with migrant workers, in her hotel room at the AATA Conference, because her work was not selected by the conference committee. Cliff Joseph chaired the Third World Ad Hoc Committee. Charles Anderson worked with Bob Ault at the Menninger Clinic for decades.

And the history goes on, but sadly is not presented on the same scale as the more notable pioneers in art therapy.

Some of the current voices in art therapy, in my opinion, who are helping to shape an anti-racist version of what is possible for the field of art therapy are: Dr. Cheryl Doby-Copeland, Dr. Louvenia Jackson, Lindsey Vance, Martina Efodzi, Deanna Barton, Stella Stepney, Dr. Anna Hiscox, Lisa Thomas and Blanche Brown. This is based on my personal relationships and having worked with these incredible people on different projects but also on how they support each other when times prove stressful. Also, those who are part of the Multicultural Committee of AATA cultivate the sense of belongingness that is essential for developing and sustaining perseverance.

This list is not conclusive, and I am so proud of many new and/or other art therapists who are actively working to shape the anti-racist version in art therapy.

You have been an art psychotherapist for over 40 years—an incredible feat! Thank you so much for your important contributions to the field of art therapy. It really is quite an honor to interview you. In adopting an intersectional self-reflexive approach, what have been your experiences working as an art therapist in the various spaces (student, practitioner, supervisor and professor)? What do you see as the pitfalls of not addressing racism and inequality within art therapy practice? How can this fracture the therapeutic relationship?

I think many of my experiences as a student have already been described earlier, but I can add the following. Many of my assignments turned into Elinor Ulman would come back with more red ink (corrections) than the original black ink. My internship at a hospital was interesting because my night-time job was in the crisis intervention program. My job was to interview psychiatric patients coming into the emergency room (ER) during those hours (midnight to 8am), contact the doctor on call, give information about the patient, and get a disposition. Based on the information, they could be admitted to the hospital, stay in the ER for further evaluation or stay in the ER for the night for the drugs to wear off. Now, I would work with those admitted to the psychiatric unit of the hospital the next day in art therapy, as an intern. Often, I had to explain that I worked in the ER at night. On one occasion, a patient kept bothering me and I couldn't understand why. He was a young Black male, whom I had interviewed and admitted the night before. Finally, I asked him why he was always bothering me. He said, "Why are you always working? Let some of these White people work." In his way, he was concerned about me.

Early on, the Health Department didn't recognize art therapy, so I was an activity therapist (art). However, they would allow me to order art supplies. They would also give me administrative leave to attend the yearly AATA Conferences, at my own expense. I am convinced that this was a factor in my never being fired during my 33 years there. I worked with the chronically mentally ill (the term of that time), dual diagnosed (mentally ill and retarded, at that time), the co-occurring disordered (mentally ill and substance abused), substance abusers, young and old. I have worked in Adult Day Treatment, Community Outreach and Treatment Services (COATS), Children And Parents (CAP), the special education wing of an elementary school, drug court and the Department of Social Services. After my 27 years as an art therapist with the Health Department, the Director of Mental Health and Substance Abuse allowed me to be the art therapist for the whole county. So, I'd go from north to central to the south. I would form groups, work with individuals, and give in-services; I enjoyed every moment of it for two years.

There were challenges along the way, but as the only art therapist in the Health Department for 33 years, I persevered, and they kept me. In each of my roles and positions, as a trained art therapist, we had art therapy wherever I was detailed. I had one supervisor early on who called art therapy "fluff," but as she got to know me and my passion for my field and saw its value, she became an advocate for me and art therapy.

As a supervisor, I have been put in some challenging positions. I filled in as chair of the Adult Day Treatment for two years, then I was told I would have to interview for the permanent position, which I did. As part of the interview, it was made clear that I might have to do some difficult actions, and I told them, "As long as it is not against the will of God." As a supervisor, I feel it is my responsibility to know my employees, encourage them to move forward, with training, and be supportive of them when necessary, and challenge them as well.

As a professor, I take seriously the role and the obligation to educate the students in many ways. There is the usual curriculum of readings and research, homework, response art, but also other related experiences. That can include field trips, assigning experiences in other cultures of at least two hours. I also share my experiences and bring in books, articles and videos to highlight and/or expose racism and to show positive points.

Not addressing racism and inequity within art therapy practice does nothing to move the issues forward. Who would you be protecting, yourself or the client? It may be uncomfortable, but not all therapy is pretty. When trying to establish trust in the relationship, holding back or not addressing difficult issues does not help anyone. Also, if a client feels you're not able to or ready to probe deeper into these issues, they may not feel you can handle their care.

Microaggressions can both be subtle and overt. They are "subtle, stunning, often automatic, and nonverbal exchanges which are 'put downs'" (Pierce et al., 1978, p.66). Have you ever experienced any sort of microaggressions? Did you recognize it immediately? What were the circumstances, what was the microaggression, and how did you deal with it?

The Adult Day Treatment was closing, and I had been the Program Chief for a few years. As it was a good program and the employees had worked with me and we had worked well together, I decided to have a closing program as a thank you to the employees. I had it catered, I hired a jazz band and I had plaques made for all the staff. I invited other staff in the building, and our administration, and the Director of Mental Health. A good time was had by all; however, the Director of Mental Health did not give a speech or thank us for the time we had all put into the program. On leaving, the Director said to me, "You really know how to throw a party."

My supervisor from the Health Department came to visit my program. I can't remember what the initial conversation was about, but she said to me, "I get the feeling that if a fire broke out, you would get everybody out, then call the fire department, then call me." I said yes, isn't that what I'm supposed to do? Seemingly, she felt I should call her for directions first.

I had a supervisor tell me that I should enter a room as if I owned it. She seemed genuinely sincere, but I had to tell her that what worked for her as a White woman would not work for me as a Black woman. She had no clue that the reception would be quite different for me.

I had learned to just ignore some of the statements that just did not make sense to me. At other times, I would briefly respond if I felt it was warranted.

Race, racism and inequality have always been at the consciousness of most Black people and other minoritized communities. However, I think with the Trump era, the Black Lives Matter movement, the COVID-19 global pandemic and the protests following the murder of George Floyd in 2020, more of the problems surrounding race and White privilege were brought into the collective consciousness. Do you think the field of art therapy has evolved in the way issues of racism, inequality and White supremacy are handled? What's your hope for how the field of art therapy can emerge from this moment, and what are the responsibilities of art therapy supervisors and professors to work to improve the way their supervisees and students confront and dismantle racism?

I think the field of art therapy is evolving; however, I cannot expect that to happen in a vacuum. All the situations mentioned above have impacted all of us. I know the Board of Directors of AATA hired The Ivy Group to address diversity, equity and inclusion issues in our organization, the AATA. This is planting the seed with many and shows, at least, some acknowledgment of the importance of the issue, as well as an attempt to make some positive changes. However, the membership and other art therapists will have examined the issues already and be willing to work on them continuously. Racism, inequity and White supremacy, yes, I think the field of art therapy is evolving to handle these issues, but they have been around for much longer than our focus to address them. But remember that the journey of 1000 miles begins with the first step, and we have many steps towards it.

My hope for how the field of art therapy can emerge from this moment is that sensitivity to these issues propels art therapists to want to eradicate them for their clients, peers and themselves. In doing so, the art therapists strengthen themselves to be advocates for themselves and others.

I cannot expect this to happen if I am not willing to be part of the solution. When I allow myself to be involved, that is the best I can do to work towards a better understanding of the issues and have more determination to fight them.

I think art therapy supervisors and professors can encourage their supervisees and students to explore different relationships, which are important, and so get to know different people. Mix and mingle, be courageous enough to step out of your comfort zone. Learn more about others, from personal experiences, rather than just reading about others or seeing movies and TV programs. It makes confrontation and dismantling racism more plausible if you are aware of it from experience or a closer understanding of what others may experience.

We owe a debt to the many social justice advocates and activists fighting for equality in previous generations and currently. The late John Lewis comes to mind, as he fought for social justice: "Never be afraid to speak up and speak out. Together we can build a more perfect union" (Lewis, 2018). How do we as art therapists "speak up and speak out" and create a practice responsive to the sociopolitical aspect of identity and its relationship to racial trauma and inequalities, and effect real change?

Art therapists must maintain some knowledge of current events to be responsive and ready to advocate for those unable to speak up or speak out. While not all art therapists are comfortable speaking out, they can still motivate others and be supportive of those who can. When art therapists are knowledgeable, they can be more proactive, and in doing so, they model behaviors that our clientele may need to see. In addressing racial trauma and inequalities, provide an open and comfortable atmosphere so that the conversation can flow. The art therapist must be prepared to be a part of these difficult conversations. The art therapist must operate from a position of healing rather than of anger or frustration. The art therapist (we) must be the change we want to see in the field/world.

We know that the process of art therapy creates an ideal environment that promotes and enables reflection and healing. What effective tools or interventions or techniques have you used to work with clients who have experienced racial trauma and oppression to enable and facilitate their ability to heal?

I usually start with where they are currently and work backwards from there. Create an art piece to show how you're feeling right now, and what brings you to treatment. Then I focus on the positive and start with the fact that they are here to work on their issues. I want them to see that their survival is a strength, as is their willingness to come to treatment and work on their pain. Usually, I am thinking of other prompts that will allow the participants a continued open and respectful environment to disclose and work on their painful issues.

What can art therapists do to become more culturally responsive to the needs of minoritized clients in their service, and what does it mean to be an effective ally or co-conspirator as part of dismantling racism and moving towards healing? What action or show of support would you say the field of art therapy can provide in realizing a future of hope that advances the social justice movement?

I advocate for all of my clients, but my marginalized clients usually need more, and I am willing to go beyond the session, if necessary. I explore and research the resources in the area and make clients aware so they can reach out for additional assistance. An example of this is the following: I worked with a Black woman with a long history of mental illness. The pharmacy would constantly put barriers in her way of getting her medication. On one occasion, she informed me that she had been without her medication for seven days. Neither her outside therapist nor her psychiatrist were responding to her calls about the situation. I also called them but did not get in touch with them. My next call was to the county's core service agency. I explained the situation and was instructed to have the client call a specific number to get a three-day supply of her medication. Then, the next day the pharmacy called and told her to come and pick up her medication. She called me to let me know she had finally got her medication and told me that her therapist wanted to know who I was. That doesn't matter, I expect them to do their job and help their client. I will also do as much as I can for my clients, especially when inequality is so blatant.

There is so much going on in the country and in the world, and "racial battle fatigue" is a real thing. How do you take care of yourself and stay positive during these times? How do you stay motivated to continue your work as an art therapist?

I pay it forward; just as people have nurtured me, supported me and encouraged me, I reach out to new art therapists, students (interns) and my peers. My motto is that I never ask anyone to do something I am not willing to do myself. I talk to others; I encourage others and I am an ear when necessary. Most of all, I am just passing through this life, and I want to make sure that those taking my place are ready and able to be the very best that they can possibly be. We owe that to those who will be in treatment with us.

Interview with Charlotte Boston, MA, ATR-BC, LCPAT

What have been some of your challenges as a Black female art therapist navigating your educational and professional path in art therapy? How did you navigate intersectional invisibility? Did you have any mentors and support along the way?

Educationally, I've had feelings of inadequacy, not feeling fully accepted, feeling in the shadows, and having to be a spokesperson for all things Black. In the beginning stages of my art therapy journey, I felt hungry to learn everything I could about art therapy, it was so new to me, and I felt like I belonged in the art therapy family. Reflecting now on my experiences more than 30 years later, I felt that I came up with my own solutions to address cultural issues at my practicum site. I was the only Black person in my class and was often uncomfortable during the times when my white classmates would look to me for answers about how to deal with the Black clients they worked with. They shared their experiences, sometimes in tears, about being cursed out or facing resistance with Black clients. They would come to me outside class and sometimes in discussion in class with these incidents. They wanted my recommendations on how to work with them. I did my best to explain, but sometimes resented being the spokesperson for my race. I felt they needed to examine themselves and their biases and do the work themselves. They expressed how uncomfortable and sometimes offended they were with the Black clients. They didn't perceive that what they said or how they said it meant any harm or would aggravate the populations with whom they worked.

We didn't have access to multicultural art materials, crayons and paints when I was in school for art therapy. My goodness, I don't recall even being familiar with a multicultural color palette. We didn't have professors of color in my undergraduate fine art education for anyone to even notice, or take action to correct it. Most of my professors were competent, but I often felt something was missing. When I chose my art therapy program, I wanted to be where the art therapists who were writing about it were teaching. At my art therapy placements, where there were often a small percentage of diverse clients, I noticed the absence of culturally diverse magazines and I found myself bringing in my *Essence* or *Ebony* magazines so there would be some materials available for diverse clients to choose from. It didn't occur to me to ask or expect this of my supervisors, but they were happy that I recognized this and contributed to the art supplies. When paint was used for brown and Black skin tones, I helped them to blend colors.

As I learned about art therapy, the "mothers" of art therapy, the various theoretical approaches and all the assessment techniques, I questioned how well they would work with Black and diverse populations, as these approaches didn't seem to have people of Color in mind. I questioned but never challenged this. It was my intention at the time to use art therapy techniques in the inner-city neighborhood I grew up in. I felt using art as an expression for the ills of the inner city would be helpful and healing. I felt that art therapy would be a safe and constructive tool to decrease the drug use, violence and destruction of property that was destroying my neighborhood. Now in reflection, I don't feel I was assertive enough to speak up on how those theories would best work for Black people. I had a host of feelings about this and said nothing because how could I as student challenge folks who wrote the books on these theories? I felt it strange that there was no discussion that really addressed culture. I felt I had to do it myself, just as I had done before with mixing the colors. I decided that I would address this issue more directly when I graduated or presented on the issue at an art therapy conference.

There were no multicultural competencies in the curriculum and ethics when I was an art therapy student. Activities related to culture were minimal and were often oriented around food or clothing. None of what I learned or read mentioned Black or diverse art therapists. I was aware of a few Black art therapists, who graduated before me, locally. However, I did not meet a pioneer of color in art therapy until 20 years later. I learned that the first PhD in art therapy was a Black woman named Lucille Venture. She took art therapy classes with Margaret Naumburg and Hanna Kwiatkowska. Lucille knew Georgette Seabrooke Powell, who was an art therapist who worked with Elinor Ulman. This made me angry because I felt cheated. I felt the urgency to talk with both Lucille and Georgette and their experiences and find out about other Black and brown art therapists. I was disappointed that this was a missing important component of information in my art therapy education.

As a professional, I became involved in the American Art Therapy Association's multicultural committee. I felt that many clients served by art therapists were diverse, but the population of art therapists was predominantly white. It seemed obvious to me that more needed to be done to address the issue of multicultural issues in art therapy. I was more assertive by this time, as I had now been privy through my observations to how other art therapists brought attention to relevant issues in the field. Gandhi said "be the change you seek" and I was that change along with some other Black art therapists who were like minded, as well as frustrated. Over the years, I presented on multicultural issues, did workshops, published articles, taught and collaborated regarding the topic. Judy Rubin and Maxine Jung, whom I admired, would frequently encourage me to write for publication. This led to more opportunities for me to write and collaborate on other topics. By this time, my colleagues in art therapy were diverse and supported me. Professionally, however, there were two incidences that were most impactful for me since they seemed blatantly discriminatory. I was a manager for a small staff of expressive art therapists. I had previously attended a leadership training course. The organization was predominantly Black and the population at this organization that we serviced was diverse. I sent two of my staff who were white, and talked with them about the training as I thought it would be an opportunity for them to improve their leadership skills and cultural competence. They agreed to attend, and my supervisor approved my decision to send them. To cut a long story short, they reportedly witnessed something that they felt was unfair and discriminatory, and they left the training. When I challenged them, they reported me to my boss, and the leadership of the organization. It caused a formal investigation, which resulted in a week's suspension. They determined that the training/organization that I sent my staff to attend was not consistent with the organization's mission and my decision was not befitting of a leader. They gave me the option to resign or be demoted as a therapist. I was shocked, insulted and offended. I had not done anything wrong and did not feel that resigning or being demoted was appropriate in this instance, especially since a thorough investigation was not performed. After much prayer, I decided I was not leaving. You can imagine how difficult it was for me to step down as the supervisor and become a peer to those I used to supervise. I did what I felt I had to do until I could find another position.

A second incident that I felt was discriminatory occurred in another leadership position. I was the first Black person in this position, and I had board experience. I also had publication experience. I was familiar with the politics in the field and prepared for the position. I was a seasoned art therapist by this point. While in my position, my decisions were ignored and disrespected, despite being in alignment with what was appropriate. I'm sure if I had been a white person, I would not have been challenged on every front. It really bothers me that these types of incidents continue to happen even today. I had figured that with all the work I had done in the field on multicultural issues, in the ways my counterparts had done, they would be minimized. However, when I look at the things that continue to happen in the United States with racism, there's still so much work that needs to be done. I wonder if we will ever get to a point where there will be significant change and I will be able to exhale.

I am the art therapist I am because of my intention to use my skills and talents to meet a need and be of service to Black, brown, diverse populations, and to make it known that it's important to the field and the future of art therapy for it to reflect diverse populations of this world on all levels: professors, art therapists, publications.

My mentors are widely diverse and not all Black and brown. I could run down a list of many art therapists, but so I don't miss anyone, I would say my mentors are all of those with whom I've had the opportunity and pleasure to present at conferences and workshops, write for publication, teach a class or be a guest lecturer at a university, serve on the board of directors of AATA and the Art Therapy Credentials Board, brainstorm ideas over a meal, have a creative weekend making art. You all inspired me and empowered me to make a difference.

Kimberlé Crenshaw (1989) coined the term "intersectionality" to refer to the convergence and interactions of the multiple dimensions that make up cultural identity, which, in turn, influence an individual's personality and worldview. How can we apply intersectionality's intended principles in art therapy practice today?

It must start with self-examination. We must first do our own self work—if we do not examine our own biases, on an ongoing basis, we are doomed to fail, doomed to build the trust and respect needed to provide a competent service for clients. Art therapists need to be in therapy. We must not function on assumption in our interactions with our clients. When we don't examine our own biases, it impedes treatment. Some employers now include "bias training" as a part of their onboarding process and it's incorporated in annual competencies for employees.

When I was getting my master's degree in art therapy in the mid-90s in our History of Art Therapy course, I learned about pioneers such as Margaret Naumburg and Edith Kramer. And similar to your experience, it was not until later, after my studies, that I began to learn more about pioneers like Lucille Venture and

Georgette Seabrooke Powell. Who are some of the important and inspirational Black female pioneers in the art therapy field? Is there enough known about them? If not, how can their contributions be more visible? What current voices of art therapists do you feel might be among us helping to shape an anti-racism vision of what is possible for the field of art therapy?

There are several Black female pioneers of color featured in a film I co-produced, *Wheels of Diversity in Art Therapy: Pioneers of Color*. It includes information on Sarah McGee, Georgette Seabrooke Powell and Lucille Venture. I am currently leading a study group of art therapists to examine Lucille Venture's dissertation, and efforts are underway to have it published so that all may have access to it. In addition, the inspirational Black women I think about are ones to watch and most have been published and have presented at AATA conferences, done research and/or conducted workshops as Black female pioneers: Lindsey Vance, Deanna Barton, Cheryl Doby-Copeland, Gwendolyn Short, Stella Stepney, Louvenia Jackson, Paula Hammond, Rhonda Johnson, Genia Young, Tuesdai Johnson and Ama Kyere. These are a few of the current voices I'm aware of who are helping to shape an anti-racist vision of what is possible for art therapy.

For their contributions, another *Wheels of Diversity* film should be done, more could be published, art therapy programs could have them as guest lecturers and presenters in other forums. They may even consider becoming part of faculty at an art therapy program.

You have been an art psychotherapist for over 30 years, and I thank you so profoundly for the work you've done thus far around multicultural art therapy. In adopting an intersectional self-reflexive approach, what have been your experiences working as an art therapist in the various spaces? What do you see as the pitfalls of not addressing racism and inequality within art therapy practice? How can this fracture the therapeutic relationship?

Pitfalls in not addressing racism and inequality will cost therapists good rapport, respect and trust with clients in this current atmosphere where there's a great need for mental health services for diverse cultures and a lack of time to build rapport. They would not seek treatment. Not addressing racism and inequality in the supervisory relationship is a disservice to supervisees. Systemic racism, whether subtle or blatant, still exists on an organizational level within healthcare and education. The cost results in a supervisee being unprepared, and ignorant of how to be aware of themselves and their clients. As art therapists, we prepare to advocate for our clients, to call out people or systems that perpetuate racist and unequal practices. Sometimes, we must advocate for ourselves or our co-workers. I believe the art therapy field would suffer and not attract the diverse art therapy faculty and student population it so greatly needs.

Microaggressions can both be subtle and overt. They are "subtle, stunning, often automatic, and nonverbal exchanges which are 'put downs'" (Pierce et al., 1978, p.66). Have you ever experienced any sort of microaggressions? When were you first aware of it? Did you recognize it immediately? What were the circumstances, what was the microaggression, and how did you deal with it?

Yes, I've experienced microaggressions in some spaces, but I do recall it as an undergraduate in a predominantly white university from white professors and some white students. I didn't see it as a microaggression—that's the politically correct term now I guess—it was blatant racism to me. In my work environment, even in the military environment, with all their layers of culture, and in some art therapy roles, I saw it as eye rolling, stares, not responding to a greeting or a question, condescending comments. My usual response as an undergraduate was to give the same back to them since it was often from female peers. I'd make a bold physical stance—hand on my hip posturing, or get closer in their personal space, stare back, roll my eyes. If it was a professor, I would report them. As a professional in the workplace, if I had the opportunity, I would look at them and ask, "There must be something I can help you with because you are giving me so much attention," or similar comment, or say "God bless you" and bat my eyes. Lately I haven't experienced any microaggressions, but it may be due to my work environment being more diverse, and the inclusion of bias training in our annual competencies.

Race, racism and inequality have always been at the consciousness of most Black people and other minoritized communities, but with the Trump era, the Black Lives Matter movement, the global pandemic and the protests following the murder of George Floyd in 2020, more of the problems surrounding race and White privilege have been brought into the collective consciousness. Do you think the field of art therapy has evolved in the way issues of racism, inequality and White supremacy are handled? What's your hope for how the field of art therapy can emerge from this moment, and work to improve the way racism is confronted and dismantled?

The field of art therapy is evolving on these issues. There are now multicultural competencies established in the American Art Therapy Association and there are currently members on its board of directors who have been trained in diversity, equity and inclusion issues. In addition, multicultural competencies are embedded in the art therapy program curriculum.

The article "Advancing multicultural and diversity competence in art therapy: American Art Therapy Association Multicultural Committee 1990–2015" (Potash *et al.*, 2015) shared the 25-year history of this committee's work to "provide education, networking, and mentoring activities for all art therapists, as well as support for art therapists of color" (p.2). Past chairs provided a historical account of this committee's history. In my chapter on art therapy and multiculturalism in *The Wiley Handbook of Art Therapy*, I outlined:

> information and guidelines on improving multicultural competency for art therapists. Its purpose is to facilitate the efforts of art therapists to explore their identity as cultural beings and to provide a context for culturally sensitive considerations when using art therapy interventions... Unless one is willing to examine his or her own prejudices, biases, cultural assumptions, family origins, beliefs and traditions, cultural roadblocks may lead to ineffective treatment and poor client rapport. (Boston, 2016, p.822)

In this chapter, I also discussed the national initiatives on multicultural competencies. I defined what it is to be a culturally sensitive art therapist and included tools that can support this effort. It's a process where you will be uncomfortable and outside your comfort zone. However, this is a normal process to become more culturally aware.

Race is a social concept and has wreaked havoc on the lives of Black people and many others. The word race seems to be loaded with so many meanings that some folks are not always certain about its meaning and tend not to want to discuss it. In the context of art therapy practice, what does it mean and how does it impact how we as art therapists practice? What do you see as the consequences of not addressing racial trauma and inequality in the art therapy room?

We have seen, from the things you mentioned earlier, that race is still a "sensory" concept, even in art therapy. If there are differences that can be seen or heard, these are targets used to oppress and stereotype. The consequences of not addressing racial trauma and inequality in an art therapy session would jeopardize whether you would have anyone in session. The safe environment has not been established. Clients would not feel acknowledged, welcomed or valued. If racism was allowed in the art therapy group, and the art therapist did not address it and advocate for equality, the group in whole or part may walk out or not create art at all.

We know that the process of art therapy creates an ideal environment that promotes and enables reflection and healing. In your experience as an art therapist, what effective tools, interventions and techniques have you used to work with clients who have experienced racial trauma and oppression to enable and facilitate their ability to heal?

I work from a strengths-based approach, with concrete themes focused on comfort and safety. During the intake, I make sure I listen carefully and take the time to allow them to share their story as this helps me to determine related themes and consideration of art materials unique to them.

What can art therapists do to become more culturally responsive to the needs of minoritized clients in their service? What does it mean to be an effective ally or co-conspirator as part of the force of dismantling racism and moving towards healing? What action or show of support would you say the field of art therapy can provide in realizing a future of hope that advances the social justice movement?

Art therapy programs need to establish an ongoing recruitment of students from diverse cultures in a similar manner as has been done for college sports. Graduate scholarships and/or work/study programs for diverse graduate students should be provided. Mentoring diverse students is still needed and another necessary component that would be valuable, as I mentioned earlier.

There is so much going on in the world, and "racial battle fatigue" is a real thing. How do you take care of yourself and stay positive during these times? How do you stay motivated to work?

I do my best to practice regular self-care: I pray and meditate, create art, exercise regularly, get proper rest, schedule time off, go to an exhibit, stay connected with my broadly diverse art therapy friends and colleagues, and we plan time together to gather and/or create. I also choose my battles. I'm motivated to work because I believe in art therapy and its power to heal. As a Black woman who has experienced discrimination, and who is aware of the continuing inequalities and discriminatory practices towards other BIPOC people, I feel obligated to advocate for change because the need continues.

Note: In her interview, Charlotte Boston uses "white" with a lower case "w," and BIPOC for Black, Indigenous and People of Color.

DISCUSSIONS

- What are the highlights learned from these interviews?
- What is your understanding of the complexities of identity in counseling across cultures?

EXPLORING YOUR INTERSECTIONAL IDENTITIES: DISCUSSIONS AND ART THERAPY EXERCISE

Who are you? How do you see yourself?

Purpose and goal: To examine our multiple identities. Cultural identity is composed of several sociocultural factors. Age, religious/spiritual orientation and gender. Intersectionality demands self-reflexivity, and it offers art therapists a way of identifying and dealing with racial, ethical and cultural complexities and issues of power in a variety of perspectives (Talwar, 2010).

Title: Exploring your intersectional identities

Materials: Picture of yourself, collage materials, fabric materials, glue, markers, found objects that speak to you, paints, brushes, colored pencils.

Instructions:

- All of us come with our own cultural backgrounds, privilege, biases, cultural awareness, cultural worldview, racial/ethnic identity, which all contribute to microaggressions within the counseling relationship. Types of inequality include class, racial, gender, (dis)ability, educational (college educated/non-college-educated).

- On a separate piece of paper, share who you are and how you define yourself. Think in terms of your background, beliefs, gender identity, privilege, ethnic identity, education, (dis)ability and ableism, professional affiliations, employment, family background, economic status, and so on. Write them down as well as creating a piece of artwork representing all these parts of you.

- Social identities include race, gender, class, religion, sexual orientation and age. Create an image that reflects on "Who am I?" "How do I see myself?" What are the aspects of your social identities you relate to the most? What are the aspects of social identities you don't relate to? What aspects of your social identities are privileged, and which are oppressive/inequitable? Are any of your privileges or oppressions "invisible?" How do all these multiple identities intersect with your race?

- You can use the blank face below to start you off, or you can create your own (you can download this at https://library.jkp.com/redeem using the code CQXSRUU).

- This art exercise can be done individually, or in class in a group. This exercise can also be created during a therapeutic session with your client.

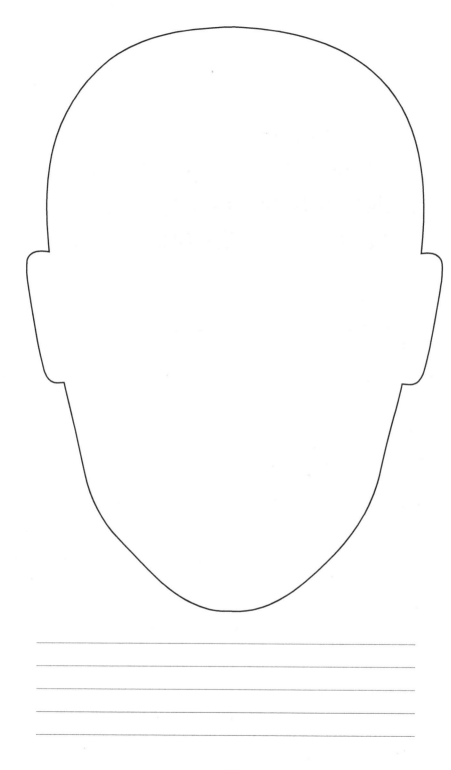

Chapter 7

Theoretical Frameworks for Understanding Racism, and Interventions and Implications for Art Therapy Clinical Practice

MY IROKO TREE OF IDENTITY AND PATHWAY TOWARDS HEALING

This is an updated version of an art therapy exercise that I first presented at the 2019 New Jersey Counseling Association Conference.

Instructions

This art exercise requires honest self-reflection:

- Draw a tree (make sure you make room for the roots, branches, leaves, a thick trunk).

- Make a heap next to your tree.

- Draw a pathway leading to your tree.

- On the roots, draw:

  - your race, ethnicity, culture, heritage/history—think about your family of origin

  - where you come from—hometown, state, geographic location, country

  - your experiences, customs observed by family and people who have shaped your identity (grandparents, parents, teachers, etc.). What has anchored you? What makes you feel secure, supported and protected? Who "sees" you?

- On the trunk, draw your:
  - skills
  - educational experience/background—for you and your family of origin
  - socioeconomic class—you and family of origin. Any changes?
  - occupation
  - age, gender, marital status—family history. Any divorces/separations/remarriages
  - religion/spirituality—family history and what has accounted for any changes, if any.
- On the branches, draw:
  - parts of your identity you still want to develop
  - what you still want to accomplish/your hopes and dreams
  - your relationship with your own racial/ethnic/cultural group
  - your relationship with the dominant power racial/ethnic/cultural group.
- On the leaves, draw:
  - those who have been significant in a positive way/those who have been important in your life and identity
  - parts of your identity that have garnered you privilege.
- On the heap/pile, draw:
  - parts of your identity that seem fragmented. Parts of your identity that are overwhelmed
  - parts of your identity that have caused you oppression/discrimination
  - parts of your identity that you feel are difficult for you to discuss, particularly with those who don't share this identity with you
  - parts of your identity that are most misunderstood
  - aspects of your identity where you feel powerless.
- On the gates, draw:

- things that need to be kept out—biases, stereotypes, White supremacy, racism, unconscious bias, racial microaggressions, intolerance, and so on.

- On the path, draw:

  - ways towards healing

  - what work you are willing to do to heal or contribute to the healing process within yourself, with other groups and communities, and globally

  - what makes you anti-racist, and how you show up as an ally for marginalized/minoritized groups

  - what work you are doing to become a culturally responsive art therapist.

Does this tree represent your cultural identity and pathway to racial healing, inclusive of your family heritage?

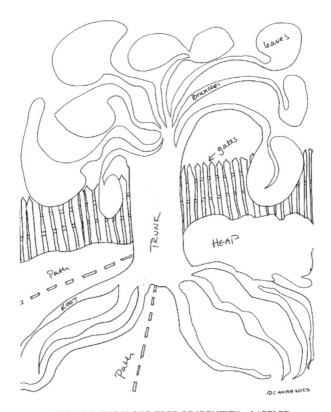

FIGURE 7.1: THE IROKO TREE OF IDENTITY—LABELED

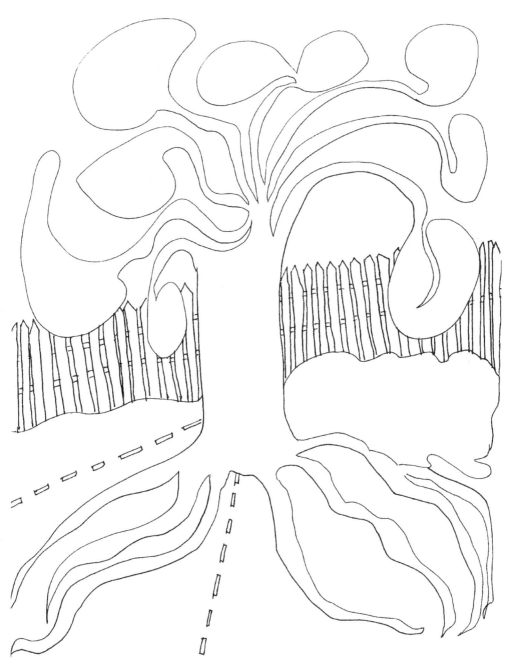

FIGURE 7.2: THE IROKO TREE OF IDENTITY—ACTIVITY

My Iroko Tree of Identity and Pathway Towards Healing—exercise explained

A brief history and origins of the tree of life

The tree has for centuries been used as a visual metaphor to represent your life. For instance, the tree of life has been an underlying archetype in religion, politics and mythology in many cultures and traditions (Giovino, 2007). The concept of the Tree of Life may have originated in Central Asia and was then adopted by several other cultures and became a widely used metaphor (Knutsen, 2011). As a very young child, the Iroko tree was always a symbol of life, strength and stability for me, believed to also have healing qualities. This was a tradition passed down to me and my siblings from our Nigerian grandparents through their stories, folktales, and the books we read. Here we are also using the tree to represent different parts of identity: racial identity, the growth in racial, ethnic and cultural (REC) identity, and most importantly ways to work towards racial healing, represented by the path.

I have seen examples of other tree of life exercises, notably the Tree of Life tool developed by Ncube (2006) in Zimbabwe in her Regional Psychosocial Support Initiative (REPSSI) work to support vulnerable children in Southern Africa through their experiences with grief and loss, and to hear and share stories of hope and strength. Ncube joined with David Denborough (Dulwich Center Foundation) to add a narrative therapy approach to the work she was already doing in Africa (Lock, 2016). Lock (2016) posits that the Tree of Life "draws on the metaphor of a tree, taken from Zimbabwean folklore and collective narrative practice to support groups and communities to overcome difficult life experiences" (p.2). Denborough (2012) stated, "The Tree of Life is a collective narrative tool that aims to promote a feeling of identity and connectedness and allows an opportunity for people to re-author their stories" (p.2). The Tree of Life exercise I have in this chapter is similar in that it explores people's life experiences but it significantly differs in its focus on individuals exploring themselves as racial beings and from a perspective of racial healing. Individuals working on My Iroko Tree of Identity and Pathway Towards Healing exercise can simultaneously work on their REC history and identity, process difficult racial experiences or experiences of privilege, as well as explore pathways towards racial healing.

Ncube (2006) needs more recognition for the development of the Tree of Life tool, and I salute, recognize and appreciate the work she has done, paving the way for my work with racial identity and racial healing in My Iroko Tree of Identity and Pathway Towards Healing exercise.

By doing this exercise, you start to get a sense of your REC history, exploring who you are as a racial cultural being, who you are within those aspects of your racial ethnic and cultural history that has shaped your life—and, most importantly, what you are going to do to facilitate racial/ cultural healing in your own life. For professional art therapists and mental health professionals and for art therapists-in-training, how does this exercise lead you to become a more culturally responsive art therapist?

Section I: Exploring internalized racism
Racial socialization: Explore how you learned about racism

Racism has been and continues to be ingrained in all aspects of American life, including its laws and traditions (Carter, 2007). How does racism get internalized by people? Singh (2019) stated that "internalization of racism is a key mechanism of how this system of oppression works" (p.33). In sociology, socialization is defined as the process of internalizing the norms and ideologies of society (Clausen, 1968). Macionis (2013) defines socialization as "the means by which social and cultural continuity are attained" (p.126). In essence, socialization is how one learns to function in the world. In her model, Bobbie Harro (1996) identifies five stages of socialization.

Cycle of socialization (Harro, 1996)—five stages (discovering your racial socialization)

1. *Stage 1: The beginning:* Societal norms are already set when you are born and there are clear messages that being White is superior and being a Black and person of Color is inferior (Singh, 2019).

2. *Stage 2: First socialization:* Parents, families, loved ones, teachers and others teach you racial scripts. Whether consciously or unconsciously, the individual learns rules of how to be in the world, and ways to be a racial being within a White privileged world (Singh, 2019).

3. *Stage 3: Institutional and cultural socialization:* The institutions you attend, such as schools, reinforce White privilege in your first racial socializations (Singh, 2019).

4. *Stage 4: Enforcements:* Within your network and groups, you experience the rewards and punishments of the system of racism (Singh, 2019).

5. *Stage 5: Results:* You believe stereotypes you encounter about other racial groups, and you shape your behavior to match what you feel is expected of your racial group. In this stage, Black people and people of Color endure the poor treatment they receive because of their racial identity (Singh, 2019).

REFLECTION, ARTWORK AND DISCUSSION

1. What did you learn about racism from your family? Was it positive or negative? Create a piece of artwork that expresses how you feel now about that experience.

2. What did you learn about racism from different spaces in your life, including your school, friends' homes and other spaces? Think about those experiences and feelings about what you learned or didn't and create a piece of artwork about this.

3. What did you learn from your parents, family, loved ones and teachers about racism?

4. Reflect on your life experience. What clear messages did you get that being White was superior and being Black and a person of Color was inferior?

5. Reflect on who taught you about how to be in a world where White privilege was dominant.

6. What do you see are the stereotypes of Black people and other culturally diverse groups?

7. Create a piece of artwork relating to one of the above questions. How do you move towards a space of healing?

Section II: Exploring and understanding racial identity

What is your racial identity? In order for art therapists to really understand how racism works, it's important for you to know your racial identity and your racial identity development. *Racial identity* is a social construct and generally refers to a group that is thought to share a racial heritage/ancestry. For instance, my father is Nigerian-Igbo, and so shares a racial heritage with Nigerians, Igbos and Africans from Sub-Saharan African people. However, your *racial identity development* refers to the processes, statuses, stages or schemas you experience in learning about your racial identity. So, as my father's racial identity unfolded through time and experiences, particularly his experiences during the Nigerian-Biafran civil war—as we see in his excerpts (Chapter 2)—he understands all too well what it means to be an Igbo man in Nigeria and has claimed his racial identity. My father completely feels that his identity as an Igbo man is part of the many important identities he has and cherishes. My racial identity development has been a combination of my Nigerian (Igbo) heritage, my British (Oxfordshire) upbringing, and my experiences living as a Black woman in America. I strongly endorse social justice advocacy for minoritized and marginalized people living in the United States.

You as a racial cultural being

TOM REDD'S STORY CONTINUES: "WE DON'T WANT YOU HERE"

I think I was about eight years old or so when I realized I had a racial identity. At the time, I was oblivious regarding racism. I had come from an all-Black school to a predominantly White all-boys private school, and some White kid used the "N" word while we were all in the classroom. I was the only Black boy in the class. I really didn't know what it meant at the time, and I was so confused. However, I instantly understood that there was something almost salacious and horrible about it. I knew that it wasn't a nice word and it was viler than any curse word because I noticed that everyone else really looked stunned, and some sniggered to hide just how uncomfortable they were. The boy then went on to say, "We don't want you here." From the reaction of the classroom teacher, it was definitely a bad word and the offender was sent immediately to the principal's office. Later, I heard the boy in question got suspended for three days and had to have a bunch of meetings with his parents. I think I had a meeting with the principal, my teacher and parents, and I just remember the principal being extremely apologetic. It was weird. I think the boy's parents eventually transferred him to a different school. After the incident, I started to look at things differently. I can say that I went through a lot of moments within my experiences of confusion, anger and frustration, and I asked my parents a lot of questions about racism. Sadly, I hear this word repeated at least once a day and in many situations, including in everyday conversations and in jokes involving racial and ethnic stereotypes. Many seem to believe it's just a word and doesn't hurt anyone. I tend to disagree.

ARTWORK AND REFLECTION EXERCISE: YOU AS A RACIAL CULTURAL BEING

1. Reflect on the earliest time you noticed you had a racial identity.

2. What thoughts did you have about your racial identity? What thoughts did you have about your race?

3. What feelings come up from here?

4. How does this relate to you as an art therapy student? As a practitioner?

Using art materials, create a piece of art about your feelings and experiences when you first realized you had a racial identity.

Let's now look more in depth at Black American and White racial identity models, including early development of the processes of identity development models.

Racial, ethnic and cultural (REC) identity development models

The racial, ethnic and cultural identity development models highlighted are a conceptual framework to aid art therapists in understanding the REC diverse clients' attitudes and behaviors and are not a comprehensive theory of personality.

Early definitions of the process of *Black identity development models* came from Black social scientists and educators (Cross, 1971; Jackson, 1975; Thomas, 1971). *The Cross model* (Cross, 1971, 1991, 1995), which was developed during the Civil Rights Movement, is the most influential. Cross's five-stage model or psychological *nigrescence* (the process of becoming Black) processes how African Americans move from a White frame of reference to a positive Black frame of reference: *pre-encounter, encounter, immersion-emersion, internalization* and *internalization-commitment*.

1. *Stage 1: Pre-encounter:* Vandiver (2001) characterizes this stage by African Americans unconsciously or consciously devaluing their own Blackness and valuing White values and ways. The need to assimilate and acculturate to White society is high. African Americans at this stage have low self-esteem, self-hate, anti-Black identity and poor mental health.

2. *Stage 2: Encounter:* This often happens when an African American encounters a profound crisis that challenges their anti-Blackness, and then begins to shift their worldview. For example, the killing of Martin Luther King Jr. was a pivotal experience for many African Americans, similarly the killing of Trayvon Martin, and most recently George Floyd, and many others. The person in this stage experiences anger and guilt for being indoctrinated by White society.

3. *Stage 3: Immersion-emersion:* Black pride begins to develop as the person starts to distance themselves from White society and becomes immersed in Black culture. The person in this stage feels an emerging sense of Black pride, and feelings of anger and guilt decrease.

4. *Stage 4: Internalization:* The person is secure in their Black identity, more tolerant of White society, and more bicultural/multicultural (Sue *et al.*, 2019).

5. *Stage 5: Internalization-commitment:* The person has a commitment to social justice, social change and equality. The person in this stage is involved in actionable change. For example, Alicia Garza, Patrisse Cullors and Opal Tometi began the Black Lives Movement in 2013 after the acquittal of George Zimmerman in the shooting death of African American teen Trayvon Martin (Garza, 2020).

QUESTIONS AND DISCUSSIONS (PLEASE REVIEW "BROACHING" IN CHAPTER 1)

1. Would a Black client in Cross's (1995) model encounter stage be receptive to a White art therapist? How would the art therapist broach this client? What art materials can the art therapist utilize to facilitate broaching?

2. As an art therapist, how would you broach a client in Cross's (1995) Internalization stage?

3. As a White art therapist, how can you support your client who is in the Internalization-commitment stage of Cross's (1995) model?

A general model of racial/cultural identity and art therapy implications

Sue and Sue (1990, 1999) proposed the racial/cultural identity development model that cut across cultures, including Latinx Americans, Indigenous/Native Americans and Asian Americans, and emphasized the awareness of cultural oppression as the common unifying force. The five levels of development that highlight the experiences of oppressed people as they work to understand themselves in terms of their own culture, the dominant culture and the oppressive relationship between the two experiences are described as: *conformity, dissonance, resistance and immersion, introspection* and *integrative awareness* (Sue *et al.*, 2019). In addition, there are four corresponding beliefs and attitudes, which are an integral part of identity in understanding how a person views themselves, others of the same REC identity, others of another REC identity, and the dominant group.

The value of this model is also a helpful tool for art therapists to understand and better work with culturally diverse populations. It reminds art therapists that:

- there are differences within all members of a REC group, depending on their racial awareness, beliefs and attitudes

- culturally competent and culturally responsive art therapists must be cognizant and abreast of the sociopolitical factors that influence identity

- It makes art therapists aware of the challenges associated with each phase of REC development of minoritized people and helps guide them to best understand their clients

- other socially marginalized groups, such as women and LGBTQIA+ groups, go through a similar identity process. (Sue *et al.*, 2019)

As art therapists, the thing to remember when understanding the racial/ cultural identity development model is that identity is contextual. It is not a comprehensive theory of personality development. Identity is not static or linear and it is possible for people to skip stages and a person can fluctuate between stages based on external events; for example, turning on the news can make us go from introspection back to resistance, immersion and so on. Human beings are very complex, and the overt behaviors may not indicate the covert thoughts—emotions, cognition and attitudes may be in some other stage. This model lacks an integration of intersectionality and does not neatly fit in to *all groups* and all contexts.

1. *Phase 1: Conformity status:* Like Cross's (1991) pre-encounter stage, those in this stage are victims of White superiority and dominant culture and values. They are oblivious to the existence of racism, normalize Whiteness, and think the dominant culture is good and positive. They are in denial of how racism works. There is a sense of self-deprecating attitudes and beliefs or neutrality regarding their own group of Color. Members of an inferior group will tend to conform to the dominant White group to avoid feeling inferior (Sue *et al.*, 2019). At this phase, individuals have internalized most of the White stereotypes about their own group—for example, Black women being "angry" or "loud," and Asian women being poor drivers, and passive. Individuals in this phase distance themselves from the stereotypes of their group and think of themselves as the exception who has "pulled themselves up by their own bootstraps." Feelings associated with this schema include obliviousness, contentment and comfort.

   Art therapy implications: Clients in this status might be happy to be working with a White art therapist and feel the need to please and seek approval. Clients may have a negative reaction to a Black and non-Black art therapist of Color. Attempts to explore racism or cultural identity issues with clients in this phase may be challenging and would expose the client's self-hatred. Art therapists should focus on task-oriented and problem-solving approaches with clients in this phase and work to re-educate the client regarding adopting positive values of their own culture. Art therapists of Color working with these clients can try to gently move the client closer to self-appreciation and may act as a role model for the client (Sue *et al.*, 2019). White art therapists must be careful not to reinforce the client's stereotypes and denial of racism. Lastly, art therapists, whether White or a person of Color, should *broach* or introduce the subject of race, ethnicity and culture during the counseling process (Day-Vines *et al.*, 2007). Acknowledgment of racial factors during the counseling process enhances counselors' credibility, rapport building and client efficacy (Sue *et al.*, 2019).

2. *Phase 2: Dissonance status:* Individuals in this phase are conflicted between the stereotypes and messaging they are receiving about their own group and their experiences or real-life events that question race and its meaning in America. There is usually a traumatic event that pushes an individual into the dissonance phase. The killing of George Floyd in 2020 was one such traumatic event. The individual begins to have a sense of pride about their own group and questions, "Why should I feel ashamed of who and what I am?" (Sue *et al.*, 2019). They are now aware of the harm the dominant group can do to their own group and become suspicious and mistrustful of the dominant group. Feelings in this schema may include suspicion, confusion and anger.

    Art therapy implications: In this phase, clients may work better with an art therapist with a better understanding of their cultural group. Art therapists should acknowledge racial and identity factors and broach with the client to enhance self-exploration of race, ethnicity and culture during the counseling process (Day-Vines *et al.*, 2007).

3. *Phase 3: Resistance and immersion status:* The individual in this phase is pro their own group and upholds the views and values of their own group and rejects the dominant society values and culture (Sue *et al.*, 2019). The individual is unapologetically proud of their group and has a sense of adventure in discovering their own culture's history and an appreciation for their own group. In this phase, "Black is beautiful" and "Black Lives Matter." There is anger and hostility towards White society and individuals in this phase see them as the "enemy." Phrases

such as "the White devil" are symbolic of the hatred towards White society. Feelings associated with this schema may include anger, feeling unsafe around White people. Feelings also include a sense of belonging and comfort with your own race, and avoidance of White people.

Art therapy implications: Clients in this status prefer art therapists of their own race. However, the fact that a counselor shares the same racial background as the client doesn't always mean that therapy will be effective. Broaching and the art therapist's self-disclosure become very important in this status.

4. *Phase 4: Introspection status:* Individuals move to this stage because of their awareness of the stress and pathology associated with the level of hatred they feel for White society. The need for individual autonomy is present in this phase. There is some conflict and dis-comfort, but there is an attempt to reach out to other groups, and there is less anger towards White society. There are some positive experiences with White people, and individuals start working with White anti-racists to challenge racism. The individual starts looking at their intersectional identities, including gender and social class. Feelings in this schema are complex and include excitement and anxiety.

Art therapy implications: Although the client may prefer an art therapist of their own race, they are open to working with art ther-apists of other races. In this status, art therapists should work with clients on self-exploration approaches to help clients enhance their sense of identity (Sue *et al.*, 2019).

5. *Phase 5: Integrative awareness status:* Individuals in this phase have a high sense of autonomy and an integrated self-concept and positive self-image and esteem that involves pride for their racial identity and culture (Sue *et al.*, 2019). The individual in this phase views racism as a sickness and sees that White people are also victims. There are a range of feelings in this schema that include clarity and motiva-tion, as well as sadness and anxiety. It is possible to have a range of opposing emotions at the same time.

Art therapy implications: Clients in this status prefer art therapists who are knowledgeable about social justice and advocacy issues that effect change. Clients prefer art therapists who understand and accept their worldview. During this stage, clients prefer an art therapist who is an ally and more a co-conspirator than someone who is performative.

QUESTIONS AND ART MAKING

The value of the REC identity framework is that it is a useful hands-on tool to assist art therapists in working with culturally diverse clients (Sue *et al.*, 2019).

1. In Tom Redd's story, at what stage of Cross's Black identity development was he in his racial development model?

2. Look at both the REC development and the racial/cultural identity development models. What stages are similar? What stages are different, and why?

3. As a Black therapist or therapist of Color, what stage are you currently at in your racial identity development based on Cross's (1995) model? Have there been any extenuating factors that have contributed to your current stage?

4. Create a piece of artwork that explains where you currently are in the schema of your racial identity development.

5. What are some of the challenges a Black art therapist might encounter with an Asian client in the Conformity status or Cross's Pre-encounter stage? What therapeutic challenges may arise? How could the art therapist successfully deal with the challenges to be effective with the client?

6. What art therapy interventions would you use if you were a White art therapist, and your client was in the Resistant and immersion status of identity development?

7. As an art therapist, how would you work with a client in the Integrative awareness status?

8. As a Black art therapist or art therapist of Color, where do you think you are in Cross's (1995) model, and Sue's (1990) model? Create a piece of artwork that expresses the stage you're at.

CASE STUDY: "MARTIN," A (SECOND-GENERATION) JAPANESE AMERICAN MAN

Martin is a 23-year-old Japanese American. He reports, "I was born in America, but my parents came here from Japan when my older brother was four years old. I was born two years after they came to America, and I see myself as American. I have worked to fit into the White culture. I really tried to convince myself that I did not experience any discrimination or prejudice; however, I did hear rumblings from my parents about experiencing some discrimination and not being respected by White people. My parents identify as Japanese. They are adamant that they are not Asian, or Chinese, or Korean, but Japanese. They do not have anything against those other cultures but are clear that they are Japanese. I also identify as Japanese. I must admit that I have tried to distance myself from identifying as a person of Color. I am just Japanese, and don't identify as a minority or as a marginalized group."

The other day he was at a restaurant, sitting with his colleague, who is a Black woman, and he noticed that the White waitress who walked past them several times did not come to greet them, offer them water or take their order. Instead, the waitress sat two sets of groups who came later than them and started serving them. Martin stated, "I was so embarrassed, as it was ridiculously clear that they had overlooked us. It wasn't until my Black friend called to the waitress that we were indeed visible and present, that she then gave us water and later asked for our orders." Martin also noticed that the other two White groups that were sitting and served before him and his Black colleague had finished their dinner before their own entre came out.

Martin stated, "That day, for the first time, I felt like a second-class citizen. Since that day, I lost my naivety to the notion that I wouldn't be treated as 'a person of Color.' I had been in a bubble that made me deny, or even think about, the existence of discrimination or racism. I had experienced something with my Black friend that was painful. I am now painfully aware that there is no escaping from my ethnic heritage. I just feel very powerless against this and society's obsession with racist behavior."

Case study analysis and discussion

In this case study, it appears that Martin was going through a period of racial awakening that had significant implications for his racial, ethnic and cultural identity. Martin did not identify himself as part of the marginalized group in America. He identified as Japanese, and not Asian. His previous belief system about assimilating and "fitting" into White American culture was challenged by his feelings of invisibility and feeling like a "second-class" citizen. His illusions of fitting in with White Americans were shattered when he was treated like an ethnic minoritized person, like his Black friend, and he cannot change his ethnic heritage. Additionally, Martin had been taught to believe that White society was superior and held all the power and privilege.

DISCUSSION QUESTIONS

1. As an art therapist, how would you work with Martin? What are the problems in this case?

2. Using the REC identity model, where was Martin at the beginning of the case study and where was he at the end? What took place for a shift to happen?

3. What was Martin's locust of control and responsibility? (Review Chapter 1.)

White racial identity development

JOHN BLUE'S WHITE RACIAL IDENTITY AWAKENING

I grew up in a small town in Western Maryland with a population of approximately 1200 people. The demographic was all White, except for a couple of Black kids whose parents were temporarily stationed at a nearby military installation. These families would typically stay a couple of years and then be deployed somewhere else. The town was founded by a couple of families, of mostly German ancestry, who had a strong dislike for anyone from the outside, including my family, who had moved up from Baltimore shortly before I was born. Although my family was White, the town still considered us outsiders because we were not born there; we were "White trash" but, nonetheless, White.

It was probably somewhere between kindergarten and second grade when I saw how racism worked. There was a Black kid, Tim, who held his own in the initial fights with the White kids, was good at sports, and easy to get along with. I had bonded somewhat with Tim because I had felt like an outsider coming from Baltimore. Tim was grudgingly accepted as much as a Black, athletic kid could be by the local kids, and everyone wanted him on their team because he was great at sports. One day, he ended up out-playing a White kid named Joe who was used to winning, in a pick-up game. Words were exchanged and pushing happened, typical stuff. Then Joe called Tim the N-word. We all stopped. Tim just looked at him—the word was familiar, adults had used it at home and outside, and it was clear that Joe had power from just that one word. Tim just walked away.

Tim could have beaten Joe up, but it wouldn't have mattered. He was marked as different, more different than me because he was Black. I felt ashamed watching it happen, as it felt like I was kicked in the stomach. This clearly changed everything for me, and for me and Tim's "bond." I may have tried to say or do something, but I was still White, and besides, the incident was over, just like that. The die was cast, and it was clear that Tim would never be accepted, even with his athletic prowess. He endured the rest of the year and then his family moved away.

QUESTIONS, REFLECTIONS AND ART MAKING

1. As a person of your own race, what does it mean to be White? Do White people think of their Whiteness? Why do you think it's hard for White people to talk about what it means to be White?

2. In John Blue's story, he was aware that he was "White trash." What does this mean? Are there levels to Whiteness?

3. In what ways do you think White people have been bruised or "harmed" by racism?

4. Dealing with racism requires self-reflection, non-defensiveness and a personal commitment to anti-racist action. Create a piece of artwork illustrating what you think it means to be White. If you are White, how do you accept your own Whiteness?

Racism has been a consistent and firmly embedded part of American history and culture with significant consequences for many African Americans (Jones, 1997; Sue *et al.*, 2007a). For most African Americans, the Civil Rights Movement did not eradicate racism in America (Cose, 1993), and many continue to experience inequality in various facets of their daily lives (Smith *et al.*, 2007). Individual, institutional and societal racism is ever present and subsequently morphs into White supremacist beliefs, attitudes and behaviors (Sue *et al.*, 2019).

Janet Helms (1995) updated her 1990 white racial identity development model that assumes that racism is a central part of being a White American, and developing a healthy White identity requires abandonment of racism and defining a non-racist White identity (Helms, 2015). Helms proposes six White racial identity statuses: *contact, disintegration, reintegration, pseudo-independent, immersion/emersion* and *autonomy.* Helms's model is the most applied; however, we will be focused on the model proposed by Sue *et al.* (2019) which has used the work by Sue and Sue (1990), and also integrates some of the formulations of other models such as Helms and Hardiman. White art therapists are encouraged to explore how to better work with clients from diverse backgrounds.

The seven phases of White racial identity development

Being a White person in this society means chronic exposure to ethno-centric monoculturalism as manifested in White supremacy (Hays, 2014). It is difficult, if not impossible, for anyone to avoid inheriting the racial biases, prejudices, misinformation, deficit portrayals and stereotypes of their forebears (Cokley, 2006). To believe that one is somehow immune from inheriting such aspects of White supremacy is to be naive or to engage in self-deception. White people denying their racial power and Whiteness is one of the greatest barriers to racial understanding and healing.

Sue and Sue (1990) proposed a seven-step White racial identity development model:

1. *Naivete phase:* This phase is like Hardiman's models. The child has a lack of awareness of biases and there is naivety and neutrality for all races. A child is innocent, but between the ages of three and five they begin to associate positive rewards with their group and negative ones with other groups. This was illustrated by the doll test conducted by psychologist Kenneth and Mamie Clark in the 1940s, who asked participants aged three to seven to identify the race of the dolls and pick the one they preferred. The majority of the participants picked the White doll and ascribed positive characteristics to it.

2. *Conformity phase:* People in this phase feel that "people are people," "we are all the same under the skin" and a person's differences are not important. There is minimal awareness of self as a racial being. There are contradictory and compartmentalized beliefs—the person can deny they are racist but still believe that minoritized people are inferior. Therapists in this phase state their color-blindness and feel that the problem is with the marginalized population. Art therapists in this phase are less likely to broach with their marginalized clients.

   Clients in this phase may find broaching off-putting and may present obstacles and resistance to multicultural therapy. Clients may sabotage the therapeutic process by obstructing any positive change. They may start being chronically late for the session or not showing up for the sessions, as a sign of anger towards the art therapist. They may change topics during the session to avoid processing unpleasant and painful feelings relating to their racial identity or racism. They may also avoid taking any responsibility or acknowledging or confronting unpleasant insights regarding race. It is important to note that some of these client resistances can be likened to how students can act or behave during multicultural training.

3. *Dissonance phase:* The individual is forced to acknowledge their own prejudges and biases, particularly when major events occur, such as racist acts. However, a person may hear or see a racist act and not say anything about it in this phase (Sue *et al.*, 2019). There is inconsistency in this phase, which sometimes produces feelings of guilt, anger, shame and sadness—as they realize that they play a part in the existence of racism. White people feel that they are powerless at this stage to do anything. White art therapists in this phase are likely to avoid any significant racial issues, and are also less likely to broach the subject of race, ethnicity or culture to their clients—they prefer to redirect their clients to discuss more generic and *etic* topics. Therapists may broach with their clients only minimally in this phase (Day-Vines *et al.*, 2007). Clients in this phase will be less receptive to process any racial, ethnic or cultural issues.

4. *Resistance and immersion phase:* The individual begins to be aware of what racism is all about. Racial self-hatred may be likely as the individual questions and challenges their own racism, that of others, and society. They recognize societal and institutional oppression and experience anger at others and at institutions, and guilt regarding society's role in racism. Clients in this phase require guidance from their art therapists to process their feelings of guilt for societal and institutional racism and their anger towards White supremacy, as well as their feeling of helplessness to make a difference. Therapists may broach mechanically because they lack the "verbal dexterity to talk explicitly about the client's REC concerns" (Day-Vines *et al.*, 2007, p.108).

5. *Introspective phase:* The individual vacillates between accepting his Whiteness and rejecting White society. However, they no longer deny that they are part of the oppressive systems and that they benefit from White privilege (Sue *et al.*, 2019). There are feelings of isolation, loss, confusion and disconnectedness. The individual actively engages in cultural experience with diverse groups. Clients in this phase need to process their vacillating and conflicting feelings about their Whiteness and the power they have. Art therapists at this stage are beginning to broach with clients regarding issues of race, ethnicity and culture.

6. *Integrative awareness phase:* The individual forms a *non-racist* White identity. They are comfortable with members of many diverse groups. Clients in this stage work to be allies for marginalized groups. In this

phase, allyship may look more performative than actionable; therapists tend to broach effectively, "by helping clients make connections
between their presenting problems and REC issues" (Day-Vines *et
al.*, 2007, p.108).

7. *Commitment to anti-racist action phase:* The individual is aware of
their own White privilege, accepts it, and starts to work to define it
in an *anti-racist* manner. This phase is characterized by social action.
Developing a non-racist and anti-racist White identity/reduction of
prejudice for art therapists requires the therapist to be non-racist
and delve deeper into being anti-racist. Clients in this phase will do
well with art therapists also in this phase of anti-racism. Therapists
are much more comfortable broaching REC issues with their clients.
Therapists work to maintain "a social justice focus that addresses
barriers that impede client progress and well-being" (Day-Vines *et al.*,
2007, p.108). Art therapists must support and empower their clients
to be allies for marginalized groups to effect change through social
and political action.

DISCUSSION QUESTIONS AND ART MAKING

It is important to remember that the higher the phase of White identity
development the individual is in, the greater the reported multicultural counseling competence. However, those in the lower phase of White identity
development are more likely to exhibit increased levels of racism. It is also
important to note that individuals are not neatly in one stage and that moving
from stage to stage is not linear and may illicit some grief for the individual.

1. As a White art therapist, where do you think you are in your racial
identity development?

2. As an art therapist, how would you work with a client in the Conformity phase?

3. Your White client comes into your office with tears in her eyes, upset,
and is finding it hard to speak after she heard the news about yet
another police shooting of an unarmed Black person. When she finally
speaks, she says, "This is horrible. Enough is enough. I want to do
something about this. I know I have power and privilege with my
Whiteness. How can I use this to take action and effect change?"
What phase of White identity development is your client at, and as
an art therapist, what can you do to assist this client?

Section III: Critical race theory and art therapy considerations

Daily racial microaggressions experienced by Black people and people of Color are the result of the racist ideology of White supremacy. Its effects can be best understood by utilizing the paradigm of critical race theory (CRT), which posits that racism permeates all aspects of societal laws and institutions, and oppression based on race cannot be separated from the ethos of White supremacy. Bell (1995, 2008) developed CRT as a race-based critique to address covert and subtle forms of racism within the legal system. However, Richard Delgado, Kimberlé Crenshaw and Derrick Bell are the founders of modern CRT. It is important to note that CRT has now become a symbol of divisiveness and "negative" teaching, which has prompted some elected officials in various parts of the United States to propose policy aimed at reducing or eliminating its instruction at all levels of education (Eyerman, 2023). Further, in January 2023, Florida governor and presidential candidate Ron DeSantis called CRT "false history," while he suggested that its teaching was used to "denigrate the founding fathers, denigrate the American Revolution" (Nelson, 2023). The overarching goal of CRT is not anti-Whiteness, but rather to address racism, White supremacy and dominant societal practices, and call attention to the voices of marginalized racial and ethnic groups that are often silenced (Haskins & Singh, 2015). It is called CRITICAL because it asks us to critically look at systems in order to best understand the origins of racial inequality and dismantle inequities at the root cause.

The five core tenets of CRT are introduced here to provide an important context for discussion relative to art therapy interventions and considerations for clinical practice.

1. *The permanence and intersectionality of race and racism* (Haskins & Singh, 2015). Racism is real and occurs daily and is woven into the fabric of America. It is ingrained legally, culturally and psychologically and intersects with sex, class, national origin and sexual orientation (Bell, 1994; Crenshaw, 1991; Solorzano, 1997). Institutional racism is defined as privileged access to information that results in the loss of power and voice (Bell, 1994). Art therapists must move away from the naive notions that racial incidents only occur outside art therapy settings and come to understand that race and racism are endemic in this field. In addition, art therapists must understand that the therapeutic relationship is a microcosm of society and, thus, they must broach with their clients in an effort to explore their culture and the complexities of race and ethnicity and their daily experiences of oppression.

2. *Color-blindness* (Haskins & Singh, 2015). This tenet critiques liberalism

and color-blindness and challenges the traditional claims of meritoc-racy (Delgado & Stefancic, 2012). It highlights oppressive systems that accompany institutional and systemic practices that minimize racism and perpetuate segregation. Discrimination is still a factor in many institutional spaces and art therapists must be aware of this and that current laws and institutions uphold the impact of oppression and White privilege (Taylor, Gillborn & Ladson-Billings, 2009).

3. *Counter storytelling/unique voices of Color* (Haskins & Singh, 2015). African Americans, Latinx, Native Americans, Indigenous people, Native Alaskans and Asian Americans have unique voices and need to be heard. CRT highlights the importance of marginalized individuals to have their voices heard and speak out. It allows individuals to challenge claims of meritocracy and color-blindness (Delgado & Ste-fancic, 2012)—and name their own reality through stories provided by marginalized individuals, with an opportunity to preserve them-selves mentally and emotionally. In this book, Chapter 4, Special Study: Results and Findings, illustrates the importance of naming one's own experiences in order to move towards healing. It is vital for art therapists to listen to the voices of their marginalized clients, and work to validate their stories and empower them. Art making can be used effectively to facilitate and validate clients' stories of racism and experiences of oppression.

4. *Interest convergence* (Haskins & Singh, 2015). This encourages indi-viduals to be cautious in examining and interpreting the civil rights victories for individuals from marginalized communities. It is the idea that Whites in powerful positions have benefited from racism, and White-privileged folks have no incentive to eradicate racism (Delgado & Stefancic, 2012). CRT challenges traditional claims of objectivity, meritocracy, race neutrality and color-blindness. An inaction and unwillingness to recognize, discuss and challenge racist behaviors and systemic discrimination that furthers the agenda of dominant White culture must be challenged and does not advance the field of art therapy.

5. *Whiteness as property* (Haskins & Singh, 2015). This last tenet indi-cates that economic, social and educational value is associated with being White (Harris, 1993). Whiteness excludes people of Color and Black Americans with educational rights and denies them access to equitable schooling and non-discriminatory school experiences (Ladson-Billings & Tate, 1995). According to Harris (1995): "Whiteness

as property has carried and produced a heavy legacy. It is a ghost that has haunted the political and legal domains in which claims for justice have been inadequately addressed for far too long... It has warped efforts to remediate racial exploitation. It has blinded society to the systems of domination that work against so many by retaining an unvarying focus on vestiges of systemic racialized privilege which subordinates those perceived as a particularized few—the Others... In protecting the property interest in whiteness, property is assumed to be no more than the right to prohibit infringement on settled expectations, ignoring countervailing equitable claims predicated on a right to inclusions" (p.290). Art therapists must work on more inclusive practices for their African American clients.

Art therapists must embrace the racial, ethical and cultural identities of their clients. They must be proactive in destroying the systemic culture that sustains racist ideas and practices. Art therapists must create and facilitate a climate of inclusion and respect the differences of their clients, developing a climate that nurtures and values diverse clients and promotes understanding and healing.

QUESTIONS, DISCUSSIONS AND ART MAKING

1. Do you believe that race is real and permanent? Why or why not? What art therapy interventions would you utilize to validate your clients' racial, ethnic and cultural experiences, and how would you empower them?

2. Of the five tenets of CRT, which one is the most important to you and why?

3. As an art therapist, how would you utilize art making in conjunction with the Counter storytelling CRT tenet with Native American/Indigenous/Native Alaskan clients? What art techniques would you use?

Section IV: Clinical considerations and recommendations for art therapists developing cultural responsiveness when practicing with clients

Multicultural and Social Justice Counseling Competencies (MSJCC) provide a more detailed theoretical and culturally contextual framework and recommend interventions at both individual and systemic levels (Ratts *et al.*, 2016). Art therapy standards have also included guidelines to providers for the competent practice of client advocacy. Multicultural counseling and therapy (MCT) means understanding the worldviews and lived experiences of diverse groups in our society. Cultural competency requires an understanding of the history of discrimination and oppression experienced by minoritized groups in our society. Art therapists must acknowledge the reality of racism, homophobia and sexism. Ignoring this reality because of the discomfort it brings prevents any movement towards change.

To become culturally responsive practitioners, art therapists must:

- critically reflect on their own racial, ethnic and cultural backgrounds, and understand where they are in their own REC identity and places of privilege

- confront systems of oppression and challenge each other by using a trauma-informed, anti-Black-racist, social justice approach

- pay attention to their own biases and beliefs and how these affect the therapeutic process, and be aware of their clients' racial, ethnic and cultural developmental phase or status

- not allow defensiveness to negate their clients' voices and experiences, but listen to their clients and their narratives of oppression

- remember that although they might feel that they are not racist, no individual or group is immune to the inherent biases of U.S. society

- listen to the client, and do not feel as if they are the one being unfairly accused

- if the client is of a different racial, ethnic culture from them, broach the subject of race at the beginning of the session, and revisit it throughout the session

- be aware of their own racial, ethnic and cultural development, and where their belief systems and worldviews have oppressed others, look to ways to empower their clients

- broach racial, ethical and cultural issues with their clients during the therapeutic sessions. This means open dialogue to discuss and work through some of your differing values and beliefs. Art therapists must never be silent or dismissive about their clients' pain and oppression

- understand that they may still be reaping the benefits of past oppressive practices, and be aware of past and current legislations that affect their marginalized clients

- encourage their clients to work on their own healing and be empowered to create a world they want.

REFLECTION, ARTWORK AND DISCUSSION QUESTIONS

1. What emotions have you been experiencing thus far?

2. Are those emotions obstructing you from understanding the text?

3. What does it mean to you personally and as an art therapist to be culturally responsive and competent?

4. What does your broaching style look like?

5. What changes are you willing to make?

Summary

This chapter cast a new light on the notion of knowing YOU as a racial being and your racial identity development journey. Racism is an integral part of our life in the United States, and so White people inherit all the stereotypes and racist attitudes and behaviors and benefit from a White supremacist society. Art therapists should be aware of where they are in their racial identity development as well as their clients' status. It is important for everyone to explore their racial identity development. In all counseling dynamics it is vital for broaching to occur. Becoming a culturally competent art therapist requires action and change.

Chapter 8

Healing and the Way Forward

If you assume that there is no hope, you guarantee that there will be no hope. If you assume that there is an instinct for freedom, that there are opportunities to change things, then there is a possibility that you can contribute to make a better world.

—NOAM CHOMSKY[1]

As art therapists, how do we address racial trauma and anti-Black racism in treatment options and theory? Healing requires moving beyond mere coping to address the root of the problem and foster thriving (French *et al.*, 2020). To heal, we must know what wounds to heal, ways to be a true ally and co-conspirator to those who have been marginalized, and ways to heal from within.

According to Singh (2019), healing from racism requires:

- recognizing the wounds that racism has caused, and the cost of racism

- unlearning the stereotypes of racial messages that have been internalized about our own race and other races. An ongoing commitment to *education* that involves actively seeking out information and deepening our understanding of racism. Reading books, watching movies, having conversations with someone of another race, culture or ethnicity. And, taking *action* that actively resists racism and oppression

- action, practiced throughout our lifetime

- passing on that healing, and giving others in our life the opportunity to heal as well.

---

1   https://chomsky.info/199702__

Section I: What wounds need healing?

We have discussed racism and its cost throughout this book. Art thera-pists must recognize the lived experiences of Black people and that many marginalized group members experience daily oppression, and their stories are filled with minimization, invisibility, discrimination, trauma and pain. Their realities of racism are generally ignored by many in positions of power and by well-intentioned White people, due to the discomfort that challenging those realities may cause them. In Chapter 4, we heard the stories from Randolph, Jackson, Dwayne, Lewis, Phillip and James of their daily experiences of covert and overt racial microaggressions, which served to undermine their humanity through racial hostility, questioning of their competence, ascription of intelligence and assumption of inferiority. We heard the specific examples of what wounds need to be healed. We also heard from Tom Redd in Chapters 2 and 7, and Irene Hendricks in Chapter 1. These daily racist acts and racial microaggressions are often invisible to well-intentioned White Americans.

Art therapists must recognize the assumption of criminality experienced by African Americans, and Black men especially. The following narrative provided by Jackson, a Black male anesthesiologist, describes day-to-day experiences with microaggressions that serve to devalue his humanity through an assumption of criminality.

A co-worker of mine, a Black anesthesiologist, told me a story about a female nurse who I also know and like, a White lady, very cool seeming, always friendly and doesn't give you any impression in the workplace that she has any animosity or apprehensiveness about Blacks or anyone else. He had been working with her for years. He was talking about how it was Halloween and they were all dressed up; they were joking and complimenting one another on the little costumes they were wearing at work, and had just a wonderful time during the day. Then in the evening, it was dark and they were in the parking garage and they walked into each other. He spoke to her and there was sheer terror in her face—she did not recognize who he was, a man that she had worked with on a regular basis for years and years and years, whom she had worked with all that day, laughing and joking together, was petrified of him in that parking garage, startled, jumped, and he had to say, "It's me, it's me." But that didn't change anything, and that really affected him, and he said thank God she did not have a weapon or pistol that she was licensed to carry or something because the story the next day would have been how this doctor must have gone crazy and tried to rape his co-worker in the parking lot. That would have been the story. So that was another startling reminder that even in that professional environment, when you are removed from that environment, you are still very much a Black man, and that carries with it whatever it carries with it for that particular individual. (Jackson)

The excerpt highlights the experiences of a Black American anesthesiologist who was harmed by racial microaggressions that labeled him as "untrustworthy," "dangerous," "unqualified" and "unintelligent." One of the ways to dismantle racism is to illuminate its detrimental consequences, and to encourage honest and open dialogue about race.

DISCUSSION STATEMENTS AND QUESTIONS

- Art therapists most respond to marginalized and minoritized people with lived experiences of racial trauma, microaggressions and inequality.

- Art therapists must be clear in their own biases and not impose those biases on their clients within the therapeutic relationship.

- Art therapists must avoid the misuse of power and the language pathology in therapeutic approaches. (Bullimore, 2011)

1. As an art therapist, how can you provide *emotional validation and affirmation* for clients experiencing racism in the same way that Jackson did? How do you validate the stories of Black men who have these experiences, and make them feel "seen?"

2. As an art therapist, how would you guide them and generate the healing process through art therapy? What art techniques can you use to facilitate this healing?

Section II: True racial allyship—being a co-conspirator or accomplice

Allies are individuals or people in groups of social power and dominance that include Whites, males and heterosexuals, who actively work to disarm or eradicate oppression and discrimination through action and support of non-dominant groups. Allies work to end inequality and social disparities for marginalized groups such as Black people and LGBTQIA+ individuals. Sue *et al.* (2019) state that "allyship development involves internal and painful self-reckoning, and a commitment to external action" (p.132). As indicated by Sue and Sue (1990) in their seven-step White racial identity development model, developing a commitment to anti-racist action, where White allies are motivated by a desire to end inequality and racism, is a major step towards social justice. True allies do not work solely motivated by their White guilt and so do not require accolades and recognition for the anti-racist work that they do. True racial allyship requires active support of others who have and are experiencing discrimination, racial and social injustice and inequality. In essence, if you have privilege of any kind, you use it to dismantle and challenge prejudice and oppression. Being a White racial ally requires that you not only challenge and condemn racism, but take action and speak out against it with your White relatives, friends and colleagues, and you advocate for Black people and other diverse groups. For example, some White Americans stood up against racism and aligned themselves to the Civil Rights Movement in the 1960s, and the Black Lives Matter movement (Parker, Horowitz & Anderson, 2020). If you are a Black American or part of a culturally diverse group, you can be an ally for other culturally diverse people by speaking out against policies that harm them. For instance, in my work as an art therapist, counselor, supervisor and educator, I advocate for other culturally diverse populations by speaking out against racism. I live in Maryland, and I've done a lot of racial justice work here, which has included being the founding member and first president, in 2018, of the social justice division for a counseling organization in Maryland. In the words of the late John Lewis, I have made "some good trouble."

Going further in your racial allyship is becoming a *co-conspirator* or *accomplice*, which means making more of a commitment to take action and collaborate with those with White privilege and power to challenge oppressive acts, change racist policies and work towards systemic change. It is being anti-racist and actively confronting and dismantling the sociopolitical climate that is rooted in racist ideas. We've had several protests that vocally condemn violent acts of police brutality on Black Americans. The Black Lives Matter movement was built to protest against police brutality. Further, we've had protests that brought down Confederate flags and statues that honored Confederate leaders and colonizers. White co-conspirators must work in solidarity with Black people to "conduct culturally responsive professional practice, research, training and institutional transformation" (Spanierman & Smith, 2017, p.607). They must be allies and act towards social change. Albert Einstein stated, "The world is a dangerous place to live, not because of the people who are evil, but because of the people who don't do anything about it."

Dr. Martin Luther King Jr. stated, "We will have to repent in this generation not merely for the hateful words and actions of the bad people but for the appalling silence of the good people."

ART EXERCISE AND DISCUSSION

Art materials: Paper, colored pencils, markers, magazines, glue, scissors, paints, yarn.

Purpose: To reflect on ways to become a racial ally.

- Reflect on a time when you have been a racial ally. What were the circumstances? What did you do? Do you think you could have done more?

- Reflect on the quotes by Albert Einstein and Dr. Martin Luther King Jr. What are your interpretations of them? How does this affect the way you advocate for your clients?

- Do you envision your allyship moving into co-conspirator or accomplice status? What do you think this might look like?

- Create an art piece that illustrates what true allyship or being a co-conspirator looks like.

Section III: Who is a culturally competent art therapist? What competencies are important for culturally responsive practice?

Culturally responsive art therapy encompasses culturally specific perspectives in mental health. Art therapists must work to see beyond Western therapeutic concepts, and not assume that mental disorders appear in all cultures and society; they should operate in a way that challenges these assumptions. This essentially means that any contact between an art therapist and client could be regarded as cross-cultural in nature, whether it involves working with clients who are marginalized on the basis of their race, ethnicity, culture, gender and other identities (Sue *et al.*, 2019). Healing strategies—as a Black person, a person of Color or a White person—have been discussed in previous chapters. Here is a reminder of what art therapists need to do:

- Demonstrate cultural awareness, and consider and take into account the cultural context and manifestations of disorders to limit inaccurate diagnosis and inappropriate treatment (Sue *et al.*, 2019) (Chapters 1, 5).

- Talk honestly and meaningfully about racism and social injustices. They must not be color-blind, and should use *broaching* to aid clients with their presenting problems (Day-Vines *et al.*, 2007). Their strengths rest in their diversity and ability to make the invisible visible (Chapters 1, 2).

- Demonstrate a willingness to work with clients of diverse background and have a way of being that accommodates cultural humility. They must acknowledge and validate clients' experiences of racism. Cultural humility when working with marginalized clients is correlated to successful therapeutic engagement and better treatment prognosis (Chapters 2, 7).

- Explore their internalized racism (Chapter 7).

- Examine their racial identity development and connect with people who are also awakening to their identities as racial beings (Chapter 7).

- Understand the history of racism, and how microaggressions can manifest in the therapeutic relationship (Chapters 2, 3, 4).

- Understand what it means to be an agent of social justice, and find ways to advocate for their marginalized and culturally diverse clients (Chapter 5).

- Understand what true allyship is and what being a co-conspirator looks like (Chapter 8).

- Operate from a culturally responsive and anti-racist lens, in order to provide clients with treatment that explores their experiences, encourages healing and enhances the quality of their lives (Chapter 7).

- Assist clients in building a path towards empowerment, action and healing (Chapters 1, 2, 5, 6, 7).

DISCUSSION QUESTIONS

1. Reflect on a time when you were not culturally competent. After reading this book, what could you have done differently?

2. Knowing these healing strategies, do you feel more culturally responsive as an art therapist? Which areas of healing require more work for you?

Section IV: Ways to increase cultural awareness and unlearn anti-Black racism

- Be involved with interactions with people from varying cultural backgrounds, becoming immersed in or learning more about communities that you know very little about.

- Read books that enhance awareness and knowledge on different cultural backgrounds and similarities.

- Attend seminars and training programs that promote cultural diversity.

- Attend museums, plays, movies and other events that highlight racial and cultural issues.

- Encourage workplace/school diversity and inclusion efforts.

- Travel to destinations that provide exposure to cultural diversity.

- Maintain a weekly art journal for continued self-reflection and self-care.

- For educators/lecturers/professors, infuse multicultural issues in all courses.

- For those teaching the diversity/REC courses, focus teaching on books and articles by diverse authors, discuss students' varying cognitive, emotional and behavioral responses to the teaching, and lean instructions towards racial healing.

Suggested resources to enhance cultural awareness

In some areas of the United States, books are being banned and we are now being forced to not learn or talk about Black history, about slavery and its consequences which continue today. Black history is part of American history and we must never forget.

BOOKS

- *The Wretched of the Earth* by Frantz Fanon (1961)

- *The Rage of a Privileged Class* by Ellis Cose (1993)

- *Our Kind of People: Inside America's Black Upper Class* by Lawrence Otis Graham (1999)

- *Caste* by Isabel Wilkerson (2020)

- *Race Talk and the Conspiracy of Silence* by Derald Wing Sue (2015)

- *Sister Outsider: Essays and Speeches* by Audre Lorde (2015)

- *Thick* by Tressie McMillan Cottom (2019)

- *All That She Carried* by Tiya Miles (2021)

- *In My Grandmother's House* by Yolanda Pierce (2021)

- *The Conversation: How Seeking and Speaking the Truth about Racism Can Radically Transform Individuals and Organizations* by Robert Livingston (2021)

- *Let Us Descend* by Jesmyn Ward (2023)

- *Go Back to Where You Came From: And Other Helpful Recommendations on How to Become American* by Wajahat Ali (2022)

- *There was a Country* by Chinua Achebe (2012)

- *Forgotten War* by Henry Reynolds (2013)

- *Dark Emu. Black Seeds: Agriculture or Accident?* by Bruce Pascoe (2014)

- *That Deadman Dance* by Kim Scott (2012)

- *Invisible Asians* by Kim Park Nelson (2016)

- *Girl in Translation* by Jean Kwok (2010)

- *The Covenant of Water* by Abraham Verghese (2023)

- *All Boys Aren't Blue* by George M. Johnson (2020)

- *Lawn Boy* by Jonathan Evison (2018)

MOVIES ABOUT AFRICAN AMERICAN HISTORY, STORIES AND AMERICA'S COMPLICATED HISTORY WITH RACE

- *Rustin* (2023)

- *Origin* (2023)

- *American Fiction* (2023)

- *When They See Us* (miniseries, 2019)

- *Hidden Figures* (2016)

- *12 Years a Slave* (2013)

- *Crash* (2004)

- *American History X* (1998)

- *A Time to Kill* (1996)

- *Black Like Me* (1964)

ARTISTS AND THEIR WORKS

- Adrian Piper—called out racial oppression in her work.

- Favianna Rodriguez—highlighted the immigrant justice movement.

- Kerry James Marshall—painted what it means to be Black in America.

REFLECTION AND DISCUSSION

1. Can you add to the list of suggested resources to enhance your cultural awareness?

2. What current art exhibitions, plays and movies will you attend or have you attended? What are their messages regarding racial and cultural issues?

3. Reflect on some ways you can better educate yourself about racism.

4. What racial communities are you unfamiliar with? How do you intend to become familiar with them?

Section V: Healing artwork

Reflect on your healing journey throughout this book. Create a piece of artwork that reflects where you were in the beginning, middle and now. What areas are positive and solid? Which areas are weak? For the solid areas, what do you need to do to maintain them? For the weak areas, what do you need to do to strengthen them?

Who in your life do you think you need to share this healing journey with? You can name as many as you want.

Section VI: The way forward for art therapists, and the field

Art therapists and the field of art therapy should make a lifelong commitment to address individual, institutional, societal injustices and be aware of their own biases that may unintentionally discriminate against others/ their clients. Here are a few suggestions for the path forward for art therapy:

- Provide ongoing *individual* training on multicultural implications for the practice and teaching of art therapy.

- Engage in *supervision* that speaks to REC topics for culturally diverse individuals and how better to serve them and their needs.

- Undertake more research on racial trauma, microaggressions and inequality in the art therapeutic context. For example:

    - Continued use of art-based research and qualitative methods for marginalized and culturally diverse clients.

    - More exploration of how Black art therapists respond to racial trauma, racial microaggressions, and the effects on their mental health.

    - Culturally responsive supervision on the efficacy of art therapy practice with culturally diverse clients.

- At graduate level study, infuse REC topics and issues in courses, and advocate for diversity and social justice courses to be taught in schools.

RACIAL HEALING: FEEDBACK FROM STUDENTS

As a professor, tasked to teach the master's degree level Diversity and Social Justice in Counseling course, I asked some of my students to express their experiences taking the course and their journey towards racial healing.

Personal perspective from Black male, Terry Sidney, counseling student-in-training, January 18, 2024

Walking into the classroom of the Diversity and Social Justice in Counseling course was like entering my own private room filled with wrapped boxes of hidden truth. Notice, I didn't say unknown truth, but truth that had been suppressed, ignored or simply unacknowledged. Opening those boxes ignited a confluence of emotions related to race, ethnicity and culture. Diversity and social justice were often a deferred dream historically in my family. Older generations feared White privilege, and younger generations challenged it fiercely. I exist somewhere right in the middle of both.

I often think that what it truly means to be Black has been lost by constantly trying to assimilate into a Eurocentric society, to the point our Blackness has been so watered down that much of our heritage doesn't even exist anymore.

However, as I opened the many different boxes filled with concepts and contexts presented to me in this class, I tried to honestly respond in conversations, fully aware that many of my classmates' experiences were different from mine. I likely would have more in common with their parents. Mostly because I believe that the world we live in today gives the impression of unification, diversity and equal opportunity, but on peeling back the layers, we find ourselves dealing with the same old issues of White supremacy, only now the assaults are more subtle.

In summary, I feel that I gained much insight into my own perspectives on the racial climate that exists in the world today. The benefit of that is an increased sensitivity and empathy for other REC identities and their lived experiences, so, as future counselors, we are able to have multicultural sensitivity with our clients and increase positive outcomes.

This Diversity and Social Justice class has enlightened me to the reality that my biases do matter; even when I ignore them, I still need to be intentional about not letting them enter the counseling therapeutic relationship.

Personal perspective from White male, David Casson, counseling student-in-training, January 15, 2024

FIGURE 8.1: "RACIAL HEALING" BY DAVID CASSON (COLLAGE ON PAPER, 10" X 8")

My experiences with the Social Justice and Diversity in Counseling course were ones I hope to truly never forget. From the very beginning, I remember feeling more overwhelmed than I initially believed I would. Being one of two White people in the class initially gave me some anxiety about discussing powerful and emotional topics regarding racism, discrimination, prejudice and White privilege, in particular. Most of all, I was afraid to speak at times in the beginning because I feared the idea of accidentally offending anyone by saying the wrong thing or not speaking up about specific topics or ideas. However, after a few sessions, I started to realize the importance and necessity of speaking about these topics. Dr. Anah did a superb job of ensuring that every person's voice mattered and this was valuable for the progression of numerous insightful discussions about literature and personalized experiences related to social justice and diversity. This encouraged me to speak more in class than I typically do as a student and allowed me to challenge and push myself to contribute to class discussions despite my insecurities and anxieties that would arise at times.

I became increasingly more comfortable with the class, made friends with my peers in class, and looked forward to coming back every Tuesday afternoon. I truly learned more than I ever knew about race, social justice, diversity, intersectionality and the forces that perpetuate the many systems that run our societies in our everyday lives. As a White man who is privileged in more ways than one, I found that Dr. Anah's class opened my eyes and showed me how necessary it is to be aware of privilege and how to use it in my anti-racist work—validating the experiences of marginalized clients and learning to empower them through social action. As a counselor-in-training, I felt that this class taught me invaluable counseling skills, crucial information about a multitude of diverse groups and populations, and how those who possess power and privilege must use these concepts to advocate and empower all who are oppressed and limited through our societal foundations built on systemic racism, discrimination, prejudice and oppression of marginalized and minoritized groups and populations. These were my greatest takeaways from this course, and I am eternally grateful for the opportunity to engage in such a rich and insightful class that also focused on the importance of discussing what racism is, understanding, and healing from racism, in order to dismantle it. The education I received from Dr. Anah and my peers was life-changing. Thank you.

Personal perspective from Black female, Kyla P. Hunter, counseling student-in-training, February 6, 2024

FIGURE 8.2: "RACIAL HEALING" BY KYLA P. HUNTER (COLLAGE ON PAPER, 11" X 14")

This collage represents my interpretation of racial healing through the lens of my experience in the Diversity class at Johns Hopkins University.

At the beginning of my time in Dr. Anah's class, I had a limited Black and White view of the world, represented by the clouds at the bottom of the collage. The first steps to racial healing were about embracing who I am and being true to the significance of my story, which I discovered through our My Culture Paper. Through the empirical readings and rich conversations in class, a gift brought to us by the diversity of our class, my climb continued. With each step forward, my thirst for knowledge grew, and I discovered the history of other cultures different from my own. I could feel the mental shift that comes with racial consciousness.

I showed cultural appreciation for identities different from my own as I immersed myself in the stories of others who were different. Collaborating and connecting, we collectively began to understand better the inner workings of racism and its effects as we picked out the patterns in racism. I became devoted to lifting the stories of others and saw the power of change.

I felt transformed as I reached the top of the mountain and the end of our Diversity class. Today, I have a clearer understanding of racism and the way it hurts *all* people. I am at a place where I can see myself authentically appreciating every aspect of who I am and those who came before me. History has a new meaning, and, most importantly, I can see the beauty of cultures and the people tied to them in a new way. As I look forward and stride towards the subsequent phases of racial healing, I hope to encourage others as we become accomplices to radical change, creating an unimaginable but possible future.

The materials used for this project were magazine clippings, personal images, newspaper clippings, tape, iridescent construction paper, 11" x 14" white poster board and gold marker.

Summary

Multiculturalism in the field of mental health has had a renaissance in the past decade given the sociopolitical climate that has disproportionally affected marginalized groups. Like any other helping professionals, art therapists are expected to be aware of these social changes. The art therapy profession must evolve to better serve the needs of Black and other minoritized clients, and enthusiastically embrace art therapy theories that highlight and celebrate non-traditional approaches. I believe that the field of art therapy has made some positive steps for diversity, with the art therapy curriculum, research and art therapists using their voices to facilitate social change. However, more work is needed to improve cultural responsiveness in the field. The field of art therapy needs to continue its efforts regarding inclusion, diversity and equity. Healing from racism is an ongoing process, it is both transformational and affects social change. We must always acknowledge the stain of centuries of inequality and oppression in our country and around the world. But, be guided by healing, ongoing love, care and understanding—not hate—to disarm racism.

Glossary

Acculturation: Changing from your culture to the dominant one. This process typically happens with immigrants moving to a dominant culture and assimilating to that culture.

Advocacy: Counselors who take action to facilitate the removal of external and institutional barriers to clients' well-being.

African American: Refers to Americans having ancestors from Sub-Saharan Africa who were born in the United States. This book sometimes uses Black Americans and Black people interchangeably with African American.

Anti-Blackness: Insists on the dehumanization of Black people.

Anti-racism: Being self-aware and conscious about race and racism, and engaging in action that challenges and dismantles White supremacy and ideology.

Anti-racist: Someone who supports anti-racist policies and works to express those ideas, and participates in actionable change at individual and systemic levels.

Apartheid: South Africa's policy of segregation and discrimination based on race.

Art-based research: The use of any art form at any point in the research process to enhance the results of the inquiry and outcomes of the study.

Art therapy: A mental health profession that utilizes the creative process of art making to improve the well-being of people. Art making is used within a professional therapeutic relationship, by people experiencing trauma, difficulties in life, and those seeking professional development (Malchiodi, 1998). The aim of art therapy is not to produce aesthetically pleasing products to be judged by external standards, but rather to help achieve insight, self-awareness, communicate feelings, reduce stress and resolve conflicts and issues through the creative process involved in the artistic self-expressions (Liebmann, 1990).

Black people: People with ancestors from Sub-Saharan Africa. In this book, this term is used interchangeably with African Americans and Black Americans. In this sense, it includes Black people from Africa, West Indies, Caribbean and South America who have migrated to the United States.

Broaching: Addressing race, gender, class and other sociocultural issues within the therapeutic relationship.

Cisgender: An individual's gender that matches the sex they were assigned when born.

Collage: Visual representations composed on paper, via the process of using fragments of found images from photos, pictures, magazines and other media and gluing them to a flat surface to create a piece of artwork.

Coping mechanisms: For the purpose of this book, these are strategies, either positive or negative, that people use to deal with their experiences of racial microaggression. They are ways in which African Americans assign meaning to a race-related stressful event and determine resources for addressing those stressors.

Cultural humility: A term applied when therapists take a multicultural and open stance on ongoing learning when working with their culturally diverse clients.

Culturally competent: A term applied when therapists have the self-awareness of their own values and bias, and skills and knowledge to work effectively with Black and other culturally diverse clients.

Culturally responsive: A term applied when therapists are responsive to the cultural values, assets and strengths of their clients in empowering ways that facilitate and effect change.

Decolonization: In this book, dismantling institutional and social values that are shaped largely by Eurocentric and patriarchal theory.

Discrimination: The behavioral component of prejudice and social comparisons manifested in negative attitudes towards an individual or a group (Jones, 1997).

Dissonance: Discomfort with difference.

Dreamer: An immigrant brought to the United States at an early age without proper documentation.

Emic: Considering the cultural differences of an individual client, and being culturally specific when treating and diagnosing them.

Empowerment: "Includes counselor actions that tend to focus on the individual or group counseling environment and on assisting clients in recognizing and addressing socio-political barriers to well-being" (Toporek, Lewis & Crethar, 2009, p.262).

Ethnicity: Belonging to a group who share the same descent or cultural background.

Ethnocentric monoculturalism: A therapist's belief in the superiority of their own cultural values and beliefs, and imposing those standards to marginalized groups.

Ethnoracial: The various ways people distinguish themselves based on color and ancestry.

Etic: Treating and diagnosing culturally diverse clients from a Western and EuroAmerican orientation and culturally specific worldview.

European American (EuroAmerican): In this book, used as another term for White.

Immigrants: Individuals who migrate (move) from their country of origin and now reside in the United States.

Informed consent form: Given to clients by the therapist to ensure they understand the process and expectations of therapy, and if they give permission and consent to the treatment.

Intersectionality: The interconnected nature of social categorizations such as race, class and gender as they apply to a given individual or group, regarded as creating overlapping and interdependent systems of discrimination or disadvantage.

Latinx: Gender-inclusive term to refer to Spanish-speaking individuals with ancestry in Mexico, Cuba, Puerto Rico, Dominican Republic and non-Spanish-speaking individuals from South and Central American countries living in the United States.

Locus of control: Refers to what people believe about the degree of control they have over circumstances of their life.

Locus of responsibility: Refers to the degree of blame or responsibility the individual places on themselves or the system.

Microaggressions: Daily brief and denigrating messages and assaults directed towards marginalized groups and communities that are harmful.

Oppression: The systematic subjugation of subordinated groups by privileged groups with social power. The limiting of personal and intellectual freedoms of those in subordinate groups, creating disparities affecting the well-being and development of individuals and members of these groups, leading to feelings of self-deprecation and fear; it is widespread social injustice suffered by the oppressed due to everyday practices of a society (Prilleltensky & Gonick, 1996).

Power: A complex, multi-dimensional, multi-level process embedded within relationships for a single purpose: control (Foucault, 1980). It is a process that contributes to the production and maintenance of privilege.

Privilege: Unearned access to beneficial resources available to some people, but usually at the expense of others (Harvey, 2000). Privilege is the culmination of the interactions between three forms of relational power dynamics to decide: who is taken seriously, who receives attention and who is accountable to whom and for what (Johnson, 2006).

Professional men: Men who have achieved a master's degree or greater and who have earned professional degrees, which include degrees in law, medicine, journalism, counseling, psychology and several other fields.

Race: For the purposes of this book, a socially constructed concept used, historically, to organize groups of people based on skin color in order to create and perpetuate oppression and uphold White privilege.

Racial microaggressions: "Verbal, behavioral and environmental indignities, whether intentional or unintentional, that communicate hostile, derogatory or negative racial slights and insults that potentially have harmful or unpleasant psychological impact on the target person or group" (Sue *et al.*, 2007b, p.273).

Racial trauma: Emotional and physical harm caused by repeated encounters of racism, primarily experienced by Black people.

Racism: Oppression and marginalization of Black people and people of Color based on the socially constructed concept of race in order to sustain White privilege. It is rooted in the ideology composed of beliefs in the racial superiority of Whites through individual behavior and institutional and societal policies and practices that have dire consequences for African Americans and other minoritized people (Jones, 1997). It perpetuates acceptance of negative stereotypes of minoritized groups.

Racist: Someone who supports racist policies and negative stereotypes to oppress minoritized people through their silence, actions or expressed racist ideas and behaviors.

Refugee: An individual forced to flee their home due to war, poverty, persecution or other atrocities.

Social justice: "The idea of a just society, which gives individuals and groups their due. Social justice as a general concept is based on the idea of human rights. Thus, a broad definition of social justice would be the way in which human rights are manifested in the everyday lives of people at every level of society. Whereas equal opportunity and human rights are applicable to everyone, social justice targets the marginalized groups of people in society—it focuses on the disadvantaged" (Holcomb-McCoy, 2007, p.17).

Social justice advocacy: Professional practice, research or scholarship focused on identifying and intervening in social policies and practices that have a negative impact on the mental health of clients who are oppressed and marginalized on the basis of their social status (Steele, 2008). It includes the direct service of clients' personal needs, and increasing their sense of personal power (Toporek *et al.*, 2009).

Social justice counselor advocate: Someone who works with or on behalf of the client, to help mitigate oppressive and discriminatory practices that deny the client equal treatment and access to services (Chang, Hays & Milliken, 2009).

Social justice for mental health professionals: "Scholarship and professional action designed to change societal values, structure, policies, and practices, such that disadvantaged or marginalized groups gain access to these tools of self-determination" (Goodman *et al.*, 2004, p.795).

Structural change: Change to cultural or institutional barriers that impact well-being, and change that ensures laws, policies and practices are just for all (Ratts, 2009).

Subtle racism: Similar to racial microaggressions in that it is covert, indirect and ambiguous racism experienced daily by Black people that causes harm or an assault on their self-identity and well-being.

White privilege: The unearned, first-class status and advantages of White people.

White supremacy: The belief that White people are superior to Black people and other culturally diverse groups.

Worldview: People's attitudes, values, morals and beliefs and racial realities that affect how they think, perceive events, behave and make decisions.

References

Acuff, J. (2018). Confronting racial battle fatigue and comforting my blackness as an educator. *Multicultural Perspectives, 20*(3), 174–181.

Ahmadi, M., Sharifi, A., Dorosti, S., Ghoushichi, S. J. & Ghanbari, N. (2020). Investigation of effective climatology parameters on COVID-19 outbreak in Iran. *Science of the Total Environment*. Retrieved from www.sciencedirect.com/science/article/pii/S0048969720322221.

Alleyne, A. (2004). Black identity and workplace oppression. *Counseling and Psychotherapy Research, 4*(1), 4–8.

American Art Therapy Association. (2013). *Ethical Principles for Art Therapists*. [Brochure]. Alexandria, VA: Author. Retrieved from www.americanarttherapyassociation.org/upload/ethicalprinciples.pdf.

American Art Therapy Association. (2017). Definition of Art Therapy. Retrieved from www.arttherapy.org/upload/2017_DefinitionofProfession.pdf.

American Art Therapy Association. (2023). *Statement denouncing hate, discrimination & violence*. American Art Therapy Association (AATA) Conference, San Diego, CA. (October 25–29, 2023).

American Counseling Association. (2014). *ACA Code of Ethics*. Alexandria, VA: Author.

Anah, C. (2014). *Experiences of Racial Microaggressions and Coping Skills Among African American Professional Men*. Dissertation.

Anah, C. (2016a). Racial microaggressions: Consequences of "assumption of criminality" on African American men. *MCA Quarterly Newsletter, Compass Points, 9*(20), 6–7.

Anah, C. (2016b). Baltimore Uprising/Freddie Gray: An artist's creative journey towards clarity and healing. American Art Therapy Association (AATA) Conference, Baltimore, MD. Digital Poster (Thursday, July 8, 2016).

Anah, C. (2017). The relevance of social justice advocacy today. *PerceptA Therapeutic Blog*. Retrieved from http://perceptatherapeutic.com/?p=1730.

Anah, C. (2018a). Art therapy and social justice intersectionality: Interview with Dr. Chioma Anah and Molly Watkins. *Counselors for Social Justice Newsletter*.

Anah, C. (2018b). Still I rise: Reflections of an artist's journey as social activist. American Art Therapy Association (AATA) Conference, Miami, FL. Paper Session (November 3, 2018).

Anah, C. (2019a). A call to action: Social justice advocacy is fundamental to art therapy and counseling. Making Space: Art and Social Justice Advocacy with Dr. Anah. *Canadian Art Therapy Association online magazine, ENVISAGE, 2*(2), 19–20.

Anah, C. (2019b). Art & social activism. *Canadian Art Therapy Association online magazine, ENVISAGE, 2*(1), 5–7.

Anah, C. (2019c). Who are you really? Exploring the identity and roles of professional counselors as social justice advocates. Paper presented at the New Jersey Counseling Association (NJCA) Conference, Brookdale Community College in Lincroft, NJ.

Anah, C. (2020). The legacy of King: Counselors as advocates for social justice in 2020. *ENVISAGE, 3*(1), 14–15.

Anah, C. (2023). Land Acknowledgement.

Anah, C. & Anah, R. S. (2023–2024). Interview with my father: Biafra before, during, and after. Unpublished manuscript.

Ani, M. (1994). *Yurugu: An African-Centered Critique of European Cultural Thought and Behavior.* Trenton: African World Press.

Ansley, F. L. (1989). Stirring the ashes: Race, class and the future of civil rights scholarship. *Cornell Law Review, 74*(6), 993–1077.

Art Therapy Credential Board. (2016). *Code of Ethics, Conduct, and Disciplinary Procedures.* Retrieved from https://atcb.org/ethics/

Awais, Y. J. & Yali, A. M. (2013). A call for diversity: The need to recruit and retain ethnic minority students in art therapy. *Art Therapy: Journal of the American Art Therapy Association, 30*(3), 130–134.

Banaji, M. R. & Greenwald, A. G. (1995). Implicit gender stereotyping in judgments of fame. *Journal of Personality and Social Psychology, 68*(2), 181–198. https://doi.org/10.1037/0022-3514.68.2.181.

Baumann, A. A., Kuhlberg, J. A. & Zayas, L. H. (2010). Familism, mother-daughter mutuality, and suicide attempts of adolescent Latinas. *Journal of Family Psychology, 24*, 616–624.

BBC World Service Africa. (2023, September 21). Ghana's leader repeats slavery reparations demand. BBC News. Retrieved from www.bbc.co.uk/news/world/africa/live.

Bell, D. (1992). *Faces at the Bottom of the Well: The Permanence of Racism.* New York, NY: Basic Books.

Bell, D. (1994). *Confronting Authority: Reflections of an Ardent Protester.* Boston, MA: Beacon Press.

Bell, D. A. (1995). Who's afraid of critical race theory? *University of Illinois Law Review, 1995*(4), 893–910.

Bell, D. A. (2008). *Race, Racism, and American Law* (6th edition). Boston, MA: Aspen Publishers.

Bell, L. A. (1997). Theoretical Foundations for Social Justice Education. In M. Adams, L. A. Bell & P. Griffin (eds), *Teaching for Diversity and Social Justice: A Sourcebook* (pp.3–15). New York, NY: Routledge.

Bell, M. P., Berry, D., Leopold, J. & Nkomo, S. (2021). Making Black Lives Matter in academia: A Black feminist call for collective action against antiblackness in the academy. *Gender, Work and Organization, 28*(S1), 39–57. https://doi.org/10.1111/gwao.12555.

Bemak, F. & Chung, R. C.-Y. (2007). Training Counselors in Social Justice. In C. C. Lee (ed.), *Counseling for Social Justice* (2nd ed., pp.239–257). Alexandria, VA: American Counseling Association.

Beutler, B. (2017). Trump's chaos is causing lasting damage. *New Republic.* Retrieved from https://newrepublic.com/article/142065/trumps-chaos-causing-lasting-damage.

Bonilla-Silva, E. (2017). *Racism Without Racists: Color-Blind Racism and the Persistence of Racial Inequality in America* (5th ed.). Lanham, MD: Rowman and Littlefield Publishers.

Boston, C. (2016). Art Therapy and Multiculturalism. In D. E. Gussak & M. L. Rosai (eds), *The Wiley Handbook of Art Therapy* (pp.822–828). Malden, MA: Wiley-Blackwell.

Boyd-Franklin, N. (1989). *Black Families in Therapy: A Multisystem Approach.* New York, NY: The Guilford Press.

Breiding, M., Smith, S. G., Basile, K. C., Walters, M. L., Chen, J. & Merrick, M. T. (2014). Prevalence and characteristics of sexual violence, stalking, and intimate partner violence victimization—National Intimate Partner and Sexual Violence Survey, United States, 2011. *Morbidity and Mortality Weekly Report, 63*, 1–18.

Brondolo, E., Rieppi, R., Kelly, K. P. & Gerin, W. (2003). Perceived racism and blood pressure: A review of the literature and conceptual and methodological critique. *Annals of Behavioral Medicine, 25*, 55–65. doi:10.1207/S15324796ABM2501_08.

Bullimore, P. (2011). The Relationship Between Trauma and Paranoia: Managing Paranoia. In M. Romme & S. Escher (eds), *Psychosis as a Personal Crisis: An Experience-Based Approach* (pp.74–85). London: Routledge.

Butterfield, F. (1995). *All God's Children: The Bosket Family and the American Tradition of Violence.* New York, NY: Knopf.

Caldwell, J. C., & Vera, E. M. (2010). Critical incidents in counseling psychology professionals' and trainees' social justice orientation development. *Training and Education in Professional Psychology, 4*(3), 163–176. https://doi.org/10.1037/a0019093

Carr, P. R. (2016). Whiteness and white privilege: Problematizing race and racism in a "color-blind" world, and in education. *International Journal of Critical Pedagogy, 7*, 51–74. doi: 10.1007/978-3-658-14721-1_52.

Carter, R. (2007). Racism and psychological and emotional injury: Recognizing and assessing race-based traumatic stress. *The Counseling Psychologist, 35*(1), 13–105.

Center for American Progress. (2017, April 26). 100 ways, in 100 days, that Trump has hurt Americans. Retrieved from www.americanprogress.org/article/100-ways-100-days-trump-hurt-americans.

Chambala, A. (2008). Anxiety and art therapy: Treatment in the public eye. *Art Therapy: Journal of the American Art Therapy Association, 25*(4), 187–189.

Chang, C. Y., Hays, D. G. & Milliken, T. (2009). Addressing social justice issues in supervision: A call for clients and professional advocacy. *The Clinical Supervisor, 28*, 20–35.

Chung, R. C.-Y. & Bemak, F. P. (2012). *Social Justice Counseling: The Next Steps Beyond Multiculturalism.* Thousand Oaks, CA: Sage Publications.

Clack, A. R. (2018). *Women of Color Talk: The Psychological Narratives on Trauma and Depression.* Sicklerville, NJ: Clark Associates.

Clausen, J. A. (1968). *Socialisation and Society.* Boston, MA: Little Brown and Company.

CNN. (2023, June 29). Read the opinion: Supreme Court decision on Affirmative Action and college admissions. Retrieved from https://edition.cnn.com/2023/06/29/politics/read-affirmative-action-supreme-court/index.html.

Cokley, K. (2006). The Impact of Racialized Schools and Racist (Mis)Education on African American Students' Academic Identity. In M. G. Constantine & D. W. Sue (eds.), *Addressing Racism* (pp.127–144). Hoboken, NJ: Wiley.

Constantine, M. G. (2007). Racial microaggressions against African American clients in cross-racial counseling relationships. *Journal of Counseling Psychology, 54*(1), 1–16.

Constantine, M. G., Hage, S. M., Kindaichi, M. M. & Bryant, R. M. (2007). Social justice and multicultural issues: Implications for the practice and training of counselors and counseling psychologists. *Journal of Counseling & Development, 85*, 24–29.

Constantine, M. G., Smith, L., Redington, R. M. & Owens, D. (2008). Racial microaggressions against black counseling and counseling psychology faculty: A central challenge in the multicultural counseling movement. *Journal of Counseling & Development, 86*(3), 348–355.

Constantine, M. G. & Sue, D. W. (2007). Perceptions of racial microaggressions among black supervisees in cross-cultural dyads. *Journal of Counseling Psychology, 54*(2), 142–153.

Corey, G., Corey, M. & Callanan, P. (2015). *Issues and Ethics in the Helping Professions* (9th ed.). Pacific Grove, CA: Brooks/Cole.

Correll, J., Wittenbrink, B., Park, B., Judd, C. M. & Goyle, A. (2011). Dangerous enough: Moderating racial bias with contextual threat cues. *Journal of Experimental Social Psychology, 47*(1), 184–189.

Cose, E. (1993). *The Rage of a Privileged Class.* New York, NY: HarperCollins.

Council for the Accreditation of Counseling and Related Educational Programs. (2016). *2016 CACREP accreditation manual.* Alexandria, VA: Author.

Crenshaw, K. (1989). Demarginalizing the intersection of race and sex: A black feminist critique of antidiscrimination doctrine, feminist theory and antiracist politics. *The University of Chicago Legal Forum, Volume 1989* (1, 8), 139–167. https://chicagounbound.uchicago.edu/cgi/viewcontent.cgi?article=1052&context=uclf

Crenshaw, K. (1990). Mapping the margins: Intersectionality, identity politics, and violence against women of color. *Stanford Law Review, 43*(6), 1241–1299. https://doi.org/10.2307/1229039.

Crenshaw, K. (1991). Mapping the margins: Intersectionality, identity politics, and violence against women of color. *Stanford Law Review, 43*, 1241–1299.

Cross, T. & Slater, R. B. (2000). The alarming decline in the academic performance of African American men. *The Journal of Blacks in Higher Education, 27*, 82–87.

Cross, W. E. Jr. (1971). The Negro-to-Black conversion experience: Towards a psychology of Black liberation. *Black World, 30,* 13–27.

Cross, W. E. Jr. (1991). *Shades of Black: Diversity in African American Identity.* Philadelphia, PA: Temple University Press.

Cross, W. E. Jr. (1995). The Psychology of Nigrescence: Revising the Cross Model. In J. G. Ponterotto, J. M. Casas, L. A. Suzuki & C. M. Alexander (eds), *Handbook of Multicultural Counseling* (pp.93–122). Thousand Oaks, CA: Sage.

Day-Vines, N. L., Cluxton-Keller, F., Agorsor, C., Gubara, S. & Otabil, N. A. (2020). The multidimensional model of broaching behavior. *Journal of Counseling & Development, 98,* 107–118.

Day-Vines, N. L., Wood, S. M., Grothaus, T., Craigen, L. *et al.* (2007). Broaching the subjects of race, ethnicity, and culture during the counseling process. *Journal of Counseling and Development, 85,* 401–409.

Delgado, R. (1984). The imperial scholar: Reflections on a review of civil rights literature. *University of Pennsylvania Law Review, 140*(4), 1349–1372.

Delgado, R. & Stefancic, J. (2001). *Critical Race Theory: An Introduction.* New York, NY: New York University Press.

Delgado, R. & Stefancic, J. (2012). *Critical Race Theory: An Introduction* (2nd ed.). New York, NY: New York University Press.

Denborough, D. (2012). A storyline of collective practice: A history of ideas, social projects and partnerships. *International Journal of Narrative Therapy and Community Work, 1,* 40–65.

Din-Dzietham, R., Nembhard, W. N., Collines, R. & Davis, S. K. (2004). Perceived stress following race-based discrimination at work is associated with hypertension in African Americans: The metro Atlanta heart disease study, 1999–2001. *Social Science and Medicine, 58,* 449–461. doi:10.1016/S0277-9536(03)00211-9.

Dolezsar, C. M., McGrath, J. J., Herzig, A. J. M. & Miller, S. B. (2014). Perceived racial discrimination and hypertension: A comprehensive systematic review. *Health Psychology, 33*(1), 20–34.

Dovidio, J. F. & Gaertner, S. L. (2000). Aversive racism and selective decisions: 1989–1999. *Psychological Science, 11,* 315–319.

Du Bois, W. E. B. (1995). In D. L. Lewis (ed.), *W.E.B. Du Bois: A Reader.* New York, NY: Henry Holt.

Du Bois, W. E. B. (2007). *The Souls of Black Folk.* New York, NY: Cosimo Classics.

Dumas, M. J. (2016). Against the dark: Antiblackness in education policy and discourse. *Theory into Practice, 55*(1), 11–19. https://doi.org/10.1080/00405841.2016.1116852.

Duran, E. (2019). *Healing the Soul Wound: Trauma-informed Counseling for Indigenous Communities.* New York, NY: Teachers College Press.

Elkins, D. E. & Deaver, S. P. (2015). American Art Therapy Association, Inc.: 2013 membership survey report. *Art Therapy Journal of the American Art Therapy Association, 32,* 60–69. doi:10.1080/07421656.2015.1028313.

Ellison, R. (1952). *Invisible Man.* New York, NY: Random House.

Erikson, K. (1976). *Everything in its Path: Destruction of Community in the Buffalo Creek Flood.* New York, NY: Simon & Schuster.

Eyerman, R. (2023). Race in the culture wars. *Religions, 14*(721), 1–11.

Fielding, L. (2021). *Trans Sex: Clinical Approaches to Trans Sexualities and Erotic Embodiments.* New York, NY: Routledge.

Fondacaro, M. R. & Weinberg, D. (2002). Concepts of social justice in community psychology: Toward a social ecological epistemology. *American Journal of Community Psychology, 30*(4), 473–492. https://doi.org/10.1023/A:1015803817117.

Foster, K. M. (2005). Diet of disparagement: The racial experiences of Black students in a predominantly White university. *International Journal of Qualitative Studies in Education, 18*(4), 489–505.

Foucault, M. (1980). *Power/Knowledge: Selected Interviews and Other Writings.* New York, NY: Pantheon Books.

Franklin, A. J. & Boyd-Franklin, N. (2000). Invisibility syndrome: A clinical model of the effects of racism on African American males. *American Journal of Orthopsychiatry, 70*(1), 33–41.

Fraser, N. (2006). Social justice in the knowledge society: Redistribution, recognition, and participation. Retrieved from https://ediscipinas.usp.br/pluginfile.php/7136753/mod_resource/content/1/Fraser_1997_Social%20Justice_Redistribution_Recognition_Representation.pdf.

Fredrickson, G. (1987). *The Black Image in the White Mind: The Debate on Afro-American Character and Destiny, 1817–1914*. Hanover, NH: Wesleyan University Press.

French, B. H., Lewis, J. A., Mosley, D. V., Adames, H. Y. *et al.* (2020). Toward a psychological framework of radical healing in communities of color. *The Counseling Psychologist, 48*(1), 14–46. https://doi.org/10.1177/0011000019843506.

Frostig, K. (2011). Arts activism: Praxis in social justice, critical discourse, and radical modes of engagement. *Art Therapy: Journal of the American Art Therapy Association, 28*(2), 50–56. doi:10.1080/07421656.2011.578028.

Galarraga, M. (2022). Creating an inclusive and equitable space for LGBTQIA+ clients. American Art Therapy Association. Retrieved from https://arttherapy.org/blog-creating-an-inclusive-and-equitable-space-for-lgbtqia-clients.

Galinsky, T. J. (2023). Diorama for exploring the sexual self. *Art Therapy: Journal of the American Art Therapy Association, 40*(4), 197–204.

Ganim, B. (1999). *Art and Healing: Using Expressive Art to Heal Your Body, Mind, and Spirit*. New York, NY: Random House, Inc.

Garza, A. (2020). *The Purpose of Power: How We Come Together When Things Fall Apart*. New York, NY: Penguin Random House.

George, J. (2023). Microaggressions and repair: An experimental study of racial microaggressions and repair in art therapy. Paper presentation at the 2023 American Art Therapy Association Conference, San Diego, CA.

Ghiselin, B. (1952). *The Creative Process*. Berkeley, CA: University of California Press.

Gingras, B. (2010). Double consciousness and racial self in Zitkala-Sa's American Indian stories. *Undergraduate Review, 6*, 83–86.

Giovino, M. (2007). *The Assyrian Sacred Tree: A History of Interpretations*. Fribourg, Switzerland: Academic Press.

Gipson, L. (2015). Is cultural competence enough? Deepening social justice pedagogy in art therapy. *Art Therapy: Journal of the American Art Therapy Association, 32*(3), 142–145.

Goodman, L. A., Liang, B., Helms, J. E., Latta, R. E., Sparks, E. & Weintraub, S. R. (2004). Training counseling psychologists as social justice agents: Feminist and multicultural principles in action. *The Counseling Psychologist, 32*, 793–837.

Granello, D. H. & Wheaton, J. E. (1998). Self-perceived multicultural competencies of African American and European American vocational rehabilitation counselors. *Rehabilitation Counseling Bulletin, 42*(1), 2–15.

Halpern, J. (2015). Darren Wilson explains why he killed Michael Brown. *The Washington Post*. Retrieved from www.washingtonpost.com/news/morning-mix/wp/2014/11/25/why-darren-wilson-said-he-killed-michael-brown.

Hammond, W. R. & Young, B. (1993). Minority student recruitment and retention practices among schools of professional psychology: A national survey and analysis. *Professional Psychology: Research and Practice, 24*, 3–12.

Hamrick, C. & Byma, C. (2017). Know history, know self: Art therapists' responsibility to dismantle White supremacy. *Art Therapy: Journal of the American Art Therapy Association, 34*(3), 106–111.

Hanks, N. (1990). Lecture on arts and public policy transcript: Maya Angelou. Retrieved from www.americansforthearts.org/sites/default/files/Hanks1990MayaAngelou.pdf.

Harper, S. R. (2012). Race without racism: How higher education researchers minimize racist institutional norms. *The Review of Higher Education, 36*(1), 9–29.

Harrell, S. P. (2000). A multidimensional conceptualization of racism-related stress: Implications for the well-being of people of color. *American Journal of Orthopsychiatry, 70*(1), 42–57.

Harris, A. (2019). The Central Park five: "We were just baby boys." *The New York Times*. Retrieved from www.nytimes.com/2019/05/30/arts/television/when-they-see-us.html.

Harris, C. (1993). Whiteness as property. *Harvard Law Review, 106*, 1709–1795.

Harris, C. (1995). Whiteness as Property. In K. Crenshaw, N. Gotanda, G. Peller & K. Thomas (eds), *Critical Race Theory: The Key Writings that Formed the Movement* (pp.276–291). New York, NY: The New Press.

Harro, B. (1996). The Cycle of Socialization. In A. A. Singh (ed.), *The Racial Healing Handbook* (pp.34–38). Oakland, CA: New Harbinger Publications.

Harvey, J. (2000). Social privilege and moral subordination. *Journal of Social Philosophy, 31*(2), 177–188.

Harwood, S. A., Huntt, M. B., Mendenhall, R. & Lewis, J. A. (2012) Racial microaggressions in the residence halls: Experiences of student of color at a predominantly White university. *Journal of Diversity in Higher Education, 5*(3), 159–173.

Haskins, N. H. & Singh, A. (2015). Critical race theory and counseling education pedagogy: Creating equitable training. *Counseling Education & Supervision, 54*, 288–301.

Hays, P. A. (2014). Finding a Place in the Multicultural Revolution. In M. E. Gallardo (ed.), *Developing Cultural Humility* (pp.49–59). Thousand Oaks, CA: Sage Publications.

Helms, J. E. (1990). *Black and White Racial Identity: Theory, Research, and Practice.* Westport, CT: Greenwood Press.

Helms, J. E. (1995). An Update of Helms's White and People of Color Racial Identity Models. In J. G. Ponterotto, J. M. Casas, L. A. Suzuki & C. M. Alexander (eds), *Handbook of Multicultural Counseling* (pp.181–198). Thousand Oaks, CA: Sage.

Helms, J. E. (2015). Taking action against racism in a post-racism era: The origins and almost demise of an idea. *The Counseling Psychologist, 43*, 134–145.

Henfield, M. S. (2011). Black male adolescents navigating microaggressions in a traditionally white middle school: A qualitative student. *Journal of Multicultural Counseling and Development, 39*(3), 141–155.

Herold, B. (2024). *Disillusioned: Five Families and the Unraveling of America's Suburbs.* New York, NY: Penguin Random House.

Holcomb-McCoy, C. (2007). *School Counseling to Close the Achievement Gap: A Social Justice Framework of Success.* Thousand Oaks, CA: Sage Publications.

Hornsman, R. (1986). *Race and Manifest Destiny: Origins of American Racial Anglo-Saxonism.* Cambridge, MA: Harvard University Press.

Human Rights Watch. (2017). World report 2017: Events of 2016. Retrieved from www.hrw.org/report/2017/01/12/world-report-2017/events-2016.

Jackson, B. (1975). Black identity development. *Journal of Education Diversity, 2*, 19–25.

Jackson, L. (2020). A colorful canvas. American Art Therapy Association. Retrieved from https://arttherapy.org/blog-a-colorful-canvas.

Jefferson, T. (1787/1954). *Notes on the State of Virginia.* Joseph Meredith Toner Collection. Boston, MA: Lilly and Wait.

Johnson, A. G. (2006). *Privilege, Power, and Difference* (2nd ed.). Boston, MA: McGraw-Hill.

Johnson, T., Deaver, S. P. & Doby-Copeland, C. (2021). Art therapy students of color: The experience of seven graduate students. *Art Therapy: Journal of the American Art Therapy Association, 38*, 50–56. https://doi.org/10.1080/07421656.2020.1862603.

Jones, C. P. (2000). Levels of racism: A theoretical framework and a gardener's tale. *American Journal of Public Health, 90*(8), 1212–1215.

Jones, J. M. (1997). *Prejudice and Racism* (2nd ed.). Washington, DC: McGraw-Hill.

Kaiser, D. H. (2017). What do structural racism and oppression have to do with scholarship, research, and practice in art therapy? *Art Therapy: Journal of the American Art Therapy Association, 34*(4), 154–156. doi: 10.1080/07421656.2017.1420124.

Kapitan, A. & Kapitan, L. (2023). Language is power: Anti-oppressive, conscious language in art therapy practice. *International Journal of Art Therapy, 28*, 65–73. https://doi.org/10.1080/17454832.2022.2112721.

Kendi, I. X. (2019). *How to be an Antiracist.* New York, NY: Random House.

Kinney, E. (1971). Africanisms in the Music and Dance of the Americas. In R. Goldstein (ed.), *Black Life and Culture in the United States.* New York, NY: Crowell.

Kivel, P. (1996). *Uprooting Racism: How White People Can Work for Racial Justice.* Philadelphia, PA: New Society Publishers.

Kluger, R. (1975). *Simple Justice: The History of Brown v. Board of Education and Black America's Struggle for Equality.* New York, NY: Vintage Books.

Knutsen, R. (2011). *Tengu: The Shamanic and Esoteric Origins of the Japanese Martial Art.* Folkestone, Kent: Global Oriental.

Kozlowska, K., Walker, P., McLean, L. & Carrive, P. (2015). Fear and the defense cascade: Clinical implications and management. *Harvard Review of Psychiatry, 23*(4), 263–297.

Kozol, J. (2005). *The Shame of the Nation.* New York, NY: Three Rivers Press.

Kuhlberg, J. A., Pena, J. B. & Zayas, L. H. (2010). Familism, parent-adolescent conflict, self-esteem, internalizing behaviors and suicide attempts among adolescent Latinas. *Child Psychiatry and Human Development, 41*, 425–440.

Ladson-Billings, G. & Tate, W. F. (1995). Toward a critical race theory of education. *Teachers College Record, 97*, 47–68.

Last words of George Floyd. Transcript filed in district court in the state of Minnesota, 7/7/2020. Retrieved from www.mncourts.gov/mncourtsgov/media/High-Profile-Cases/27-CR-20-12951-TKL/Exhibit207072020.pdf.

Lewis, J. (2018). Twitter post. June 27, 2018.

Liebmann, M. (1990). *Art Therapy in Practice.* London: Jessica Kingsley Publishers.

Liebmann, M. (2004). *Art Therapy for Groups: A Handbook of Themes, Games, and Exercises.* New York, NY: Brunner-Routledge.

Lock, S. (2016). The tree of life: A review of the collective narrative. *Educational Psychology Research and Practice, 2*(1), 2–20.

Lord, T. Y. (2010). The relationship of gender-based public harassment to body image, self-esteem, and avoidance behavior. *Dissertation Abstracts International: Section B: The Sciences and Engineering, 70*(8-B), 5171.

Macionis, J. J. (2013). *Sociology* (15th ed.). Boston, MA: Pearson.

Magnis, N. E. (1999). Thomas Jefferson and slavery: An analysis of his racist thinking as revealed by his writings and political behavior. *Journal of Black Studies, 29*(4), 491–509.

Malchiodi, C. (1998). *The Art Therapy Sourcebook.* Lincolnwood, IL: Lowell House.

Martin, R. S. (2023). WTH?!? Ark. Gov. Sarah Huckabee Sanders CLAIMS Black History Course SPREADS "HATE." YouTube video, 16:17. Retrieved from www.youtube.com/watch?v=87yTV-A_unc.

Mauro, M. K. (1998). The Use of Art Therapy in Identity Formation: A Latino Case Study. In A. R. Hiscox & A. C. Calisch (eds), *Tapestry of Cultural Issues in Art Therapy* (pp.134–153). Philadelphia, PA: Jessica Kingsley Publishers.

McCall, L. (2005). The complexities of intersectionality. *Signs: Journal of Women in Culture and Society, 30*(3), 1772–1800.

McNiff, S. (2004). *Art Heals: How Creativity Cures the Soul.* Boston, MA: Shambhala.

Miller, G. V. F. & Travers, C. J. (2005). The Relationship Between Ethnicity and Work Stress. In A. G. Alexander-Stamatios & C. L. Cooper (eds), *Research Companion to Organizational Health Psychology* (pp.87–101). Northampton, MA: Edward Elgar Publishing.

Mills, C. W. (2017). *Black Rights/White Wrongs: The Critique of Racial Liberalism.* Oxford: Oxford University Press.

Moon, B. (1994). *Introduction to Art Therapy: Faith in the Product.* Springfield, IL: Charles C. Thomas.

Morrison, T. (1975). *A Humanist View.* Presentation at Portland State. Part of a lecture presentation on the theme of the American Dream. Transcribed by Keisha E. McKenzie.

Morrison, T. (1993). *The Power of Questions: Toni Morrison.* An Interview with Charlie Rose, PBS.

Nadal, K. L., Whitman, C. N., Davis, L. S., Erazo, T. & Davidoff, K. C. (2016). Microaggressions toward lesbian, gay, bisexual, transgender, queer, and genderqueer people: A review of the literature. *Journal of Sex Research, 53*(4–5), 488–508.

Ncube, N. (2006). The Tree of Life Project: Using narrative ideas in work with vulnerable children in Southern Africa. *International Journal of Narrative Therapy and Community Work, 1*, 3–16.

Nelson, J. (2023). Ron DeSantis wants to erase Black history. Why? *The New York Times.* Retrieved from www.nytimes.com/2023/01/31/opinion/ron-desantis-black-history.html.

New York Times (2023, June 29). Affirmative Action: Rejection of Affirmative Action draws strong reactions from right and left. Retrieved from www.nytimes.com/live/2023/06/29/us/affirmative-action-supreme-court.

Obama, B. H. (2013). President Obama's remarks on Trayvon Martin. Retrieved from https://obamawhitehouse.archives.gov/the-press-office/2013/07/19/remarks-PRESIDENT-TRAYVON-MARTIN#:~:text=1%20think%20it's%20understandable%20that,Trayvon%20Martin%20and%20his%20family.

Odegard, M. A. & Vereen, L. G. (2010). A grounded theory of counselor educators integrating social justice into their pedagogy. *Counselor Education & Supervision, 50*, 130–149.

O'Keefe, D. & Gearan, A. (2018). Trump, condemned for "shithole" countries remark. Denies comment but acknowledges "tough" language. *The Washington Post*, January 13. Retrieved from www.washingtonpost.com/politics/trump-acknowledges-tough-language-but-appears-to-deny-shithole-remark/2018/01/12/c7131dae-f796-11e7-beb6-c8d48830c54d_story.html.

Omi, M. & Winant, H. (1994). *Racial Formation in the United States: From the 1960s to the 1990s*. New York, NY: Routledge.

Park, M. (2017). The 62-second encounter between Philando Castile and the officer who killed him. Retrieved from www.cnn.com/2017/05/30/us/philando-castile-shooting-officer-trial-timeline/index.html.

Parker, K., Horowitz, M. & Anderson, M. (2020). Amid Protests, Majorities Across Racial and Ethnic Groups Express Support for the Black Lives Matter Movement. Pew Research Center. Retrieved from www.pewresearch.org/social-trends/2020/06/12/amid-protests-majorities-across-racial-and-ethnic-groups-express-support-for-the-black-lives-matter-movement.

Payne, H. (1993). *Handbook of Inquiry in the Arts Therapies: One River, Many Currents*. London: Jessica Kingsley Publishers.

Pearlman, L. A. & Mac Ina, P. S. (1995). Vicarious traumatization: An empirical study of the effects of trauma work on trauma therapists. *Professional Psychology, 26*(6), 558–565.

Pearson, A. R., Dovidio, J. F. & Gaertner, S. L. (2009). The nature of contemporary prejudice: Insights from aversive racism. *Social and Personality Psychology Compass, 3*, 1–25.

Pierce, C., Carew, J., Pierce-Gonzalez, D. & Willis, D. (1978). An Experiment in Racism: TV Commercials. In C. Pierce (ed.), *Television and Education* (pp.62–88). Beverly Hills, CA: Sage.

Pierce, C. M. (1975). A report on minority children. *Psychiatric Annals, 5*(6), 224–246.

Pittman, C. T. (2012). Racial microaggressions: The narratives of African American faculty at a predominantly White university. *The Journal of Negro Education, 81*(1), 82–92.

Potash, J. S. (2023). Introduction to the special issue: Sex positive art therapy. *Art Therapy: Journal of the American Art Therapy Association, 40*(4), 169–170. https://doi.org/10.1080/07421656.2023.2283361

Potash, J. S. (2020). Antiracist approach to art therapy: Re-examining core concepts. American Art Therapy Association. Retrieved from https://arttherapy.org/blog-antiracist-approach-to-art-therapy.

Potash, J. S., Doby-Copeland, C., Stepney, S. A., Washington, B. N. *et al.* (2015). Advancing multicultural and diversity competence in art therapy: American Art Therapy Association Multicultural Committee 1990–2015. *Art Therapy: Journal of the American Art Therapy Association, 32*(3), 146–150. doi: 10.1080/07421656.2015.1060837.

President's Initiative on Race (1998). *One America in the Twenty-First Century*. Washington, DC: U.S. Government Printing Office.

Prilleltensky, L. & Gonick, L. (1996). Politics change, oppression remains: On the psychology and politics of oppression. *Political Psychology, 17*, 127–148.

Ratts, M. J. (2009). Social justice counseling: Toward the development of a fifth force among counseling paradigms. *Journal of Humanistic Counseling, Education & Development, 48*(2), 160–172.

Ratts, M. J. & Hutchins, A. M. (2009). ACA advocacy competencies: Social justice at the client/student level. *Journal of Counseling and Development, 87*, 269–275.

Ratts, M. J., Singh, A. A., Nassar-McMillan, S., Butler, S. K. & McCullough, J. R. (2016). Multicultural and social justice counseling competencies: Guidelines for the counseling profession. *Journal of Multicultural Counseling and Development, 44*(1), 28–48.

Ratts, M. J., Toporek, R. L. & Lewis, J. A. (eds). (2010). *ACA Advocacy Competencies: A Social Justice Framework for Counselors.* Alexandria, VA: American Counseling Association.

Reja, M. (2021). Trump's "Chinese Virus" tweet helped lead to rise in racist anti-Asian Twitter content: Study. ABC News. Retrieved from https://abcnews.go.com/Health/trumps-chinese-virus-tweet-helped-lead-to-rise-racist/story?id=76530148.

Robinson, E. (2010). *Disintegration: The Splintering of Black America.* New York, NY: Doubleday.

Rowe, M. P. (1990). Barriers to equality: The power of subtle discrimination to maintain unequal opportunity. *Employee Responsibilities and Rights Journal, 3*, 153–163.

Sangal, A., Vogt, A., Kashiwagi, S., Meyer, M. & Powell, T. B. (2023). June 29, 2023 Supreme Court Affirmative Action decision. CNN. Retrieved from https://edition.cnn.com/politics/live-news/supreme-court-decisions/index.html.

Santiago-Rivera, A., Kanter, J., Benson, G., Derose, T., Illes, R. & Reyes, W. (2008). Behavioral activation as an alternative treatment approach for Latinas/os with depression. *Psychotherapy: Theory, Research, Practice, Training, 45*, 173–185.

Sex Positive Art Therapy. (2023). *Art Therapy: Journal of the American Art Therapy Association, 40*(4).

Singh, A. A. (2019). *The Racial Healing Handbook: Practical Activities to Help you Challenge Privilege, Confront Systemic Racism & Engage in Collective Healing.* Oakland, CA: New Harbinger Publications.

Singletary, G. (2022). The Black experience: The entanglement among African American males and law enforcement. *Journal of Community Psychology, 50*, 250–264.

Smith, W. A. (2010). The impact of racial trauma on African Americans. African American Men and Boys Advisory Board, Pittsburgh, PA: Heinz Endowments. Retrieved from www.heinz.org/userfiles/impactofracialtraumaonafricanamericans.pdf.

Smith, W. A., Allen, W. A. & Danley, L. (2007). Assume the position…you fit the description: Psychosocial experiences and racial battle fatigue among African American male college students. *American Behavioral Scientists, 51*, 551–578.

Smith, W. A., Hung, M. & Franklin, J. D. (2011). Racial battle fatigue and the miseducation of Black men: Racial microaggressions, societal problems, and environmental stress. *The Journal of Negro Education, 80*(1), 63–82.

Solorzano, D. (1997). Images and words that wound: Critical race theory, racial stereotyping, and teacher education. *Teacher Education Quarterly, 24*, 5–19.

Solorzano, D., Ceja, M. & Yosso, T. (2000). Critical race theory, racial microaggressions, and campus racial climate: The experiences of African American college students. *Journal of Negro Education, 69*(1/2), 60–73.

Spanierman, L. B., Poteat, V. P., Wang, Y. F. & Oh, E. (2008). Psychosocial costs of racism to white counselors: Predicting various dimensions of multicultural counseling competence. *Journal of Counseling Psychology, 55*(1), 75–88.

Spanierman, L. B. & Smith, L. (2017). Roles and responsibilities of White allies: Implications for research, teaching, and practice. *The Counseling Psychologist, 45*(5), 606–617.

Stainback, K., Robinson, C. L. & Tomaskovic-Devey, D. (2005). Race and workplace integration: A politically mediated process? *American Behavioral Scientist, 48*(9), 1200–1228.

Steele, J. M. (2008). Preparing counselors to advocate for social justice: A liberation model. *Counseling Education & Supervision, 48*, 74–85.

Sue, D. W. (2004). Whiteness and ethnocentric monoculturalism: Making the "invisible" visible. *American Psychology, 59*, 759–769.

Sue, D. W. (2010). *Microaggressions in Everyday Life: Race, Gender and Sexual Orientation.* Hoboken, NJ: John Wiley & Sons.

Sue, D. W. (2015). *Race Talk and the Conspiracy of Silence: Understanding and Facilitating Difficult Dialogues on Race.* Hoboken, NJ: John Wiley & Sons.

Sue, D. W., Bucceri, J., Lin, A. L., Nadal, K. L. & Torino, G. C. (2007a). Racial microaggressions and the Asian American experience. *Cultural Diversity and Ethnic Minority Psychology, 13*, 72–81.

Sue, D. W., Capodilupo, C. M. & Holder, A. M. (2008a). Racial microaggressions in the life experiences of African Americans. *Professional Psychology: Research and Practice, 39*(3), 329–336.

Sue, D. W., Capodilupo, C. M., Torino, G. C., Bucceri, J. *et al.* (2007b). Racial microaggressions in everyday life: Implications for clinical practice. *American Psychologist, 62*(4), 271–286. doi: 10.1037/0003-066X.62.4.271.

Sue, D. W., Nadal, K. L., Capodilupo, C. M., Lin, A. I., Torino, G. C. & Rivera, D. P. (2008b). Racial microaggressions against Black Americans: Implications for counseling. *Journal of Counseling & Development, 86*(3), 330–338.

Sue, D. W. & Spanierman, L. B. (2020). *Microaggressions in Everyday Life* (2nd ed.). Hoboken, NJ: Wiley.

Sue, D. W. & Sue, W. (1990). *Counseling the Culturally Diverse: Theory and Practice* (2nd ed.). New York, NY: Wiley.

Sue, D. W. & Sue, W. (1999). *Counseling the Culturally Diverse: Theory and Practice* (3rd ed.). New York, NY: Wiley.

Sue, D. W. & Sue, W. (2008). *Counseling the Culturally Diverse: Theory and Practice* (5th ed.). New York, NY: Wiley.

Sue, D. W., Sue, D., Neville, H. A. & Smith, L. (2019). *Counseling the Culturally Diverse: Theory and Practice* (8th ed.). Hoboken, NJ: Wiley.

Sue, D. W. & Torino, G. C. (2005). Racial Cultural Competence: Awareness, Knowledge and Skills. In R. T. Carter (ed.), *Handbook of Racial-Cultural Psychology and Counseling* (pp.3–18). Hoboken, NJ: Wiley.

Sullivan, K. & Rozsa, L. (2023). DeSantis doubles down on claim that some Blacks benefited from slavery. *The Detroit News.* Retrieved from https://eu.detroitnews.com/story/news/nation/2023/07/23/desantis-blacks-benefited-from-slavery/70452822007.

Swim, J. K. & Cohen, L. L. (1997). Overt, covert, and subtle sexism: A comparison between the Attitudes Toward Women and Modern Sexism Scales. *Psychology of Women Quarterly, 21*(1), 103–118. https://doi.org/10.1111/j.1471-6402.1997.tb00103.x.

Talwar, S. (2010). An intersectional framework of race, class, gender, and sexuality in art therapy. *Art Therapy Journal of the American Art Therapy Association, 27*(1), 11–17.

Talwar, S. (2015). Culture, diversity and identity: From margins to center. *Art Therapy: Journal of the American Art Therapy Association, 32*(3), 100–103.

Talwar, S., Iyer, J. & Doby-Copeland, C. (2004). The invisible veil: Changing paradigms in the art therapy profession. *Art Therapy: Journal of the American Art Therapy Association, 21*, 44–48.

Taylor, E., Gillborn, D. & Ladson-Billings, G. (2009). *Foundations of Critical Race Theory in Education.* New York, NY: Routledge.

ter Maat, M. (2011). Developing and assessing multicultural competence with a focus on culture and ethnicity. *Art Therapy: Journal of the American Art Therapy Association, 28*(1), 4–10.

Thomas, C. W. (1971). *Boys No More: A Black Psychologist's View of Community.* Beverly Hills, CA: Glencoe.

Thompson, C. E. & Neville, H. A. (1999). Racism, mental health & mental health practice. *The Counseling Psychologist, 27*(2), 155–223.

Toporek, R. L., Lewis, J. A. & Crethar, H. C. (2009). Promoting systemic change through the ACA advocacy competencies. *Journal of Counseling & Development, 87*, 260–268.

U.S. Census Bureau. (2014). U.S. people quick facts. Retrieved from www.census.gov/quickfacts.

U.S. Department of Health and Human Services. (2010). Healthy People 2010. Retrieved from www.cdc.gov/nchs/data/hpdata2010/hp2010_general_data_issues.pdf.

U.S. Department of Justice. National Advisory Commission on Civil Disorders, Report (1967). *Kerner Commission report on the causes, events, and aftermaths of the civil disorders of 1967.* Retrieved from www.ojp.gov.

Utsey, S. O., Chae, M. H., Brown, C. F. & Kelly, D. (2002). Effect of ethnic group membership on ethnic identity, race-related stress, and quality of life. *Cultural Diversity and Ethnic Minority Psychology, 8*, 366–377.

Utsey, S. O. & Hook, J. N. (2007). Heart rate variability as a physiological moderator of the relationship between race-related stress and psychological distress in African Americans. *Journal of Counseling Psychology, 13*, 250–253. doi:10.1037/1099-9809.13.3.250.

Valicenti, R. L. N., Fredman, L. A., German, M. & Greguska, C. (2023). Art in response to Antiracism. Panel discussion at the 2023 American Art Therapy Association Conference, San Diego, CA.

Vandiver, B. J. (2001). Psychological nigrescence revisited: Introduction and overview. *Journal of Multicultural Counseling and Development, 29*, 165–173.

Williams, D. R., Neighbors, H. W. & Jackson, J. S. (2003). Racial/ethnic discrimination and health: Findings from community studies. *American Journal of Public Health, 93*(2), 200–208.

Wyatt, S. B., Williams, D. R., Calvin, R., Henderson, F. C., Walker, E. R. & Winters, K. (2003). Racism and cardiovascular disease in African Americans. *The American Journal of the Medical Sciences, 325*(6), 315–331.

Yam, K. (2021). Anti-Asian hate crimes increased by nearly 150%, mostly in N.Y. and L.A., new report says. NBC News. Retrieved from www.nbcnews.com/news/asian-america/anti-asian-hate-crimes-increased-nearly-150-2020-mostly-n-n1260264.

Yates, C., Kuwada, K., Potter, P., Cameron, D. & Hoshino, J. (2007). Image making and personal narratives with Japanese American survivors of World War II internment camps. *Art Therapy: Journal of the American Art Therapy Association, 24*(3), 111–118.

Zinn, H. (2005). *A People's History of the United States.* New York, NY: HarperCollins.

About the Author

Dr. Chioma Anah, Ed.D., ATR, LCPC, NCC, ACS

Chioma Anah, Ed.D., ATR, LCPC (Board Approved Supervisor), NCC, ACS, holds a Doctorate in Education (Ed.D) in Counseling Psychology, is a Registered Art Therapist (ATR), a National Certified Counselor (NCC), a Licensed Clinical Professional Counselor (LCPC-Maryland), an Approved Clinical Supervisor (ACS) and a Board-Approved Supervisor in the state of Maryland. Dr. Anah is the Founder and CEO of PerceptA Therapeutic & Training Center, LLC, located in Maryland. She has over 20 years of counseling and art therapy experience, specifically using art with clients as part of a healing approach and intervention to treat cultural and racial oppression, and daily racial microaggressions. Dr. Anah's interests and research agenda primarily focus on social justice and advocacy, racial microaggressions, the psychology of anti-Black racism, African American mental health disparities, the intersection of art and social justice and art and creativity as tools for healing. Dr. Anah is a founding member, first President (2018–2019) and Executive Director (2019–2024) of Maryland Counselors for Social Justice (MCSJ). She is a professor at the Johns Hopkins University School of Education in Baltimore, Maryland.

Subject Index

Note: page numbers in italics refer to figures

abortion (right to) 91
Aburi Agreement 66
advocacy
    definition 163
    see also social justice advocacy
Affirmative Action 72–3
African Holocaust of Enslavement 65
agents of change
    art therapists roles as 165–7
    artists as 37–8
Alaskan Natives (having awareness of historical roots) 51
alcohol 103, 146–7, 150, 152, 154
allyship 221–3
alumni organizations 143
always being watched 99, 117–9, 134, 138, 139, 141
Angelou, Maya 35
anger 133–4
"angry Black man" stereotype 86, 98, 112–3
anti-Black racism 58
anti-Blackness (definition) 19, 58
anti-racist White identity 213
Arbery, Ahmaud 22
armoring 102, 143–4, 152, 153
art as healing intervention 37–8
art materials 48
art therapists
    Black female pioneers 178–9, 188
    denial of racism by 23
    environment provided by White 49
    predominantly White 23
    unique position to facilitate healing 44
    unique role of 23
art therapy
    ability to challenge universal discourse 166
    client-centered approach 38

overview 23
power of 22–3
art therapy programs
    feedback from students 228–32
    lack of diversity in 15
artists as agents of change 37–8, 165–7
artworks
    "Experience as a Black woman during the time of COVID-19" 40–1, 40
    "Experiences of being a Black woman" 39–40, 39
    George Floyd killing 41–2, 42
    "Invisibility" 87
    "Myth of meritocracy" 83
    "No such thing as a single-issue struggle" 175
    "Our struggle is the struggle of a lifetime" 35
    "Racial healing" (Casson) 229
    "Racial healing" (Hunter) 231
    "Racial Microaggressions" 76
    "We are not all the same" 81
ascription of intelligence
    definition 79
    in racial microaggressions study 98, 108–10
Asian Americans, hate crimes against 51
assumption of criminal status see criminality assumption

Barton, Deanna 179, 188
"be the first" 150
biases, therapists understanding own 44, 167
"birthers" 81
Black female pioneers in art therapy 178–9, 188
Black identity development models 202
    see also racial identity

Black Lives Matter movement 70, 222
Black people, diversity among 27, 42–3
"boogeyman" (Black men seen
    as) 98, 110–1, 122, 128
Boston, Charlotte 184–91
broaching
    dangers of not 49
    definition 45
    four dimensions of 46–7
    in Irene Hendricks case study 45–7
    Multidimensional Model of Broaching
        Behavior (MMBB)
        46
Brown, Blanche 179
Brown, Michael 70, 80
Brown v. Board of Education (1954) 69
burden to fight negative stereotypes 130–1
burden to represent a whole race 127–30, 136

cardiovascular health 88
case studies
    racial identity development 207–9
    "second-class citizen" 168–9
    Tom Redd's story 56–7, 60, 201
    "Trump is going to deport
        all of you" 169–70
    white racial identity development 209–10
case study (Irene Hendricks)
    approaches used with 38
    art work and process 47–8
    background 36
    broaching in 45–7
    "Experience as a Black woman during
        the time of COVID-19" 40–1, 40
    "Experiences of being a Black
        woman" 39–40, 39
    George Floyd killing impact 41–2, 42
    introduction and assessment 44–5
    locus of control 47
    locus of responsibility 47
    therapeutic process 42–3
Castile, Philando 80–1
"Caucasian" 28
"Central Park five" 79
changing persona 103, 131, 147–8, 152
Civil Rights Act (1964) 69, 70
client-centered approach 38
Clinton, Bill 70
collaborative action 222
collective trauma 61
colonialism 64–7
color-blindness 72–3, 82, 123–4
Columbus, Christopher 64
competency frequently questioned 109
consent, informed 44

constant surveillance 99, 117–9,
    134, 138, 139, 141
control, locus of 47
coping mechanisms
    alcohol 103, 146–7, 150, 152, 154
    armoring 102, 143–4, 152, 153
    being a "chameleon" 103, 131, 147–8, 152
    in collages 107
    documentation 148
    family/social support network 102,
        142–3, 150, 152, 154, 156
    food 103, 146, 152, 153, 156
    hope 149
    humor 103, 125–6, 144–5
    luxury items 147, 152, 153, 156
    mentoring/mentorship 102, 144, 150, 156
    music 103, 145–6, 153
    negative coping 103
    numbing feelings 103, 148
    prayer/spirituality 102, 143, 156
    self-care 103, 147, 148, 153, 156
    vacationing 147, 156
COVID-19
    called the "China" virus 50–1
    "Experience as a Black woman during
        the time of COVID-19" 40–1, 40
    inequality during 168–9
    police brutality during 41
creative process 42–3, 47–8
criminality assumption
    definition 79–81
    as racial microaggression 110–2, 141
critical race theory
    core tenets of 214–6
    overview 214
Cross's five-stage model of psychological
    nigrescence 202–3
cultural awareness (increasing) 225–7
cultural competence
    Art Therapy Multicultural and
        Diversity Competence 43
    and awareness of own worldview 63
    calls for more 24
    definition 43
    Multicultural and Social Justice
        Counseling Competencies
        (MSJCC) 43, 216–8
    what art therapists need to do 223–4
cultural responsiveness 44, 63, 216–8, 223–4
cycle of socialization 199

Deferred Action for Childhood
    Arrivals (DACA) 49–50
denial of the existence of racism 72–3
DeSantis, Ron 71, 73, 74
diabetes 88

diorama 93
discrimination (definition) 69
dismantling White supremacy 62-4
distortions of the existence of racism 72-3
diversity
    among Black people 27, 42-3, 81, 175
    see also intersectionality
divorce 136
Doby-Copeland, Cheryl 179, 188
documentation (as coping mechanism) 148
doll test (Clarks) 211
"Don't Say Gay" Bill (2022) 71
double consciousness 58-9
double-blind 59
Dred Scott case 68

education
    and ascription of intelligence 109
    responsibility of schools 157
    see also schools
Efodzi, Martina 179
Einstein, Albert 167, 222
emic position 44, 63
environmental microaggressions 83-4
Equal Employment Opportunity
    (EEO) laws 69
Ethical Principles for Art Therapists
    43, 61, 165, 167
excelling in field (as coping
    mechanism) 143-4
"exception to the rule" 123
external control (EC) 47

facial hair 112-3, 134
fake persona at work 103, 131, 147-8,
    152
family/social support network 102,
    142-3, 150, 152, 154, 156
Floyd, George see George Floyd killing
food/meals as coping mechanism
    103, 146, 152, 153, 156
fraternity support network 98, 140, 143

gender-based microaggressions 90-2
George Floyd killing
    anxiety levels after 36
    in case study (Irene Hendricks) 41-2
    increase in number of clients after 61
    last words 21
    vicarious trauma from 60
GI Bill (1947) 69
Gumbel, Bryant 113, 136

Hammond, Paula 188
Hausa Tribe 65

HBCU Alumni Organization 143
HBCUs (historically black colleges
    or universities) 109, 143, 144
healing
    art as intervention for 37-8
    feedback from students 228-32
healing cont.
    overview of requirements for 219
    wounds that need 220-1
health status (racial
    microaggressions and) 88
hierarchical beliefs about race 55
high blood pressure 88
Hiscox, Anna 179
hope 149
humor as coping mechanism
    103, 125-6, 144-5
Hurricane Katrina 70

identity see racial identity
Igbo Tribe 65, 66
immigrants unlikely to report abuse 50
Indigenous people (having awareness
    of historical roots) 51
inequality (definition) 25
inferiority complex 127
informed consent 44
institutional racism 214
intelligence see ascription of intelligence
internal control (IC) 47
internalized racism 199-200
intersectionality
    art therapy exercise 192-3
    author's identities 174
    Black women in art therapy 175-91
    interview with Charlotte Boston 184-91
    interview with Gwendolyn Short 176-84
    overview 173-4
interviews
    Charlotte Boston 184-91
    Gwendolyn Short 176-84
invisibility of African Americans 58, 86-7

Jackson, Louvenia 179, 188
Jefferson, Thomas (on slavery) 56
Johnson, Rhonda 188
Johnson, Tuesdai 188
Joseph, Cliff 178
Jung, Maxine 186

Kerner Commission 69-70
King, Martin Luther Jr. 222
Kramer, Edith 178
Kyere, Ama 188

land acknowledgment 51–2
language
    norms and values maintained by 16
    terminology used in book 27–9
Latinx individuals (issues affecting) 50
Levy, Berny 176
LGBTQIA+ clients 93–4
locus of control 47
locus of responsibility 47
"loud Black woman" stereotype 40
Lumumba, Patrice 64
luxury items 147, 152, 153, 156

"maafa" 65
McGee, Sarah 178
Marshall, Kerry James 38
Martin, Trayvon 29, 70, 80
mentoring/mentorship (coping
    mechanism) 102, 144, 150, 156
meritocracy myth 82–3, *83*
metaphors *see* visual metaphors
microaggressions *see* gender-based
    microaggressions; racial
    microaggressions; racial
    microaggressions study; sexual-
    orientation microaggressions
microassaults 78–9
microinsults 78, 79–81
microinvalidations 78, 81–3
minimization of the existence
    of racism 72–3
"minority" (as disempowering term) 29
Morrison, Toni 71–2
multicultural counseling and
    therapy (MCT) 37
Multicultural and Social Justice Counseling
    Competencies (MSJCC) 43, 216–8
Multidimensional Model of Broaching
    Behavior (MMBB) 46
murders of unarmed Black
    people 22, 29, 58, 61, 70
    see also George Floyd killing
music as coping mechanism 103, 145–6, 153
My Iroko Tree of Identity and Pathway
    Towards Healing exercise 194–9
myth of meritocracy 82–3, *83*

Native Americans (having awareness
    of historical roots) 51
Nigerian civil war 65–7
nigrescence 202–3
numbing feelings 103, 148

Obama, Barack
    birthplace questioned by Trump 81

Deferred Action for Childhood
    Arrivals (DACA) 49–50
racial microaggressions against 89
speech following Zimmerman
    acquittal 29, 80
Obama effect (racial microaggression)
    100, 120–4

pathologizing cultural values/
    communication styles 79
persona (changing) 103, 131, 147–8, 152
physical effects of racial
    microaggressions 88–9
Piper, Adrian 37
Plessy v. Ferguson 68
police
    brutality during COVID-19 41
    in the collages 135, 138–9
    killing of unarmed Black people
        22, 29, 58, 61, 70
political correctness 158
political views of therapist 166
Powell, Georgette Seabrooke 178, 185
prayer/spirituality (coping
    mechanism) 102, 143, 156
pressure to represent a whole
    race 127–30, 136
psychological effects of racial
    microaggressions 86–8

Race Advisory Board (Clinton
    administration) 70
racial battle fatigue 58–9
racial, ethnic and cultural (REC) identity
    development models 202–3
racial healing 219
racial identity
    Black identity development models 202
    case study 207–9
    complexity of 27–8
    Cross's five-stage model of psychological
        nigrescence 202–3
    development of 200–1
    racial, ethnic and cultural (REC) identity
        development models 202–3
    Tom Redd's story 201
    see also racial/cultural identity
        development model; white
        racial identity development
racial microaggressions
    accepting the realities of 89–90
    always being watched 99, 117–9
    "angry Black man" stereotype 86, 98, 112–3
    ascription of intelligence 98, 108–10
    criminal status assumption 110–2,
        141

definition 76–7, 77
education level and 87
environmental microaggressions 83–4
"Invisibility" 87
microassaults 78–9
"microinequality" 84
microinsults 79–81
microinvalidations 81–3
non-verbal 78
Obama effect 100, 120–4
overview 77–8
perceived minimal harm of 85
physical effects of 88–9
psychological dilemmas of 84–6
psychological effects of 86–8
"Racial Microaggressions" 76
sameness/all Black men look
    alike 99, 119–20
second-class status 79, 99, 114–6, 168–9
sexual objectification 99, 116–7, 140–1
taxonomy of 78
in television commercials 77
verbal 78
racial microaggressions study
categories emerging from 98–102
collages in 104–5
combating in the workplace 157–9
coping themes 102–5, 142–8
coping themes (visual metaphors) 148–56
Dwayne's collages 136–8, 137, 152–4, 152
experiences identified 98–100
impacts identified 101–2, 126–32
instrumentation 96
Jackson's collages 135–6, 135, 151–2, 151
James's collages 140–1, 141, 156, 156
Lewis's collages 138–9, 138, 154–5, 154
meanings emerging from 98–102
participants 97–8
participants' thoughts about 159–60
Phillip's collages 139, 140, 140, 155, 155
purpose of 95, 96
Randolph's collages 133–4, 133, 148–51, 149
reactions/responses identified
    100–1, 124–6
results/findings 96–108
themes emerging from 98–102, 108–24
visual metaphors in 106–8, 132–41, 148–56
racial profiling 80
racial trauma
arousal phase 59
clinical interventions to treat 59–60
in context of art therapy 61–2
definition 59
double-blind in 59
overview 58–60
racial/cultural identity development model

conformity phase 204–5
dissonance phase 205
introspection phase 206
integrative awareness phase 206
overview 203–4
resistance and immersion phase 205–6
racism
affects everyone in negative ways 57
definitions 22, 55–7
denial of the existence of 72–3
denied by therapist 23
evolution in United States 67–71
history 64–7
obstacles to learning about 29–30
reactions to learning about 29–30
Reagan-Bush administration 70
Redd, Tom 56–7, 60, 201
refugees unlikely to report abuse 50
reliability frequently questioned 109
reparations to African countries 67
representing whole African
    American race 127–30, 136
responsibility, locus of 47
Rodriguez, Favianna 38
Roe v. Wade overturned 91
Rubin, Judy 186

"Sambo the Happy Slave" effect 131–2, 152
sameness/all Black men look alike
    (microaggression) 99, 119–20
Sanders, Sarah Huckabee 73, 74
schools
    responsibility of 157
    segregation in 69
    teaching about slavery banned in 68, 73–4
    teaching critical race theory 214
second-class status 79, 99, 114–6, 168–9
segregation policy 68, 69
self-care 103, 147, 148, 153, 156
self-doubt/inferiority complex 127
self-reflexivity (lifelong need for) 30
sexism 90–2
sexual objectification microaggression
    99, 116–7, 140–1
sexual-orientation microaggressions 92–4
Short, Gwendolyn 176–84, 188
slave trade
    dehumanization of Black people by 68
    reparations to African countries for 67
    as root of racism/White supremacy 64–5
slavery
    ban on teaching about 68, 73–4
    claims some Blacks benefited from 73
    Thomas Jefferson on 56
    "three-fifths of all other
        persons" status 68

social justice
  definition 162
  goal of 163
  implications for art therapists 171–2
  values of 162–3, 164
social justice advocacy
  art therapy as call to action 167
  definition 163–4
  principles of 167
  targets for 164–5
social justice vision 43
Social Security Act (1935) 68–9
socialization cycle 199
spirituality/prayer (coping
    mechanism) 102, 143, 156
split of consciousness 58
Stepney, Stella 179, 188
stereotypes
  avoiding succumbing to 49
  burden of fighting 130–1
  "loud Black woman" 40
stigma about mental health treatment 61
"Stop Woke Act" (2022) 71

Taylor, Breonna 22
television commercials 77
terminology used in book 27–9
The Last Supper 140
Thomas, Lisa 179
tokenization 123
Tree of Life tool 198
true racial allyship 221–3
Trump, Donald
  called COVID-19 the "China" virus 50–1
  impact of 169–70
  questioning of Barack Obama's
      birthplace 81
  rhetoric used by 50–1, 79
12 Years a Slave (used in collage) 116, 137

Ulman, Elinor 178, 179, 185

vacations (taking) 147, 156
validating experiences of racism 49
Vance, Lindsey 179, 188
Venture, Lucille 178, 185, 188
vicarious trauma 60
visual metaphors
  coping mechanisms 148–56
  experiences of racial
      microaggressions 132–41
  overview 106–8
Voting Rights Act (1965) 69, 70, 89

"War on Drugs" 70
Wheels of Diversity in Art Therapy:
    Pioneers of Color 178, 188
"White flight" 85
White people, racism costly to 57
white racial identity development
  case study 209–10
  commitment to anti-racist
      action phase 213
  conformity phase 211
  dissonance phase 212
  Helms's model 210–3
  integrative awareness phase 212–3
  introspective phase 212
  naivete phase 211
  resistance and immersion phase 212
White supremacy
  definition 22, 56
  dismantling in art therapy 62–4
Wilson, Darren 80
workplace
  combating racial microaggressions
      in 157–9
  fake persona in 103, 131, 147-8, 152
  inequity in 84
  see also racial microaggressions study

Yoruba Tribe 65
Young, Genia 188

Zimmerman, George 29, 70, 80

Author Index

Acuff, J. 58
Ahmadi, M. 51
Allen, W. A. 58, 84, 86, 89
Alleyne, A. 87
American Art Therapy
    Association 23,
    43, 61, 165, 167
American Counseling
    Association 165
Anah, C. 31, 35, 37, 38,
    44, 51, 62, 65, 80,
    166, 167, 174, 175
Anah, R. S. 65
Anderson, M. 222
Ani, M. 65
Ansley, F. L. 56
Art Therapy Credential
    Board 165
Awais, Y. J. 24

Banaji, M. R. 91
Baumann, A. A. 50
BBC World Service Africa 67
Bell, D. 55, 68, 214
Bell, L. A. 163
Bell, M. P. 58
Bemak, F. 162, 164
Beutler, B. 76
Bonilla-Silva, E. 72
Boston, C. 190
Boyd-Franklin, N.
    55, 58, 65, 68
Breiding, M. 91
Brondolo, E. 87, 88
Bullimore, P. 221
Butterfield, F. 88
Byma, C. 23, 62

Caldwell, J. C. 163
Callanan, P. 164
Carr, P. R. 15

Carter, R. 57, 59, 60, 199
Ceja, M. 77
Center for American
    Progress 76
Chambala, A. 37, 94
Chang, C. Y. 163, 235
Chomsky, N. 219
Chung, R. C.-Y. 162, 164
Clack, A. R. 61
Clausen, J. A. 199
CNN 73
Cohen, L. L. 91
Cokley, K. 211
Constantine, M. G.
    82, 86, 89, 164
Corey, G. 164
Corey, M. 164
Correll, J. 80
Cose, E. 11, 210
Council for the
    Accreditation of
    Counseling and
    Related Educational
    Programs 165
Crenshaw, K. 173, 187, 214
Crethar, H. C. 234
Cross, T. 69
Cross, W. E. Jr. 202,
    203, 204, 207

Danley, L. 58
Day-Vines, N. L. 23, 45, 46,
    49, 61, 205, 212, 213, 223
Deaver, S. P. 15, 23
Delgado, R. 56, 68, 215
Denborough, D. 198
Din-Dzietham, R. 88
Doby-Copeland, C. 15, 23
Dolezsar, C. M. 88
Dovidio, J. F. 57, 58, 69, 79
Du Bois, W. E. B. 58, 64

Dumas, M. J. 58
Duran, E. 51

Elkins, D. E. 15, 23
Ellison, R. 58
Erikson, K. 61
Eyerman, R. 214

Fielding, L. 93
Fondacaro, M. R. 164
Foster, K. M. 69, 86
Foucault, M. 235
Franklin, A. J. 55, 58
Fraser, N. 162
Fredrickson, G. 64
French, B. H. 219
Frostig, K. 164

Gaertner, S. L. 57, 58, 69, 79
Galarraga, M. 93
Galinsky, T. J. 93
Ganim, B. 37, 94
Garza, A. 173, 203
Gearan, A. 50
George, J. 24
Ghiselin, B. 42
Gillborn, D. 215
Gingras, B. 59
Giovino, M. 198
Gipson, L. 24
Gonick, L. 235
Goodman, L. A. 164, 167, 236
Granello, D. H. 49
Greenwald, A. G. 91

Halpern, J. 70, 80
Hammond, W. R. 88
Hamrick, C. 23, 62
Hanks, N. 35
Harper, S. R. 55, 73
Harrell, S. P. 55, 86, 199

Harris, A. 79, 215
Harris, C. 215
Harro, B. 199
Harvey, J. 235
Harwood, S. A. 84
Haskins, N. H. 214, 215
Hays, D. G. 163, 235
Hays, P. A. 211
Helms, J. E. 210
Henfield, M. S. 69
Herold, B. 85
Holcomb-McCoy, C. 162, 235
Hook, J. N. 88
Hornsman, R. 65
Horowitz, M. 222
Human Rights Watch 49
Hung, M. 58
Hutchins, A. M. 163

Iyer, J. 23

Jackson, B. 202
Jackson, J. S. 87
Jackson, L. 24, 62
Jefferson, T. 56
Johnson, A. G. 235
Johnson, T. 15
Jones, C. P. 55
Jones, J. M. 55, 69, 86, 210, 234, 235

Kaiser, D. H. 15
Kapitan, A. 16
Kapitan, L. 16
Kendi, I. X. 64
Kinney, E. 64, 68
Kivel, P. 57
Kluger, R. 68, 69
Knutsen, R. 198
Kozlowska, K. 60, 69
Kozol, J. 68
Kuhlberg, J. A. 50

Ladson-Billings, G. 215
Lewis, J. 35, 162, 182
Lewis, J. A. 164, 234
Liebmann, M. 23, 37, 94, 233
Lock, S. 198
Lord, T. Y. 91

Mac Ina, P. S. 62
McCall, L. 173
Macionis, J. J. 199
McNiff, S. 37, 94
Magnis, N. E. 56
Malchiodi, C. 233

Martin, R. S. 73
Mauro, M. K. 50
Merriam-Webster.com 65
Miller, G. V. F. 82
Milliken, T. 163, 235
Mills, C. W. 55, 68
Moon, B. 23
Morrison, T. 72

Nadal, K. L. 92
Ncube, N. 198
Neighbors, H. W. 87
Nelson, J. 214
Neville, H. A. 69, 86, 87
New York Times 72

Obama, B. H. 29, 80
Odegard, M. A. 162
Omi, M. 70
O'Keefe, D. 50

Park, M. 81
Parker, K. 222
Payne, H. 23
Pearlman, L. A. 62
Pearson, A. R. 58, 69
Pena, J. B. 50
Pierce, C. 55, 76, 77, 84, 86, 181, 189
Pittman, C. T. 89
Potash, J. S. 25, 62, 92, 190
President's Initiative on Race 70
Prilleltensky, L. 235

Ratts, M. J. 43, 47, 163, 164, 167, 216, 236
Reja, M. 51
Robinson, C. L. 69
Robinson, E. 27
Rowe, M. P. 84
Rozsa, L. 73

Sangal, A. 68
Santiago-Rivera, A. 50
Singh, A. 22, 56, 199, 214, 215, 219
Singletary, G. 60
Slater, R. B. 69
Smith, L. 222
Smith, W. A. 58, 59, 60, 84, 86, 87, 88, 210
Solorzano, D. 76, 77, 78, 84, 86, 89, 214
Spanierman, L. B. 57, 77, 222

Stainback, K. 69
Steele, J. M. 163
Stefancic, J. 68, 215
Sue, D. W. 26, 29, 31, 37, 43, 44, 47, 48, 49, 50, 54, 56, 63, 72, 77, 78, 79, 80, 81, 82, 83, 84, 85, 86, 87, 89, 91, 93, 108, 124, 126, 127, 157, 163, 203, 204, 205, 206, 207, 210, 211, 212, 221, 223, 235
Sue, W. 78, 89, 203, 210, 211, 221
Sullivan, K. 73
Swim, J. K. 91

Talwar, S. 23, 24, 43, 62, 166
Tate, W. F. 215
Taylor, E. 215
ter Maat, M. 24
Thomas, C. W. 202
Thompson, C. E. 69, 86, 87
Tomaskovic-Devey, D. 69
Toporek, R. L. 164, 234, 235
Torino, G. C. 37
Travers, C. J. 82

U.S. Census Bureau 90
U.S. Department of Health and Human Services 88
U.S. Department of Justice National Advisory Commission on Civil Disorders 69
Utsey, S. O. 87, 88

Valicenti, R. L. N. 24
Vandiver, B. J. 202
Vera, E. M. 163
Vereen, L. G. 162

Weinberg, D. 164
Wheaton, J. E. 49
Williams, D. R. 87, 88
Winant, H. 70
Wyatt, S. B. 88

Yali, A. M. 24
Yam, K. 51
Yates, C. 51
Yosso, T. 77
Young, B. 88

Zayas, L. H. 50
Zinn, H. 64